D1559366

POSSESSED WITH GREATNESS

THE HEROIC TRAGEDIES OF CHAPMAN

AND SHAKESPEARE

POSSESSED WITH GREATNESS

THE HEROIC TRAGEDIES OF

CHAPMAN AND SHAKESPEARE

RICHARD S. IDE

THE UNIVERSITY OF NORTH CAROLINA PRESS

Chapel Hill

*Both the initial research and the publication of this work
were made possible in part through grants from the National Endowment
for the Humanities, a federal agency whose mission is to award grants to support
education, scholarship, media programming, libraries, and museums, in order
to bring the results of cultural activities to a broad, general public.*

Library of Congress Cataloging in Publication Data

Ide, Richard S
Possessed with greatness.

Bibliography: p.
Includes index.
1. English drama—17th century—History and
criticism. 2. Chapman, George, 1559?–1634—
Tragedies. 3. Shakespeare, William, 1564–1616—
Tragedies. 4. Chapman, George, 1559?–1634—
Characters—Heroes. 5. Shakespeare, William,
1564–1616—Characters—Heroes. 6. Chapman,
George, 1559?–1634—Characters—Soldiers.
7. Shakespeare, William, 1564–1616—Characters—
Soldiers. 8. Heroes in literature. 9. Soldiers
in literature. 10. Epic literature. I. Title.
PR658.T713   822'.3'09352   79-25864
ISBN 0-8078-1429-6

For

GORDON AND MARION IDE

CONTENTS

Contents

ACKNOWLEDGMENTS

I have tried to make my scholarly debts manifest in the following pages, but I feel obliged to single out in particular the works of E. D. Hirsch and Rosalie Colie, suggesting the theoretical and methodological stance I have assumed, the works of Jean Jacquot, Millar MacLure, Raymond Waddington, and Eugene Waith relating to Chapman, and those of Leeds Barroll, Reuben Brower, Paul Jorgensen, and Matthew Proser relating to Shakespeare. I have tried to take into account the immense bulk of historical and literary scholarship relevant to my topic and to the specific works I discuss, but space restrictions and common sense require that I often pass on widely accepted ideas without notation and pass over familiar scholarly disputes not directly related to my argument. My apologies to those scholars whose works I have overlooked and to those of the majority whose works I have read and profited by but failed to mention.

My thanks to the University of Wisconsin Graduate School for two summer research fellowships and to the Andrew Mellon Foundation and Duke University, where I was a Mellon postdoctoral fellow in 1976–77. I would also like to thank the Director and staff of the Huntington Library and Art Gallery in San Marino, of the Perkins Library at Duke University, and of the rare book room at the Library of Congress in Washington for their gracious assistance while I was engaged in research at their institutions.

I wish to extend my gratitude to Paul M. Cubeta, who first stirred my interest in Elizabethan drama; to A. B. Chambers, Standish Henning, and Andrew Weiner for their many helpful criticisms and unflagging support; and especially to my good friends Stuart Curran, Barton Friedman, Joseph Wittreich, and Raymond Waddington, who have struggled through the manuscript at various stages of composition. I have profited immensely from their suggestions, and you the reader are the beneficiary of their pain. Although I spared Jackson Cope the burden of reading the manuscript, my indebtedness to him—my teacher, friend, and best critic —is inestimable.

Finally, I should like to thank Lewis Bateman, Gwen Duffey, and the staff at the University of North Carolina Press for their patience and for the many courtesies they have extended to me over the past two years.

INTRODUCTION

At the beginning of the Jacobean period in England, George Chapman
and William Shakespeare wrote five tragedies with a soldier as protagonist. In *Othello* (1604), *Bussy D'Ambois* (1604), *Antony and Cleopatra*
(1607), *The Conspiracy and Tragedy of Byron* (1608), and *Coriolanus*
(1609), the soldier's attempt to realize a heroic conception of self brings
him into fatal conflict with society. Although the soldier's aspiration for
excellence may be appropriate, indeed fully admirable, in some circumstances, the dramatists remove those congenial contexts from the hero,
placing him in a social and political ambience where his martial and
amatory ideals are antithetical to society's needs, values, and norms of
behavior. Typically the dramatists evoke the style and subject matter of
epic to convey the soldier's heroic idealism. The epic genre is thus used as
a metaphor expressing a heroic conception of self that is at odds with
"reality" as social consensus defines it.

For most English men of letters epic was an ethical category of literature defined primarily by its exemplary subject matter. Sir Philip Sidney
states that some "kindes" are termed according to the matter they deal
with, and since he terms Xenophon's prose account of Cyrus an "absolute heroicall Poem," "*heroick*" seems to have been such a genre.[1] George
Puttenham informs his reader that "*Museus*" compiled "a true treatise of
the life & loues of *Leander* and *Hero*, both of them *Heroick*, and to none
ill edification";[2] Christopher Marlowe may have smiled, but Chapman
took the suggestion seriously. The "heroicall poem" encompasses those
works we think of as epic but also signifies a subject matter of exemplary
heroic behavior that, as it might be found in myth and history as well as
in brief and long fictive poems, extends beyond our strict generic notion
of epic. Achilles was a "heroicall" hero, of course, but so, too, were those
"great Princes"—"Bacchus, Ceres, Perseus, Hercules, Theseus"—and so
were the historical Alexander and Caesar.[3] Mindful of this historical

conception of epic, I wish to stress two preliminary points about how the genre is used to express a heroic conception of self.

Any reference to the style and subject matter of epic evokes a broad range of generic assumptions and expectations. In Rosalie Colie's words, "a literary genre stands for a kind of subject, a kind of content, literary and intellectual; and . . . some references to a subject or content may be taken as metaphors for a whole kind."[4] In the plays discussed in this book, dramatic speaker and context will usually limit the generic evocation to relatively specific implications. Typically epic ideals of individual heroism are invoked at the expense of, or in opposition to, epic social and political ideals of founding, restoring, or reforming society. Bussy's heroic individualism at the duel, which the epic evocation aligns with the amoral self-assertion of Achilles, signals the betrayal of Bussy's Herculean quest for social reformation. More obviously, Byron and Coriolanus would destroy France and Rome in order to create societies in their own images. Nevertheless, given the fact that a tragic context is likely to delimit an epic reference, distinguishing societal values and norms of behavior from the soldier's eccentric individualism, Colie's point about the force of a generic evocation is methodologically sound.

A generic reference has this evocative power because the "kinds" reside in the public domain; they are recognized and shared by speaker and interpreter, dramatist and audience, as "abbreviations for a 'set' on the world."[5] The soldier-heroes have an epic "set" on their worlds; when they attempt to live this metaphor, "unmetaphoring [it] into actual chosen behavior,"[6] they are attempting to live a personal epic myth. Their behavior does not square with society's consensus of what kind of behavior is appropriate, valuable, and acceptable. Conflict ensues when the soldiers are unwilling or unable to compromise their firm view of the world by bringing it in line with consensus. Each of the soldier-heroes is thus a social misfit; the tragedies proceeding from the conflict between personal epic myth and social reality are of a kind, and that "mixed kind" is heroic tragedy.

The recognition that these tragedies by Chapman and Shakespeare share a generic identity serves two purposes: one interpretive, concerned with the meaning of each play, and the other more strictly critical, concerned with distinguishing the dramatists' approaches to similar subject matter and with drawing conclusions proper to a comparative study. In *Validity in Interpretation*, E. D. Hirsch, Jr., contends that the first step in a valid interpretive procedure is to make an assumption about the "genre" to which a particular "trait" is meaningfully and necessarily related as a part to the whole. This first step, governed by what E. H. Gombrich refers to as the "primacy of genres,"[7] is a valid approach to interpretation because the artist's intended meaning is formulated by the same recognizable genres governing the interpreter's perception of meaning. The Renaissance term signifying artistic intention is *idea*, the foreconceit, the informing conception that shapes the work of art and at the same time is reflected by the work of art. Although the *idea* of a specific drama can never be defined fully, it can be roughly described as the sum total of what plot, characterization, poetry, themes, scenic structure, dramatic gestures, and the like articulate and enact on stage. "Heroic tragedy" is itself a heuristic generic description that cannot subsume or fully define the *idea* of each play, but it will provide a valid, fresh approach to the play's meaning.

The rationale for presenting the heroic tragedies as a comparative study rather than as a series of discrete interpretive essays also derives from the plays' generic kinship. When two contemporary playwrights write in an identifiable dramatic genre, the critic might use that "kind" as a basis for fruitful comparison. Standards of comparison should not be prescriptive, of course, for no artist thinks of genre as a determinate set of formal, stylistic, or thematic conventions, and a specific work within a genre (or a fusion of two recognizable genres) is always a special case, an original contribution to the genre. Nevertheless, the comparative critic may draw legitimate empirical conclusions from the ways Chapman and Shakespeare chose to use heroic tragedy. In the introductory chapter, I have deliberately misplaced a series of broad empirical conclusions in order to set before the reader the interpretive and comparative contexts the mixed genre provides for these plays. In subsequent chapters, identifiable generic traits, particularly epic themes and stylistic conventions, are used as critical touchstones for contrasting the dramatists' attitudes toward the tragic soldier, his martial idealism, and the heroic tradition on which the soldier's ideals are based. This comparative context I have applied in such a way that it might broaden, but not interfere with, the interpretation of each heroic tragedy.

A second, related reason for bringing these works of Chapman and Shakespeare into pointed juxtaposition requires a brief reconstruction. My preliminary question was this: why did Chapman and Shakespeare experiment with heroic tragedy while their contemporaries, almost without exception, did not? An appeal to the traditions that might promote the use of the mixed genre simply begs the question. Other dramatists must have been aware that the two "high" genres of epic and tragedy were related by style and subject matter;[8] and the sixteenth century critical controversy about the superiority of epic or tragedy must have suggested to them the appropriateness of using the warrior as a major character and war as a central action in their tragedies.[9] Other dramatists were also aware that *Tamburlaine* and the heroic romances, *1 Henry VI* and the history plays of the 1590s, had established the soldier's place on the London stage.[10] And other dramatists, having access to Lodovico Ariosto's *Orlando Furioso* and Torquato Tasso's *Gerusalemme Liberata* in translation and Sidney's *Arcadia* and Edmund Spenser's *The Faerie Queene* in the mother tongue, must also have understood that the romantic epic was an acceptable adaptation of the classical epic, that love and war were both matters appropriate to the heroic genre.[11] Critical, theatrical, and literary traditions, in short, cannot explain why Chapman and Shakespeare were singularly disposed to characterize the heroic soldier in just this way at just this time.

Part of that explanation seems accountable to the historical and cultural perception of the soldier-hero which the two dramatists shared at the turn of the century. The old-style Elizabethan soldier, projecting in debate, pamphlet, and behavior a personal myth of honorable warrior or heroic knight, was out of touch with the social and political reality of Elizabethan society and court.[12] The Earl of Essex—the man to whom Chapman had dedicated his *Iliads* (1598) and whom Shakespeare had sped from Ireland in a prologue in *Henry V* (1599)—was typical of the proud but politically inept soldier. With Essex's abortive rebellion and subequent execution in 1601, a typical social misfit became a tragic paradigm. Significantly, Samuel Daniel's *Philotas* (1605), the only other heroic tragedy during the period, was a topical recollection of Essex's dislocation in society and at court.

What appears to distinguish Chapman and Shakespeare even from Daniel, however, was a marked interest in martial heroism and the epic tradition. This fascination with the "heroick," though no doubt intensified by the cultural perception of the soldier's dislocation, extends beyond the local habitation and name of England and Essex and might best be accounted for by personal and artistic predilection. As each dramatist's interest was acute and remained so over a period of years, it fostered continual reassessments of the martial psyche, adaptations of the soldier's conflict with society, and reassertions about the value of heroic ideals.

Each dramatist might be said to have entered into a creative dialogue with his own conceptions of martial heroism. But when these expressions came into the public domain—whether in print, on stage, or in manuscript—and were found to be as sharply divergent as they were deeply felt, Chapman and Shakespeare appear to have entered into a dialogue with each other. That is, the dramatists came to exert a negative influence on one another; each was better able to clarify his own conception of the tragic soldier and his own assessment of heroic values by distinguishing them from those of the other.

Although the intensity and directness of the negative influence vary from play to play, the relationship among Chapman's and Shakespeare's heroic tragedies would seem to exemplify that which Anne Barton has recently described: "There seems to be little doubt that in the small, closely connected world of the Elizabethan and Jacobean playwrights, the evolution of dramatic form took the shape of a dialogue among plays. Writers reacted intensely to one another's work, and in a variety of ways."[13] In the case of Chapman's and Shakespeare's heroic tragedies, the likelihood that the dramatists were reacting to one another is enhanced by their near exclusive use of the mixed genre, by their sharply divergent attitudes toward heroic ideals, and by considerable circumstantial evidence. Biographical speculation about the "school of night" or the "rival poet," historical essays documenting the competition between public and private playhouses, critical essays on the relationship of "Venus and Adonis" and "Ovids Banquet of Sence" or on *Hamlet* and *The Revenge of Bussy D'Ambois*, the potentially fertile relationship of Battista Guarini's *Il Pastor Fido*, Chapman's *The Gentleman Usher*, and Shakespeare's tragicomic romances—all intimate a contentious, intensely competitive relationship based on personal animus, disparate aesthetic values, and rival theatrical traditions.

Of the "variety of ways" in which the dramatists' heroic tragedies suggest a mutual negative influence, this book shall focus on theme and characterization. In general, I have not concerned myself with explicit verbal influence and the related "busynesse" of tracing borrowings, echoes, and allusions from play to play. For the kind of dialogue I wish to recreate—one documenting basic conceptual disagreements about the martial psyche, the heroic spirit, and the value of epic and the heroic tradition—can be formulated only by recovering the diverse attitudes, assumptions, and conceptions informing the *Iliads* and *Odysses*, *Troilus and Cressida*, and the heroic tragedies themselves. In this respect—

though the mutual negative influence is no less real for its enabling the dramatists to clarify their conceptions of a definite subject matter, type of tragic hero, and "kind" of tragic drama—Chapman's and Shakespeare's dialogue on epic is implicit in their distinctive themes, characters, and approaches to heroic tragedy.

Subject matter and conventional dating have dictated the book's structure. Chapman's interest in the soldier-hero and the heroic tradition may be traced directly to his translation of Homer's *Iliad*, seven books of which were published in 1598. Shakespeare's tragic soldiers had been partially adumbrated by Talbot in *1 Henry VI*, more fully by Hotspur in *1 Henry IV*, and to some extent by the waning world of chivalry and variegated forms of heroism in *Hamlet*. For our purposes, though, *Troilus and Cressida* is the obvious starting point. Placed side by side, Chapman's and Shakespeare's insights into "the matter of Troy" introduce pivotal distinctions in their conceptions of heroic passion and their approaches to the soldier's characterization. The heroic tragedies themselves divide into two groups. Love and amatory motifs are central to *Othello*, *Bussy D'Ambois*, and *Antony and Cleopatra*; but the final two plays—*The Conspiracy and Tragedy of Byron* and *Coriolanus*— are more strictly tragedies of social dislocation. In addition, conventional dating dictates that the central chapters alternate between works of Chapman and Shakespeare. This interlocking pattern is at once conducive to the comparative study of the heroic tragedies and suggestive of the dialogue I suppose to have existed among them.

POSSESSED WITH GREATNESS

THE HEROIC TRAGEDIES OF CHAPMAN

AND SHAKESPEARE

ULYSS.: *Possess'd he is with greatness,*
And speaks not to himself but with a pride
That quarrels at self-breath. Imagin'd worth
Holds in his blood such swoll'n and hot discourse
That 'twixt his mental and his active parts
Kingdom'd Achilles in commotion rages,
And batters down himself.
[*Tro.* 2. 3. 170–76]

I

APPROACHES TO

HEROIC TRAGEDY

THE SOLDIER'S SOCIAL DISLOCATION

The clearest model for the soldier's conflict with society and court is not found in *The Iliad* or in classical and Elizabethan dramatic annals but in real life, in the tragedy of Robert Devereux, Earl of Essex (1567–1601). Essex's rise to national eminence and sudden fall from grace traced with contemporary relevance history's hard lesson about the turns of Fortune and divine retribution. But, however predictable the moralistic censure of Essex by Francis Bacon and official propagandists, the Essex affair was an emotional issue and, above all, a poignant personal tragedy. The contemporary hero differed from the illustrious men of the *de casibus* tradition in that it was difficult to regard his tragedy with the clear eye of a political moralist.[1] Here was a scion of heroic virtue and courtly favor. Polite, compassionate, and generous, hero and scholar, courtier and poet, Essex had a striking charisma that tended to offset his immense pride and political brashness.[2] His fatal blunder and final execution, no matter how appropriate the judgment, could not but elicit sympathy from those who knew his worth and had followed his career. Essex brought tragical history to life; neither wholly praiseworthy nor wholly reprehensible, the soldier-hero was finally a pathetic figure who was unable to make the transition from casque to cushion. His tragedy was primarily one of social dislocation.

In *The Civil Wars* (1595), Samuel Daniel had commended the exemplary heroism of Essex and Montjoy:

You in whose actions yet the image shines
Of ancient honor neere worne out of date,
You that haue vertue into fashion brought
In these neglected times respected nought.[3]

Because the qualities of honorable integrity and heroic virtue revert to an antique standard of heroism out of fashion in contemporary society, the soldiers' success in reinvigorating society with time-honored values is that much more worthy of celebration. Significantly, the same opposition between "ancient honor" and degenerate society is stressed in Chapman's dedicatory preface to Essex (*Iliads*, 1598). But Chapman's celebration of the "contemporary Achilles" sounds a more strident, idiosyncratic note than does Daniel's, for Chapman—thinking not only of Essex's disfavor in high places but of Homer's small repute relative to Virgil's and of his own patronless plight—perceives that society and court are no longer amenable to virtuous instruction. The heroic soldier's social dislocation is acknowledged, his tragedy foreshadowed; with the goal of social reformation through Essex's exemplary behavior (or Chapman's exemplary translation) devoutly to be wished but unlikely to be achieved, Chapman advocates that Essex persevere in his "godlike pursute of Eternitie" if only to defy the "Pessant-common polities" of contemporary England.[4] But in spite of Chapman's pessimism, both he and Daniel alike, as they endorse an antique code of heroism against the degenerate values of social consensus, speak as "ancients" against the "moderns" at court and in society. In the late 1590s, such a reactionary stance was clearly unrealistic.

The popularity of the patriotic soldier on the Elizabethan stage, reflecting both an exuberant post-Armada jingoism and a national resolve in the face of the continuing Spanish threat,[5] could not have obscured the fact that the stage soldier and his ideals were a historical anachronism. No matter what the military manuals were asserting, the heroic knight and his chivalric ideals were hopelessly outdated. The art of warfare, the humanists' political and educational ideals, and the increasingly complex, commercial, and degenerate society in which the old-style soldier lived made his simple, forthright virtues an outmoded, if venerable, relic of the past.[6] A reactionary yearning for a return to the old values celebrated in literature or drama and symbolized by ceremony could not wish away the historical reality. Still, such a sympathy for ancient virtue might color one's perception of historical reality. With Essex's tragic mistake and execution in 1601, Daniel and Chapman faced a painful reassessment of heroic virtue and its Elizabethan exemplar; neither artist was prepared to condemn Essex without a sympathetic apology for him.

The Essex-like hero of Daniel's *Philotas* (1605) is betrayed by his own uncompromising aspiration to nobility at the same time that he is victimized by cynical schemers in a social and political ambience for which he is manifestly unsuited. Philotas exhibits a free and open nature; he is above the politic "seeming" at court, his actions proceeding from a dedication to virtue, honor, and integrity. These admirable qualities, brandished by the soldier's blunt manner and passionate speech, make him an easy prey for the base-spirited sychophants at court. At a trial clearly reminiscent of Essex's, a prejudiced Alexander and his counselors convict Philotas of capital treason for which there is no hard evidence. Daniel has taken the conflict between idealistic soldier and social consensus from *The Civil Wars* and transformed it into a tragic theme of social dislocation; his portrayal of Philotas-Essex is principally that of a heroic martyr. At the end of the drama, to be sure, Daniel toes the orthodox Elizabethan line by having a *nuntius* report that Philotas, under severe torture, has confessed his guilt, just as Essex himself had done; but the circumstances of the confession are ambiguous enough that, even if the audience were to grant the soldier's guilt (as is likely), its sympathy for the heroic victim of a hostile court survives.[7] We shall see that Daniel's sympathetic handling of Philotas-Essex, which is markedly similar to Chapman's treatment of Bussy and Byron in his heroic tragedies, approximates Chapman's own attitude toward Essex.

In Shakespeare's canon, the conception of Talbot in *1 Henry VI* seems to be closest in sympathy with Chapman's and Daniel's generous attitude toward Essex's social dislocation. Shakespeare's chivalric hero is deserted by the base-spirited Fastolfe and then fatally betrayed by the envious York and Somerset. But the characterization that most closely anticipates Shakespeare's mature conception of the tragic soldier is that of Hotspur in *1 Henry IV*. Hotspur's pride, martial wrath, compulsion for honor, scorn for politic action, and individualistic code of behavior typify the limitations, vulnerabilities, and yet attractiveness of the old-style Elizabethan soldier. According to Worcester's "schooling," Hotspur's rash actions and downright manner are social liabilities (3. 1. 178–87); values and behavior appropriate to the battlefield are dangerously inappropriate to council, court, and society. Nonetheless, Hotspur's plain-dealing with Henry IV's courtier wins audience approval, and his passionate actions are set in favorable relief against his father's craven scruple and Worcester's and Vernon's politic duplicity; indubitably, Hotspur's idealism has an attractive side. But Shakespeare's soldier is not the victim of a base-spirited society. What is unique to Hotspur is his temerity, not his heroic idealism; Prince Hal marshals the same heroic virtues when necessary and when right, displaying true martial nobility. The political order and the values of social consensus against which Hotspur rebels, moreover, receive the dramatist's and the audience's emphatic endorsement. In a way that is paradigmatic of Shakespeare's Jacobean soldiers, an obsession with heroic image leads Hotspur toward a dangerous social deviancy. As the soldier isolates himself from the normative values of social consensus, he is self-fated. After 1601, there is no reason to assume that Shakespeare's attitude toward Essex, contemporary rebel and social deviant, was any different from that toward Hotspur.

It would seem, then, that Chapman and Shakespeare shared a general perception of the soldier's perplexity, restlessness, ineptitude, and vulnerability in a social milieu. They also seem to have been in general agreement about the descriptive characteristics of the soldier's conflict with society. But in assigning causes for the conflict and in evaluating the antipathy between heroic idealism and social consensus, they reveal markedly different attitudes. Both the similarities and distinctions are reflected in the dramatists' approaches to heroic tragedy.

EXPLOITING THE MIXED GENRE

The possibilities for translating the historical and cultural perception of social dislocation into dramatic conflict were innumerable. Inept or ill at ease in a social milieu, the soldier might retreat into a world of ego with its dreams of grandeur, eventually losing touch with reality. His idealism might be perverted by the degenerate society around him, or he might stand unbending against a corrupt society and withdraw into splendid, godlike isolation. His social naiveté and volatile temperament might be manipulated by cunning realists. His ideals of heroic individualism might be set at odds with public responsibility, his personal aspirations for excellence clashing with society's needs, values, and norms of behavior. In order to exploit these potential conflicts and variations of them, the dramatists had to establish the soldier's nobility early, and then shift contexts: from war to peace, from battlefield to society, from the military to the political arena, from martial heroism to the battle of the sexes, from an individualistic code of heroism to social ethics.[8]

In Shakespeare's heroic tragedies the soldier's displacement is accompanied by actual scenic shifts and a symbolic geography. Othello is transported from Venice and the heroic expectations of act I to a pacific, amatory, and incongruously tragic setting on Cyprus. In *Coriolanus* the movement from the forum to Corioli and back to the forum suggests that the hero is at peace on the battlefield and at war—with himself and country—in a social milieu. At the outset of *Antony and Cleopatra* one is taught to associate the Herculean Antony with Rome and to lament his transformation in the vicious setting of Egypt. Shakespeare's symbolic settings and scenic shifts sharpen the audience's impression that the soldier has been displaced from a former world or a congenial world appropriate to his martial profession, and in this limited sense the dramatic technique is not essentially different from the simple contextual juxtaposition employed by Chapman. Byron's congenial world is remembered for us by numerous flashbacks to the French civil wars. Bussy's heroic activity as soldier and lover is made to recall the native noblesse of the golden age or, more accurately, the natural superiority of the age of heroes; his heroic individualism brands him a misfit in a degenerate world of petty men, bankrupt values, and Machiavellian intrigue. In short, both dramatists establish a heroic milieu and a system of values associated with it and then relocate the soldier in a setting requiring different, often antithetical, values and modes of behavior.

The tragic agon does not begin until the soldier's former heroism and nobility have been established. None of the soldiers are pretenders, and their tragedies are perceived by the audience as the result of heroic idealism displaced, misdirected, misconstrued, somehow gone awry. Typically epic evocations place the soldier's mental "set" in the heroic milieu he has left behind. Epic style may be evoked by quiet yearnings, reflexive defiance, or irrational thunder; epic subject matter may be alluded to by moral visions of social reformation, resonant pledges of heroic love, or dreamy remembrances of martial triumphs. Sometimes the soldier's appeal to the principle of honor may evoke by synecdoche an entire heroic myth, a vision of self and society in defiance of reality.[9] These epic references, diverse though they may be, are invariably used to stress the conflict between the soldier's heroic idealism and the real world of social consensus. The soldier may be unwilling to accommodate his values and standards of conduct to a new social environment, or he may simply be unable to effect a compromise he thinks is desirable and viable; but whether titanic obduracy or simple human inadequacy, the soldier's conception of self precipitates a tragic action in which he fails to achieve personal aspirations and to advance communal interests.

The tragic failure of Shakespeare's soldiers might be understood as an extension of the hero's inner conflict, one in which the soldier struggles desperately and unsuccessfully to realize his heroic image. Matthew Proser elucidates the point when he argues that the hero's private sense of self—both a "gauge to the hero's hopes, wishes, aspirations" and a determinant of his compulsion to present an appropriate public persona —is betrayed by simple human inadequacy.[10] The locus of the tragic conflict, it follows, lies in the discrepancy between the hero's conception of self and his real, limited humanity. Chapman's tragic accent falls not on human inadequacy but on the soldier's inability to express his idealism through appropriate, purposeful action. His is a tragedy of social inadequacy rather than psychological frailty. But regardless of the differences in emphasis, both Chapman and Shakespeare convey the soldier's social and psychological conflicts by juxtaposing the idealism of epic and the realism of tragedy.

For Chapman the juxtaposition is relatively rough-hewn. By misplacing the soldier's epic aspirations in social contexts where they cannot be fully realized, Chapman creates an ironic distance between the hero's idealistic intentions and his actual achievements. Bussy's epic duel and heroic love, for example, are undermined by the flimsy pretext for the fight and the sordid fact of the adulterous affair; and for most of the play Bussy's actions provide feeble support for the stunning poetry of self-assertion. In addition to creating an ironic effect, however, the soldier's pursuit of heroic ideals brings him into pointed conflict with the "real" world of social consensus. Soldier confronts society as genre confronts countergenre;[11] the more assertive the soldier's heroic idealism, the more ominous becomes his entanglement in a tragic milieu hostile to heroic values. Although the point may only be suggested here, the conflict resulting from the soldier's being misplaced in a hostile society is at base a tragedy of situation. To that large generalization we shall have to return.

In Shakespeare's heroic tragedies the juxtaposition of epic idealism and tragic realism consists principally in counterpointing the soldier's heroic conception of self with his human frailty. Naturalistic characterization allows the audience to see the vulnerable human needs and inadequacies that belie the soldier's projection of self in the epic mode of grand language and heroic action. This discrepancy results in a tragedy that is acutely psychological in emphasis. Coriolanus's assumption of self-sufficiency, for example, is undermined by a natural blood-bond of affection, a vulnerable human need for his mother's love and approbation. This psychological crux is essential to his tragedy.

Chapman calls attention to the discrepancy between idealistic intentions and real achievements and Shakespeare to that between heroic image and real self by repeated recollections of the soldier's former heroic stance. In the tragedies of Bussy and Byron, even as the heroic aspirations are debased by the contexts within which they are expressed, and even as the aspirations entangle the soldier in tragic conflict with society, Chapman alerts the audience to the debasement and entanglement by playing the epic mode of heroic idealism (the grand gestures and hyperbolic poetry) against the reality of the situation. Byron compulsively invokes the heroic memory of the civil wars when his star has sunk and all seems lost; Bussy frantically pledges heroic resolve and defiance when the politic maneuverings are darkest and honorable action is doomed. At these moments in the midst of a tragic situation, the evocation of epic seems a vain appeal to a countergenre, a futile assertion of a different vision of reality. Similarly, once the tragic agon has begun, Shakespeare will use the heightened style of epic idealism when the hero reflexively invokes a former identity to buoy his self-estimation, when a sanguine conception of self is pathetically inappropriate to the action the soldier is about to take, when actions already taken ought to be measured against an earlier manifestation of heroic idealism. When Othello resolves to murder Desdemona at the end of act 3, scene 3, for example, the histrionic gesture of falling to his knees and the sacred oaths suggest that the Moor is launching a holy war, the moment perversely recollecting the soldier's earlier campaign against the heathen Turks. The heroic evocation of this moment thus alerts the audience to the perverse conception of self Othello has adopted and, by remembering the Moor's true nobility as heroic soldier earlier in the play, establishes this hideous heroic persona as a perversion of Othello's true self.

To this point, I have been concerned with sketching the broad similarities in Chapman's and Shakespeare's use of the mixed genre. Both dramatists displace the soldier from a heroic milieu, relocating him in a perplexing social setting. Both use epic evocations to associate the soldier's conception of self with the values and achievements of the former milieu and then to stress the conflict between the soldier's personal myth

9

and the communal values as social consensus defines them. Both exploit the idealism of the heroic genre and the realism of the tragic genre in creating psychological or situational conflict. In two crucial, predictable respects, however, Chapman's and Shakespeare's use of the mixed genre differ significantly.

When Puttenham distinguishes the high genres of epic and tragedy according to artistic intention, one being the genre of praise and the other of reprehension,[12] his simplistic dichotomy calls attention to a central ethical ambiguity in heroic tragedy. As might be expected of a dramatist whose tragic accent falls on social inadequacy rather than human inadequacy, Chapman emphasizes the ethical aspect of the hero's conflict with society far more than does Shakespeare. The ethical emphasis surely reflects Chapman's earlier struggle to translate Achilles' epic heroism into an exemplary ideal for Elizabethan culture. John Steadman clarifies the problem facing the translator by directing attention to the discrepancy between the poetic heroism of the epic and the ethical heroism of Christian humanism.[13] The crux of the problem is that Homeric *areté* denotes natural superiority, physical prowess, heroic valor, and an individual aspiration for excellence, which traits are often exhibited through amoral, mindless, bloody self-assertion.[14] The pagan heroic ethos is antisocial, a-cultural, unchristian—a point the youthful Marlowe had seized upon in *Tamburlaine*, it appears, with some glee. Unless the translator were to turn Achilles into a tragic figure of reprehension, what possible ethical lesson could his epic individualism exemplify for an Elizabethan society? Homer's *Iliad* required not only a verbal but a cultural translation.

Unlike the reader of the classical epic, who could effect a cultural translation by allegorical interpretation (if pressed to do so) and unlike the writer of a Renaissance epic, such as Tasso and Spenser, who could use allegory to sanction the heroic excitement of arms and amours, the translator was restricted by his material. Still, as we shall see in the next chapter, one discovers in Chapman's paraphrases and interpretive expansions a systematic attempt to justify Achilles' behavior according to Elizabethan ethical norms. Achilles' proud, defiant, destructive isolation thus becomes a virtuous stance in the face of a society that has wronged him. Chapman's defense of Achilles requires a corollary censure of Agamemnon and the Greek camp, and this pointed ethical opposition of hero and society anticipates the situational confrontations Chapman uses in framing the tragedies of Bussy and Byron. Significantly, in *Troilus and Cressida*, Shakespeare refuses to sanction the pagan heroic ethos according to

Elizabethan ethical norms. The point is made emphatically in the Trojan council scene, where, despite all of Hector's talk, his compulsion for grandeur makes humane and ethical considerations irrelevant. Instead, the self-delusion and self-idolatry of the heroes receive the dramatic stress, anticipating in this respect the psychological emphasis in the tragedies of Othello, Antony, even Coriolanus.

To return to Chapman, matters would be much simpler if one could assume, as Ennis Rees does, that when Chapman wrote the heroic tragedies of Bussy and Byron he simply juxtaposed a reprehensible tragic hero (in Puttenham's sense) against the ethical code of Christian humanism.[15] But this will not do. The translation of Achilles' self-centered, bloody heroism in the second half of *The Iliad* no doubt gave Chapman pause (it was not published until 1611), but he still clung to the belief that there was something of value in the pagan heroic ideal and that it could not be wholly discredited on ethical grounds. Chapman's moral ambivalence is reflected in *Bussy D'Ambois*, where the conflict between heroic *virtus* and a Stoic-Christian concept of moral virtue is never satisfactorily resolved. And even in *The Conspiracy and Tragedy of Byron*, where there is no moral ambivalence whatsoever, one still cannot condemn Byron without a measure of muted admiration. In these plays, Chapman ranges his characters as if according to the Platonic hierarchies that Tasso had employed in his *Gerusalemme Liberata*: counselors, soldiers, merchants; reason, heroic passion, desire; wisdom, honor, gain.[16] Byron's heroic spirit is exalted above the base desires of his society even as it falls short of King Henry's rational ideal; and although an ethical judgment must condemn Byron's unbridled aspiration, the soldier's worth is acknowledged, the tragic waste lamented. The audience knows what Chapman's imagery continually stresses: that *in a different situation* this societal monster had been, and might again have been, apotheosized.

Just what kind of deity Byron might have been seems the special concern of Shakespeare's *Coriolanus*. And, in general, it is as revelatory as it is obvious to note that Shakespeare, having no inclination to salvage respect for heroic *virtus* in the plays under discussion, does not distinguish the soldier's fiery spirit from the basely appetitive component of the psyche; rather, he employs a more familiar, bipartite psychological model opposing reason and passion. Context defines Hotspur's martial wrath as a humourous aberration, and in *Troilus and Cressida* the "heroic passion" is portrayed as an acquisitive egomania, regardless of the idealistic delusion under which the heroes operate.

Still another potential source of tragic conflict Chapman and Shakespeare might exploit lay in the interplay of the soldier's martial and amatory ideals. The chivalric tradition had stressed love as an inspiration to martial prowess; courtly love had more generally romanticized its ennobling effects; neo-Platonism had idealized its power to cleanse man's passion in a self-effacing, consciousness-raising journey toward a transcendent ideal; Dante and Tasso, Sidney and Spenser, had established love as a heroic enterprise. But the English man of letters was also familiar with other traditions in which love was appetitive rather than virtuous, selfish rather than self-effacing, emasculating rather than inspiring, destructive rather than ennobling.[17] Women had waylaid Odysseus and Aeneas on their heroic journeys and had disarmed Mars, Hercules, and many lesser heroes. And far from being an exalted yearning for transcendence, the consuming love passion was known to blind, delude, and debilitate. A pessimist, or skeptic, or the writer of tragedy, moreover, might surmise that the transcendent ideal, which the beloved was supposed to symbolize, mirrored in reality the lover's narcissistic infatuation with self-image, that the soldier's adoration of the beloved was really a kind of self-idolatry, his "service" a kind of self-tribute.

In Chapman's *Bussy D'Ambois*, there is only a slight suggestion, based on the analogy with Hercules and Deineira, that Bussy's love for Tamyra was his Achilles' heel; Chapman's supposed misogyny is anything but a central issue in the play. A stronger suggestion, but one never fully developed, is that Bussy's strangely dispassionate attraction to Tamyra and his hasty pledge of service to her amount to little more than a pretext for heroic assertion, much as the inconsequential insults at court seem merely an excuse for the epic display in the duel. In general, though, Chapman makes virtually no distinction between the martial heroism of Bussy's duel and the heroic love of his chivalric service. Bussy's martial and amatory ideals are complementary expressions of heroic spirit; his conceptions of self as heroic soldier and heroic lover do not come into conflict.

For Shakespeare, on the other hand, the juxtaposition of amatory and martial ideals, reflecting the broad theme of private values versus public responsibility, was crucial to the delineation of tragic character and of tragic conflict. In *Othello*, for example, the crusade against Desdemona, which the Moor symbolically launches at the end of act 3, scene 3, is as much the crusade of Othello the *soldier* against Othello the *lover*, for the latter's naive idealism, psychic indulgence in contentment, and silly, irresponsible truancy have betrayed Othello's public image as honorable soldier and servant of Venice. More obviously, love and war dominate the entire plot of *Antony and Cleopatra*. The lovers' attempts to preserve both the geographical space of the empire and the psychic integrity of love's world necessitate changes in roles and compromises in ideals that are too numerous to detail here. Suffice it to state the obvious, that in *Antony and Cleopatra*, from beginning to end, Shakespeare mined the rich potential of the interplay between martial and amatory ideals.

This brief survey of Chapman's and Shakespeare's use of the mixed genre has inevitably shed light on their conceptions of the soldier-hero. Indeed, the distinctions set out at the beginning of the chapter might now be readdressed and refined, for Chapman's attitude toward Essex's pathetic dislocation and Shakespeare's attitude toward Hotspur's reprehensible deviancy appear to prejudice their conceptions of the Jacobean soldier. One must proceed with a caveat, however. A typical approach to the characterization of the soldier is not the same as the creation of a hard-and-fast character type. Byron is different from Bussy and both are different from Essex; Shakespeare's heroes are different from each other and different from Hotspur. Just as one must grant the malleable nature of the mixed genre, accommodating adaptations of the paradigmatic pattern of dislocation and conflict, so each heroic tragedy must be acknowledged to have a distinctly different *idea* informing the conception of the soldier-hero.

PRINCIPLES OF HEROIC CHARACTERIZATION

Like his narrative poetry and translation of *The Iliad*, Chapman's heroic tragedies disclose a neo-Platonic aesthetic. Chapman's dramatic *idea* is a suprastructural conception whose informing influence on plot, character, and tragic structure is felt throughout the drama. Like a deterministic god, the dramatist imposes his fore-conceit on the tragic material, creating and organizing his stage world in strict accord with that conception.[18] The neo-Platonic aesthetic creates the impression that the play does not mirror nature so much as it does the vision of the dramatist who conceived it. Characters such as Bussy and Byron appear to represent intellectual concepts; they are more like walking ideograms than mimetic, naturalistic representations of life. Poetry, often divorced from the character speaking it, appears designed to convey moral or philosophical commentary. Plot seems manipulated to advance a thesis, the dramatic principle of action being better understood as the progress of an intellectual argument than as a probable sequence of narrative events. Dramatic gestures and stylized stage business seem to function as emblematic commentary. Such a play may be termed a "drama of ideas," and its peculiar qualities, its ideational emphases, should not be explained away as poor or inferior dramaturgy. Rather, it is a different kind of dramaturgy, one that might be expected from a neo-Platonic dramatist who was of philosophical temperament and who may have been inhibited from naturalistic characterization and expression because he wrote for a children's company.

Chapman's dramaturgy encourages audience and critic to translate the narrative sequence of events into a structure of ideas. The narrative structure of *Bussy D'Ambois*, for instance, is that of a tragic quest. At Monsieur's prompting, Bussy pledges himself to the Herculean mission of social reformation; he narrowly escapes physical danger at the duel and punishment after it, but he cannot extricate himself from the entanglement of an adulterous affair that eventuates in his murder. The quest has been a failure; the plot has been straightforward and relatively simple, yet not without moments of stirring poetry, large doses of melodramatic intrigue, and some sensational stage business. The play's structure of ideas, however, is circular. The hero's philosophical reflections in his first and final moments enclose the tragic quest in an ideational context. This framing device, together with frequent choric commentary, suggests that the tragedy's narrative progression is used to figure forth the dramatist's suprastructural conception. Thus, after a philosophical defense of virtuous inaction in a sadly corrupt society, the hero pledges himself to an active pursuit of virtue that is inextricably involved with the goal of social reformation; but personal and social ideals run amok when their realization requires a spirited assertion of *virtus*, which is not only detrimental to the propagation of virtue but provokes the hostile reaction of society. At his demise the hero recants the active ideals in favor of the initial philosophy of moral virtue and self-reformation, now fully understood for the first time. This articulation of the tragedy's ideational design is only partial, of course, but it is necessary to attempt it if one values *Bussy D'Ambois* beyond its purple patches and melodramatic intrigue. For Chapman's dramatic *idea* informs and gives significance to the movement of character through plot.

Functionally, a Chapman plot may be said to subserve character.

Bussy's and Byron's psychological behavior are consistent and predictable; the heroes are static, monopathic giants who march through the sequence of events rather than develop with it. Plot has relatively little determination on the hero's growth and development and therefore functions to exhibit his conception of self, to provide contexts for heroic assertion and heroic response. The use of plot as a vehicle for character fosters a presentational characterization, and what Bussy and Byron display in various situations are various aspects of heroic *virtus*, of itself neither good nor bad, but always astonishing. The presentation of heroic spirit and heroic resolve, eliciting the "astonished" response of an audience distanced from the hero, places Chapman's conception of heroic characterization squarely in the tradition of Marlovian titanism.[19]

Given the soldier's monolithic psychic stance and single-minded pursuit of excellence, the situation in which the dramatist places the hero is crucial, not only in providing contexts for one's evaluation of the soldier's actions—patriotic, moral, exemplary, or anarchic, immoral, reprehensible—but also in precipitating tragic conflict. The soldier's conception of self and his brassy evocations of the "heroick" change little, but contexts change significantly, the soldier's actions becoming increasingly unworthy of him and the situations in which he finds himself more perilous to him. One may say, in fact, that once the static, uncompromising hero is displaced from a heroic milieu that makes ambition virtue, his moral and social conflict with an antiheroic society is assured. Though the soldier himself is by no means a complex character, his heroic actions and society's hostile reactions proceed toward a situational complexity that issues in tragedy. As the dislocation of the hero is the radical principle ensuring tragic entanglement, *Bussy D'Ambois* and the *Byron* plays are better understood as tragedies of situation than as tragedies of character.[20]

If one were to assume that tragedy ought to be a naturalistic representation of life, by that criterion a Chapman tragedy such as I have described would be judged inferior to a Shakespearean tragedy. But the "realities" that Chapman's heroic tragedies mirror are not the minds, mores, and frailties of man, such as might be conveyed in a psychological tragedy, but the structure of ideas reflected by a tragedy of situation. The distinction is illuminated especially well by those rare moments of character change and fluctuation in Chapman's heroic tragedies. For example, Bussy's conversion to moral virtue in the death scene is abrupt and, in terms of naturalistic principles of characterization, unsatisfying. Chapman subverts Bussy's heretofore uniform motivation and psychological consistency, and the turnaround in character seems both expedient and melodramatic, much as Byron's sudden turnaround at the end of *The Conspiracy*. But Bussy's conversion is nevertheless aesthetically satisfying, for it brings Chapman's ideational conflict between heroic *virtus* and moral virtue in a degenerate milieu to a coherent closure. Naturalistic principles of characterization are strained so that the drama of ideas might be served.

In broad terms, the ideas figured forth by the situational confrontations between soldier and society are variations on a theme: the tragic irreconcilability of ancient virtue in an antiheroic society. Chapman had begun his life work of translating *The Iliad* and *The Odyssey* with missionary zeal, convinced that a return to exemplary epic ideals was essential to the regeneration of a sadly diffident, morally craven Elizabethan society. As the delay in the translation of *The Iliad* perhaps indicates, the Essex tragedy dealt a shattering blow to Chapman's literary idealism, forcing upon the enthusiastic celebrator of the "contemporary Achilles" a serious reevaluation of the soldier-hero. The replication of the Essex paradigm in both *Bussy D'Ambois* and the *Byron* plays documents such a reassessment. Like Daniel's Philotas-Essex, like the Essex of the dedication to the *Iliads*, Bussy and Byron are throwbacks to the demideities of the heroic tradition (Hercules, Achilles, Alexander, et al.), now tragically misplaced in a social context where ancient virtue is a liability. That the liability should issue in tragedy evidences the initial pessimism attending Chapman's search for a new exemplary hero and exemplary heroic ideal; at best, only the rudiments of the heroic ideal are laid out in the characters of Bussy and Byron. Chapman's "complete man," clumsily delineated in the figure of Clermont, is not fully fashioned until the translation of *The Odyssey*, a full fifteen years after the Essex affair.

Shakespeare, of course, also exerts a godlike control over his tragic world, but his controlling mechanism is different from Chapman's and elicits a different quality of response from audience and critic. Unlike Chapman, who appears to manipulate character and plot in accord with a shaping conception, Shakespeare creates the illusion that his tragic characters move freely within the plot, indeed determine the plot from within, as if they were surrogate dramatists. The difference in one's impressions may be distinguished as that between a suprastructural *idea* and an infrastructural *idea*. Shakespeare's heroic tragedies draw the audience into the illusion of a real world determined by real people who initiate action and respond to events in accord with verisimilar patterns of psychological behavior.[21] By attending to logical motivation in plot and psychological consistency in characterization, the dramatist fosters the illusion of probability.

Character and plot in Shakespeare's heroic tragedies are functionally interdependent; plot subserves character no more than character subserves plot. For example, Shakespeare wishes to create an Antony whose unlikely action at Actium is understandable, and so the necessities of plot might be said to determine aspects of Antony's characterization leading up to Actium. In the fourth act of the play, however, Shakespeare changes his source by having Hercules, not Bacchus, desert Antony; at this point the dramatist takes an insignificant skirmish (which took place in Plutarch before the desertion of Hercules), magnifies it into a victory of momentous proportions, and then places it after the desertion. In this instance, the needs of character determine plot. Shakespeare's dynamic interplay of character and plot has many intriguing ramifications, but of primary relevance is the illusion of character growth and development.

One finds in Shakespeare's heroic tragedies salient turns in character used to motivate subsequent events in the plot sequence. These turns in character, invariably highlighted by iterative imagery and thematic emphases, bring to a close one pattern of behavior and signal the beginning of another. The end of the temptation scene in *Othello* is a good example. The grotesque ceremony with Iago turns upside down Othello's earlier martial and amatory ideals. Iago becomes not only the Moor's lieutenant but his "fair warrior" in what might be described as a Turkish crusade against Desdemona. Othello's turn in character motivates a behavioral sequence leading directly to the murder. After the murder, moreover, Othello's cataclysmic imagery alerts us to another turn, that of his psychic annihilation. Who did it? "Nobody. . . . Commend me to my kind lord" (5. 2. 124–25). The recognition sequence then leads painfully through Othello's growing awareness of his loss of identity, of his being "nobody," to the final turn in character at the moment of Othello's self-recognition ("O fool, fool, fool!"—5. 2. 323). The recognition then motivates the attempt to reassert his former ideals with the soldier's suicide and the lover's kiss. There is no reason to insist, of course, that only three major turns in character follow the initial revelation of the loyal soldier and faithful husband, but these or similar demarcations in the progression of character are essential to the illusion that events are motivated by real people in a real world.

Equally important, a Shakespearean tragic character, progressing from one pivotal turn to the next, is perceived by the audience as being in the process of change, of meeting challenges and initiating action from progressively different stances, of moving into conflict with himself.[22] In the heroic tragedies, turns in character invariably define the soldier's new stance in relation to his former conception of self. At these pivotal moments, thematic and imagistic emphases evoke the soldier's former heroic idealism, even as that idealism is now perceived by the audience as delusive, debased, or perverted. Shakespeare's tragic soldiers, like Hotspur, typically progress toward false conceptions of self and typically isolate themselves from the real world of social consensus. As these false conceptions lead to social deviancy, precipitating tragic conflict, the soldiers are self-fated. Theirs are tragedies of character rather than tragedies of situation.

Unlike Chapman, Shakespeare does not search for a new heroic ideal in the post-Essex period. The critique of epic heroism in *Troilus and Cressida*, where legendary heroes are demythologized into condemnable human beings, marks a rejection of the "heroick" genre insofar as it idolizes a destructive egomania in the name of heroic individualism. If the behavior of Achilles at Troy, Essex in England, or Byron in France seems heroic to some, to Shakespeare it is reprehensible, antisocial, antihumanitarian, destructive, and tragic. The search in Shakespeare's heroic tragedies is rather for a new conception of heroism that might be substituted for the defective epic ideals advanced by a tyranny of tradition and blindly embraced by contemporary "ancients" like Chapman and Daniel. To varying degrees, each of Shakespeare's soldier-heroes empties himself of heroic pretensions and conceives himself anew in the tragic forge. Improbably, the soldier's new heroic identity is grounded in human nature, that is, in the same weak, ignoble humanity he had repudiated in others and had tried to transcend in himself by living a "heroick" myth.

Shakespeare's characterization draws the audience into the inner world of the soldier-hero, where the war of heroic and humanistic values is fought. The audience sympathizes with the soldier and yet passes judgments on him, negative as the hero attempts to perpetrate a delusive heroic myth, positive as he faces the delusions squarely and reconstructs a new conception of self after a rigorous, disarming, purgative process of humiliation. For Shakespeare, true heroism and true tragic grandeur reside in the humanization of the titan and in an allegiance to the values of the heart; with this kind of hero and this quality of grandeur a sympathetic audience identifies. Both in conception and in effect, then, Shakespeare's heroic characterization is diametrically opposed to Chapman's.

This brief survey of Chapman's and Shakespeare's approaches to the mixed genre and brief sketch of their conceptions of heroic characterization have provided the broad interpretive and comparative contexts for the study of their heroic tragedies. The discussion of Chapman's *Iliads* and Shakespeare's *Troilus and Cressida* in the following chapter will narrow the focus on both interpretive and comparative contexts considerably, so that at chapter's end these preliminary observations might be recollected and sharpened.

2

TRANSLATIONS OF HONOR:

HEROIC CHARACTERIZATION IN

CHAPMAN'S *ILIADS* (1598) AND

SHAKESPEARE'S *TROILUS AND CRESSIDA*

The scraps of available information indicate that "the matter of Troy" was in vogue on the Elizabethan stage of 1598–1602. The Lord Admiral's Men had performed a play in 1598 which Philip Henslowe refers to as "troye"; Henry Chettle and Thomas Dekker were paid for their "troylles & creseda" in the spring of 1599; and the Admiral's Men had three other Troy-related dramas in the 1599 repertory: *Agamemnon*, *Troy's Revenge*, and *Orestes' Furies*.[1] Unfortunately, all of these plays are lost, and what we do possess, a fragment of an Admiral plot (ca. 1598–1602), suggests only that Shakespeare had a theatrical precedent for incorporating the Troilus and Cressida story into the chronical saga of Troy. The fragment seems to be from a classical legend and—assuming the validity of the theory that Thomas Heywood's *I Iron Age* (ca. 1612–13) was a revision of Henslowe's "troye" (1598)—indicates that at least one other play in the Troy vogue was a classical legend typical of the 1590s.[2] Of the literary sources standing behind the interest in Troy one can be more certain: undoubtedly they are Geoffrey Chaucer's *Troilus and Criseyde*, published with Robert Henryson's *Testament of Cresseid*, and William Caxton's *The Recuyell of the Historyes of Troye*.[3]

The two other accounts of Troy during this period are Chapman's translation of *The Iliad* in seven books in 1598 (with his translation of

"Achilles' Shield" later in the same year) and Shakespeare's *Troilus and Cressida* (ca. 1602). Since the appearance of Robert Presson's *Shakespeare's Troilus and Cressida & The Legends of Troy*, no one has seriously doubted that Shakespeare used Chapman's translation as a primary source for his play, though it remains commonly accepted that his debts to Chaucer and Caxton were at least as great.[4] Presson refers to Chapman's *Iliads* and Shakespeare's *Troilus and Cressida* as the "new" tradition of Troy, a tradition at least partially based on Homer himself, not solely on medieval legend, and one distinguished by its interest in characterization and its serious evaluation of Homeric heroism. To support the thesis that Shakespeare used Chapman's *Iliads* as a primary source, Presson stresses the similarities between the translation and the drama; but now, with this point established, it is possible for others to examine the distinct differences between Chapman's and Shakespeare's attitudes toward "the matter of Troy." This chapter will contrast the heroic characterization of the *Iliads* with that of *Troilus and Cressida*, disclosing Chapman's and Shakespeare's radically different perceptions of the legendary heroes and their heroic culture.

THE "GODLIKE PURSUTE OF ETERNITIE"

Chapman considered the translations of *The Iliad* and *The Odyssey* the keystone of his literary reputation, the task he was born for. Although the passage of time has dimmed Chapman's reputation as translator and we are more likely to value him as an original and thoughtful dramatist, he was indeed born for the task. The monumental project occupied Chapman off and on for the better part of two decades (ca. 1597–1616), exacting rigorous demands on his scholarly ability and poetic talent. But perhaps Chapman's unique qualification as translator was an astringent temperament, manifested in a remarkably intense, if graceless, personal resolve to complete an ambitious project, the value of which he never once doubted. He persevered despite the criticism of his peers, the chief of whom, the "detractor" of 1611, appears to have been Ben Jonson. In a word, Chapman was born for the task because he was enthusiastic. Lamentably, this enthusiasm was worn on his sleeve; it was both puerile and pretentious.

The self-consciousness of Chapman's translation is not only noticeable but often disturbing. The translator's epistles, commentaries, and marginalia display the patent aspiration of one who would put aside the provincial labors of English drama in order to make a place for himself among the international community of Renaissance literati. No doubt Chapman did prefer Homer to Virgil, but one senses that he would have warmed to the task of lambasting Julius Caesar Scaliger and other Renaissance literary critics who preferred Virgil to Homer regardless of his literary judgment. In the proud and stubborn independence Chapman trumpets in his commentary one recognizes the boyish overreacher. To be sure, Homer's works merited translation into English; but Chapman's stance as the nation's literary shepherd is irritating, and his projection of himself as Homer's first true "understander" is outrageous. Exactly what did Chapman understand? Critics have emphasized the ethical coloring of Chapman's translations[5] (and that will be my focal concern also), but he also reveled in Homer's wry wit, subtle insights into human nature, and characteristic understatement. With a schoolboy's excitement, he discovered that Homer could be read between the lines, and—one must assume—since other translators had translated only the lines, they obviously had no understanding of what Homer really meant. In Chapman's *Iliads* and *Odysses* character motivation is written in, humor explained, implied logic of speeches expostulated, implicit insights into characterization made explicit. The ethical coloring of Chapman's translations may be the most salient departure from the originals (because it is the most disturbing), but an equally pervasive violation resides in the translator's tendency to "flatten out" Homer. If one reads Robert Fitzgerald's or Richmond Lattimore's Nausikaa episode and then turns to Chapman's, the difference is astounding. Ethical coloring and character "explanation" transform Nausikaa's girlish charm into the heroic virtue of a self-conscious prude.

One should also understand Chapman's enthusiasm in a strict sense, however. Chapman considered himself to be a Platonic poet,[6] and the special "insight" of the Platonic seer enabled him to make Homeric culture relevant to contemporary England. One should recall that the dimensions of the cultural alienation facing an Elizabethan translator of *The Iliad* are immense. At face value, the heroic deeds and heroic ideals are not only unchristian but baldly amoral. Achilles' rage over the loss of a concubine, his grotesque vision of sharking up glory from the destruction of Greeks and Trojans alike, his shameful abuse of Hector's corpse—incidents such as these make it difficult for Chapman to present Achilles as an exemplary hero, thus preserving epic as the high genre of approbation. Achilles' self-enclosed world removes him from the society of men; his heroic conduct is often mindless, egotistical, and cruel. After the Grecian embassy is rebuffed at Achilles' tent, Jean de Sponde cannot avoid a character summation: "Achilles was proud and haughty by nature; hence poets describe him so often as fierce, bold-spirited, savage, headstrong, inexorable, unrestrained, bull-headed, implacable."[7] The summation of character reveals what any man nurtured on Latin literature and Renaissance morality already knew. In short, Achilles stood in great need of "translation" if Chapman were to do more than condemn his unbridled passion out of hand or to offer Homer's hero as other than the ogre the Elizabethans were accustomed to meeting in the pro-Trojan versions of him.

The publication of the *Iliads* in 1598 announced that Chapman had translated Homer's Achilles into the Elizabethan moral ethos and indeed had sanctioned him according to it. He held up Achilles' heroism as a model for contemporary imitation, claiming the prerogative of free paraphrase to reveal his understanding of Homer's "inward sence." But exactly what Chapman saw in the character of Achilles has itself been a mystery. Reviewing Chapman's translations in general, Millar MacLure finds no evidence of "neo-Platonic exegesis on 'sacred' Homer," no effort to "unfold a multiple allegory or create a symbolic system out of the Homeric poems."[8] The reason is that Homer had written profound works in which fruit and chaff, kernel and husk, were the same; as MacLure suggests, Chapman thought that the "letter" was itself sacred, or, in Waddington's terminology, Chapman regarded Homer's epics as totally mythic.[9] The mystery Chapman purported to uncover, then, lay not in the subject matter per se, but in the fact that Homer's ancient patterns of heroic behavior were of timeless relevance, indeed ought to serve as exemplary models for the nobility of Chapman's own society. It was Chapman's obligation to reveal to the eyes of the uninitiated the contemporary relevance of the "eternall Fictions," and this revelation may be partially recovered in the translator's colorings, periphrases, and additions to Homer's original text. Specifically, the 1598 *Iliads* discloses Chapman's studied, eccentric attempt to apologize for Achilles' isolation; even though some actions of the "Achilles Furens" in the latter books are unconscionable even to his Elizabethan apologist,[10] the defense of the patient man of virtue in *Iliads* is consistent and complete.

Chapman departs radically from de Sponde's translation and commentary, taking pains to portray Achilles' wrath as a "Predominant Perturbation" which, once tempered and controlled by the rational faculty, becomes a heroic passion of the mind.[11] The Achillean ideal of the *Iliads* hinges on the process of channeling passion into virtuous action, and because Chapman perhaps learned from Senecan tragedy that the intervention of the gods often served as a poetic counter for psychic turns of character, one might first look to "wise" Athena, or "she that tames hard hearts," to understand the process better.

With considerable help from de Sponde's commentary, Chapman fixed Athena's allegorical resonance early in his translation. When Agamemnon vows to take Achilles' Briseis, it sets "Pelides' soule on fire, and in his brisled brest / His rationall and angrie parts a doutfull strife possest" (*CH* 1. 1. 198–99). Achilles pulls out his sword and ponders whether to run Agamemnon through or "calme his anger's heat," but Athena is present to resolve his quandary. Her wise intercession is fortuitous. At her behest, Achilles sheathes his "*adviseles* sword" ("neque ensem trahe manu") and "*rule*[s] that part that strives" ("Sed age quiesce a contentione"—Loeb, 1:219–20; de Sponde, p. 11). Then, again embracing the advice of wisdom, Achilles decides to vent his anger only in round terms of abuse. My emphases reveal how Chapman throws the incident into an ethical context: "rule" is an interpretive coloring, "adviseles" has no textual authority at all. The translator's purpose is to make the momentary allegory clear. Achilles has tempered his wrathful passion, redirecting its fury from willful violence into just censure. As MacLure notes, the allegorical import of the episode and one whole line (199) of Chapman's translation were borrowed from de Sponde's commentary.[12] Achilles' fiery passion has been transformed into wise restraint, and to Chapman's mind in 1598, this reaction in the face of provocation as well as Achilles' subsequent calm defiance of the society that wrongs him exemplify not the "fashion of outward Fortitude" Chapman will later recognize in Achilles, but something approaching Stoic virtue. In the *Iliads*, Achilles is the positive example of channeling passion into right action; Agamemnon, we shall see, is the negative example.

In Book 1, Agamemnon's rebuff of Apollo's priest is placed in a moral context. Apollo is not simply an angry god, but a god who has been sinned against; and so Achilles does not suggest that the seer find out why Apollo is so angry ("cur tantum iratus"—Loeb, 1:64; de Sponde, p. 5), but that the seer learn and report "*what sinne* doth thus the Delphian Archer move / *To punish us*" (*CH* 1. 1. 64–65; here and throughout the chapter I have italicized only Chapman's flagrant expansions and interpretive colorings). Similarly, the seer Calchas does not urge sacrifices to appease Apollo's wrath ("placantes"—Loeb, 1:100; de Sponde, p. 9), but to "please / *Th' offended* God" (*CH* 1. 1. 98–99). At this point, Agamemnon rises with a hero's powerful passion ("ira autem valde"—Loeb, 1:103; de Sponde, p. 7). The Greek word μένεος is nonmoral, and Scapula defines it as "animi ardor," but Chapman tips the context and makes a moral judgment on Agamemnon's heroic anger; with the help of de Sponde, he translates the phrase as "*excessive* anger's *sting*" (*CH* 1. 1. 101).[13] Agamemnon is wrong from the start, and Chapman's expansions emphasize his lust and covetousness in order to establish Achilles' legitimate complaint and legitimate use of strong language. Here are de Sponde's Latin translation and Chapman's interpretive expansion:

Hunc autem torue intuens allocutus est pedes velox Achilles,
Heu impudentia indute, vulpina mente prodite
Quomodo aliquis tibi promptus obediens verbo erit Achiuorum
Vel vt ad insidias eat, vel adversus viros fortiter pugnet?
[Loeb, 1:148–51; de Sponde, p. 9]

Æacides, *observing well the urgte authoritie*
Of his proud foe with browes contract, returnd this sharp reply:
'O thou possest with Impudence, that *in command of men*
Affectst the *brute* mind of a Fox, *for so thou fill thy denne*
With forced or betrayed spoiles thou feelest no sence of shame!
What souldier *can take any spirite to put on* (for thy *fame*)
Contempt of violence and death, or in the open field
Or secret ambush, *when the heyre his hie desert should yeeld*
Is beforehand condemnd to glut thy gulfe of avarice?
[*CH* 1. 1. 152–60]

In this passage Chapman does all he can to depict Agamemnon's moral failings as those of a tyrant while at the same time nicely expanding "*fortiter pugnet*" into lines 157–58 to create sympathy for the loyal soldier under the tyrant's thumb. De Sponde, a confirmed monarchist, had commented sharply on Achilles' wrath in this passage and inveighed against his indecorous language.[14] Perhaps from reading de Sponde's commentary Chapman knew that Achilles' character was at stake and so translated the moment into a defense of Achilles. Agamemnon, not Achilles, has undermined the principles of authority and degree.

Chapman's interpretation of the quarrel as a conflict between a just, independent spirit and a lustful, covetous tyrant is consistent. Later in Book 1, Achilles vents his anger in the round terms of censure that Athena herself had advised. This is the result:

> Certe multo melius est, per exercitum latum Achiuorum
> Dona auferre, quicunque tibi contradixerit:
> Populi vorator Rex . . .
>
> [Loeb, 1:229–31; de Sponde, p. 12]

> . . . tis more safe, *with contumelious breath,*
> *To show thy manhood* gainst a man that contradicts *thy lust*
> *And with thy covetous valour* take his spoiles *with force unjust,*
> *Because thou knowest a man of fame will take wrong ere he be*
> *A generall mischiefe, nor shamst thou though all the armie see.*
> Thou souldier-eating king . . .
>
> [CH 1. 1. 233–38]

Achilles, who has tempered his wrath and sheathed his sword seconds before, emerges from Chapman's translation as a wise and temperate man of honor, indeed, a patriotic defender of the public good. This is neither a Homeric nor a Renaissance Achilles Chapman is creating, and after a look at a veritable tour de force from Book 1, some preliminary conclusions about this uniquely Chapmanesque exemplary hero may be ventured.

After Nestor has attempted to cool the quarrel, Agamemnon, though deferential to Nestor's wise counsel, accuses Achilles of ambition. Achilles interrupts him:

> Certe timidusque & vilis vocari possem,
> Si iam tibi in omni re cessero quam dicis:
> Aliis iam haec iube, non enim mihi
> Praecipe: non enim me tibi obtemperaturum puto.
> Aliud autem tibi dico, tu autem in praecordiis mitte tuis:
> Manibus quidem non ego pugnabo, gratia puellae

Neque tecum, neque cum alio quouis, cum a me aufertis quod
  dedistis.

[Loeb, 1:293–99; de Sponde, p. 15]

Thou mightst esteeme me base
And cowardlie to let thee use thy will *in my disgrace;*
To beare such burthens never were my strength and spirites
  combinde,
But to reforme their insolence, and that thy soule should finde
Were it not hurt of common good more than mine owne delight.
But I, not soothing Nestor's sute, for right's sake reverence right,
Which thou dost servilely commend but violate it quite.
And this even in thy intrayles print—I'le not *prophane* my hand
With battell *in my lust's defence*: a gyrle cannot command
My honour and my force like thine, who yet commandes our hoast.
Slave live he to the world that lives slave to his lusts engrost.
But feed it, come, and take the dame. . . .

[CH 1. 1. 302–13]

Four lines later, when Achilles warns Agamemnon to keep his covetous hands away from his ship or pay in blood, Chapman's eye seizes
on "*sanguis niger*" and renders it according to moral psychology: "thy
blacke and *lust-burnt* bloud" (CH 1. 1. 316).

The importance of the above passage, however, resides not only in the
portrayal of the tyrant's greedy lust but in the sketch of Achilles as the
protector of the public good and torchbearer of civic probity. He is a
paragon of honor, worshiping the right for its own sake and tempering
his action with concern for the public good. Achilles seeks no public
adulation; he sees the right and recognizes his moral responsibility to act
on its behalf. Ironically, such virtue isolates Achilles from the lustful
tyrant and the society that supports him.

The larger issue of Achilles' integrity leading to actions counter to the
public good, the potential danger of the individual's adamant pride and
self-assumed moral authority undermining society's well-being—indeed,
the kinds of indictments Shakespeare will make soon in his *Troilus and
Cressida*—are encountered head-on by Chapman's interpretive translation. But they are encountered by assertion only. The moral law that
guides Achilles' conduct is innate; it is valid, one is asked to assume,

because in a Senecan world of corruption society can provide no objective moral standards. Homer's wrathful dragon, whose loyalty to self is stronger than that to his society, has been transformed into the only man willing to stand up for individual and societal moral values. Achilles' defiant stance might be compared to and contrasted with his heroic ancestor's: he is a Herculean reformer, but his mode of reform is passive defiance, not active assertion.

I shall return to Achilles' honor and civic virtue in a moment, but it will be interesting first to glance at Chapman's translation of Achilles' loss of Briseis and his subsequent prayer to Thetis. Chapman fabricates a dramatic inset to enhance the pathos of the departure scene and to apologize for the frustrated tears that follow it. One encounters Achilles' Herculean fortitude in lines without a trace of textual authority:

> Shee wept and lookt upon her love; he sigh't and did refuse.
> O how his wisdome with his power did mightilie contend—
> His love incouraging his power and spirite, that durst descend
> As far as Hercules for her, yet wisedome all subdude,
> Wherein a high exploite he showd, and sacred fortitude.
>
> [CH 1. 1. 360–64]

Here as elsewhere in the *Iliads*, Achilles' wise restraint and Stoic constancy is far different from the "Bodie's fervour and fashion of outward Fortitude to all possible height of Heroicall Action."[15] The point to be emphasized, however, is that this is Chapman's version of Stoicism, not at all the Stoic ideal of apathy. Achilles' heroic passion is present, is indeed Herculean in its grandeur, and part and parcel of Achilles' "high exploite" is that he curbs, not annihilates, it. The implication—and its importance cannot be overstressed in looking forward to the discussions of Bussy and Byron—is that active and passive "exploites" are not antithetical, but complementary modes of heroism, that the wise hero will either bridle or loose his heroic passion depending on the situation.

A real character crux appears soon after Briseis's departure, when Achilles entreats his mother to convince Jove

> To fight for Ilion and expell the Greekes to sea againe,
> Or, slaughterd at their Fleete, their lives may wreake their king's

offence
And he in his acknowledgde harmes confesse my Eminence.

[*CH* 1. 1. 412–14]

The translation here is surprisingly accurate in view of the fact that
Achilles' sentiment seems viciously self-serving, and at such a point one
might expect an apologetic expansion from Chapman.[16] De Sponde comments on the passage: "Achilles seeks nothing other but that the loss of
the Greeks be transformed into the gain of his personal glory—a sentiment which should scarcely be praised, much less imitated, by a good
man."[17] Nevertheless, Chapman's silence seems to signal approval for
Achilles, for soon after he has Thetis defend her son's entreaty as "An
honorable wreake" (*CH* 1. 1. 424), and later he incorporates de Sponde's
pejorative note into the expanded text of Thetis's plea to Jove:

> that the Greekes *may let him clearelie joy*
> *Gaine of his honour in their losse*, and so augment his fame
> *By that disgrace they let him beare to their eternall shame.*

[*CH* 1. 1. 499–501][18]

The implication is that Chapman understood the Greeks' near fatal defeat at the ships as the inevitable result of their acceding to Agamemnon's
crime against Achilles. Agamemnon, after all, has won rule over beasts
(*CH* 1. 1. 238), and a base-spirited society must pay for the tyrants
it supports.

To this point, we have witnessed Chapman's considerable effort to
defend Achilles' part in the ill-fated quarrel of Book 1. Achilles' self-
imposed isolation and his judicious retreat in the face of Agamemnon's
provocation exhibit heroic restraint. A similarly significant expansion is
inserted in summary position at the end of the embassy in Book 9, where
Chapman again defends Achilles' proud stance of isolation despite the
destructive consequences for the Greeks. Ajax turns to Ulysses and ad-
vises that there can be no profit in the embassy's lingering any longer at
Achilles' tent. He blasts Achilles' proud, implacable position on the issue
of a single girl (Briseis). To Chapman's mind, of course, the simple soldier has missed the point of Achilles' defiance. To make certain that the
reader has not similarly erred, he inserts into Achilles' response to Ajax a
significant and, by now, predictable apology:

Aiax nobilis, Telamonie, princeps populorum,
Omnia mihi ex animo visus es dixesse.
Sed mihi tumescit cor ira, quoties illius
Recordor, qui me contemptibilem inter Argiuos fecit,
Atrides, tanquam aliquem immunem aduenam.
                              [Loeb, 9:644–48; de Sponde, p. 171]

Noble Telamon, Prince of our souldiers here,
Out of thy heart I know thou speakst, and as thou holdst me deare:
But still, as often as I thinke how rudely I was usd
And like a stranger for all rites fit for our good refusd,
My heart doth swell against the man *that durst be so profane*
To violate his sacred place—not for my private bane,
But since wrackt vertue's generall lawes he shamelesse did infringe,
For whose sake I will loose the reines and give my anger swinge
Without my wisedome's least impeach.
                              [CH 1. 9. 610–18]

De Sponde had condemned Achilles' adamant posture in Homer's text, beginning "Learned men in Ethics will teach that this is not the voice of wisdom. . . ."[19] Chapman needed an apologetic expansion and provided it. The tyrant has abused the public good, and Achilles stands adamant not because of a personal grudge but because he must defend virtue's general law. Achilles' individual pursuit of virtue is thus linked with universal virtue, and in Stoic terminology this means simply that an individual must govern his own actions according to the universal law of nature of which his own individual nature is a part. Here is an ethical sanction above the mutable and corrupt mores of society. It is not difficult to see, however, that such a philosophy, of which the definitions of virtue, honor, and integrity are conceived by a committee of one, is vulnerable to Shakespeare's charge of proud self-delusion in *Troilus and Cressida* or, for that matter, the Son's charge of philosophic pride in Milton's *Paradise Regained* (4. 300–308). Nevertheless, the potential danger inherent in the individual's determining his own course of action with godlike assurance of its righteousness is countered by Achilles' mere assertion of virtue and sanctioned (presumably) by the patent immorality of Agamemnon and the base society that props him up. In the translator's mind, wisdom has passed a favorable judgment on Achilles' anger; the "Predominant Perturbation" has been transformed into "just wrath"

(*CH* 1. 9. 620),[20] becoming a heroic passion of the mind, a rational passion, an *ira per zelum*.

Isolated in this way, Chapman's "translation" of Achilles runs through the *Iliads* with the force of an allegorical motif. There is much at issue beneath the surface text of Homer's Achilles, and Chapman has done his best to bring the "soule" of the hero's honorable isolation to the eyes of the Elizabethan reader. Achilles is defended on both ethical and moral grounds; he displays both personal and civic virtue. Achilles' "pursuit of Eternitie" in defiance of a "Pessant-common" society,[21] his virtuous individualism, and the personal suffering it brings, reflecting obliquely on the heroic ideals and tragic fates of Bussy and Byron (and more directly on those of Clermont), also provide an insight into Chapman's dedication of the *Iliads* to the Earl of Essex.

If the defense of Achilles was most likely considered eccentric by Chapman's Elizabethan readers, who were wont to trace their national heritage to legendary Trojan heroes,[22] the portrayal of the Earl of Essex as the contemporary exemplar of Achillean virtue probably smacked of bold partisanship.

> Most true Achilles (whom by sacred prophecie Homere did but prefigure in his admirable object and in whose unmatched vertues shyne the dignities of the soule and the whole excellence of royall humanitie), let not the Pessant-common polities of the world, that count all things servile and simple that pamper not their own private sensualities, burying quick in their filthie sepulchres of earth the whole bodies and soules of honor, vertue and pietie, stirre your divine temper from perseverance in godlike pursute of Eternitie.[23]

Despite the blatant plea for patronage both in this passage and throughout the dedicatory preface, it would be a mistake not to take these sentiments seriously. Waddington has pointed out that Chapman's "De Guinea" was written in support of Sir Walter Ralegh's expansionism[24] and, given this political bent, Chapman most likely aligned himself with the war party of Ralegh and Essex (on this issue they were in agreement) against the Lord Burghley–Robert Cecil coterie. Whether the dedication was written after Essex received the infamous "box in the ear" from the queen's hand is not crucial, for Essex's turbulent history during the period after the Azores campaign and before the Irish expedition (ca. 1597–99) is well documented.[25] For Chapman and for many of his Elizabethan contemporaries, Essex embodied an individual ideal and a political cause threatened by the petty politicians at court. That is context enough for the hyperbolic dedication.

The dedicatory passage quoted above sounds a telling Chapmanesque chord. The nobility of Achilles continued to exist in Essex, and the contemporary exemplar of heroic idealism, unique for his divine virtue and fated to be misunderstood by his barbarous world, assumes the lonely stance of a tragic hero. Essex is a giant among petty men. Indeed, the passage epitomizes the thought and tone of the entire dedicatory preface, being at once an enthusiast's celebration of the heroic spirit and a pessimist's acknowledgment of inevitable tragedy. The preface to the *Iliads* thus anticipates the Senecan backdrop that will stand behind and frame, as if an a priori assumption, the tragic fates of Chapman's dramatic heroes. Time would pass, however, before Chapman wrote his heroic tragedies, and his conception of individual heroism would become more penetrating and complex. One can safely speculate, I think, on the reasons for his changing conception. First, the pagan heroic ethos in the second half of Homer's *Iliad* and Achilles' awesome wrath do not readily translate into the Elizabethan ethical code; and second, like Achilles, Essex had moved beyond the bounds of rational, virtuous restraint. Achilles' irrational fury in the second half of *The Iliad* and Essex's impulsive blunder in 1601 forbade a partisan portrayal of them as heroic victims, such as Chapman had offered in 1598. For these reasons, although Chapman continued to believe that Homer's Achilles was the exemplary hero of an exemplary epic and that there was something of value in Essex's aspiring spirit, his initial admiration of Achillean heroism was later qualified by moral condemnation of its excesses and—in the case of Essex —a recognition of the hero's complicity in his own demise. The ambivalent portrayal of Bussy's and Byron's Achillean heroism suggests that although Chapman cannot provide a full-blown defense of the heroic spirit on moral grounds, as he did in 1598, he is nevertheless willing to offer an apologetic explanation of the extraordinary "godlike pursute of Eternitie" that is the source of the heroes' tragic grandeur.

To return to the dedicatory preface of the *Iliads*, Chapman believed that the individual's pursuit of "fame, honor, and love of the best" was a noble passion and the hallmark of a humane and civilized society; but, given the decadence of the contemporary world, the heroic exemplars of "royall humanitie," those unique embodiments of human excellence and dignity of "soule," were cast into tragic roles on the world stage. Similarly, the patronless poet who understood human excellence and shared its passion was himself a hero, and like his epic hero and tragic heroes he, too, was fated to be misunderstood, and his life was fated to be tragic.[26] Nevertheless, the heroic poet would tell the stories of his contemporary heroes as only he could interpret, translate, and recreate them. The translator of *The Iliad* considered himself not so much a celebrator of the past as a visionary interpreter of the present, a contemporary seer who could discern the manifestations of human excellence that would otherwise be hidden from his blind and decadent age. This visionary stance perhaps explains why Chapman writes of recent historical figures (Bussy, Byron, the Guise, and Chabot), translates Achilles into a contemporary ethical context, and points to Essex as the living exemplar of Achillean virtue. Like the allusion to Achilles gracing Essex in 1598, the mythological and historical allusions that later accompany Bussy and Byron are not simply descriptive analogues. They appeal to a single, shared ideal; for their possessors are archetypal embodiments of a timeless, noble, but inevitably tragic "pursute of Eternitie."

To Chapman's mind, then, the mythic form of the *Iliads* reveals an archetypal pattern of heroism centered on Achilles' virtuous retreat from the degenerate society in which he lives. Like a star in the night, the exemplary hero stands apart from and in opposition to a potentially tragic, decidedly Senecan, milieu. Society has need of ancient virtue—whether to defend the ships against Hector and the Trojans or to quell the rebellion of Tyrone and the Irish—but the exemplar of epic ideals has been rejected, and society shall pay for its mistake. Shakespeare also attempts to evaluate Achilles' isolation and probe the "soule" of epic heroism, but his *Troilus and Cressida* reveals no shimmering light of virtue at the heart of either the hero or the heroic culture of *The Iliad*.

HEROIC MYTH-MAKING AT TROY

In her seminal essay on *Troilus and Cressida*, Una Ellis-Fermor celebrates Shakespeare's unique achievement in being able to confront a vision of the "disintegration of civilization" and to reflect the "imminent dissolution" in a conscious dramatization of discord and disharmony.[27] The playwright was able to give form to the intellectual and imaginative wreckage envisioned in the material of the play—a remarkable feat and perhaps the finest achievement in what R. J. Kaufmann has called the pretragic period of "preliminary devaluation."[28] Ellis-Fermor's thesis focuses on a central question of *Troilus and Cressida*: is there, or can there be, an absolute standard of value? She finds that in 1602 Shakespeare's answer was a masterfully discordant "No."

The critical premise of Ellis-Fermor's essay is that *Troilus and Cressida* is a metaphor for the dramatist's vision. Given this premise, the critic then suggests that Shakespeare is projecting on stage his own fruitless quest for absolute standards of value and, hence, the wreckage of his own civilization. Ellis-Fermor's suggestion is mistaken, I believe, not because it is biographical fallacy, but because the subject matter of the play defines a heroic culture unlike Shakespeare's, confining his pessimistic vision within the limits of an alien dramatic world. The vision conveyed through the dramatic medium is not the "disintegration of civilization" but of *a* civilization governed by heroic ideals, not man's fruitless quest for absolute value but the heroic psyche's failure to find absolute value in the crass physicality and illusory idealism of love and war. The twin heroic quests of love and war, dominating dramatic plot and characterization from beginning to end, create just such an impression: one of limitation, of narrow-mindedness, of closed-mindedness, of a world isolated by its heroic code from normative social behavior. The heroes love when they do not want to love and war when they do not want to war because the alternative to both is loss of heroic identity. To the heroic ego this loss is tantamount to self-annihilation, and nothing— not natural law, rational judgment, religion, or political stability—will deflect the heroes from what they see as a course of self-preservation.

E. R. Dodds's distinction between the "shame culture" of *The Iliad* and the "guilt culture" of the Greek tragedians is helpful in illuminating the heroic world of *Troilus and Cressida*.[29] In a "guilt culture," such as our own or that of the Elizabethans, the individual is subservient to a god or some ultimate power; his life is a test, and he is constantly measuring himself against an external code of behavior. He is racked by anxiety; he lives in fear of God and yearns for a quiet conscience. In the "shame culture" of the heroes, however, the emphasis is on individualism, on bold action and self-assertion; life is not a test but a fulfillment of one's nature, a completion of one's personal destiny. The individual lives not in fear of God but in respect of public opinion; his goal is not a quiet conscience but self-esteem and public approbation. To varying degrees, all of the active warriors to be discussed in this study have pledged allegiance to this alien cultural ideal. The self-assertion in quest of personal fulfillment, the fierce pursuit of honor, and the extraordinary paroxysms of shame distinguish their personal code of behavior from society's normative standards. Only in *Troilus and Cressida* and in *Coriolanus*, however, are the heroes' ideals fully consonant with the ethos of society. In *Coriolanus*, the heroic culture is "written in" to the play from beginning to end; in *Troilus and Cressida*, Shakespeare creates the alien culture for his audience by "writing out" Elizabethan moral and political assumptions.

Hector's lecture on Aristotle and natural law, deliberately anachronistic, initially may seem to establish an Elizabethan perspective for judging the Trojan course of action; but the fact that the moral prohibitions are leagued with reason and promptly defied, never again to resurface, indicates that the anachronism was introduced not to reveal what is normative so much as what is irrelevant to the heroic culture. Similarly, Ulysses' speech on degree suggests that Elizabethan political idealism is equally anachronistic and irrelevant to the play's world. Believe what he will "by way of truth," Ulysses' pragmatic resolution is that the chaos of emulous egos, the raw material of the heroic society, must be controlled as in a competitive race so that the heroes might be lopped off one by one in the linear progression of time. This ordering principle, not degree, ensures that society will not wither away in a state of paralysis or destroy itself in a chaotic free-for-all.

The values of natural law, rational judgment, religion, and political stability, announced and preemptively withdrawn in such a way that forbids their functioning as satirical norms,[30] help define the closed heroic world of *Troilus and Cressida*. The play dramatizes the relationship of the heroes' psychological compulsions and the values of the heroic culture the warriors dominate, displaying Shakespeare's singular genius for intellectually and imaginatively entering into the assumptions of a civilization and pursuing them to their logical conclusions.[31] Within the limitations of the dramatic subject, Ellis-Fermor's sense of discord and disharmony is precisely to the point.

The locus of Shakespeare's pessimism, therefore, will not be found in the satirical reflections the stage world casts upon Elizabethan society, but rather in the dramatist's conception of "the matter of Troy": what is the heroism of heroic legend all about? Is it of value? Can it be forwarded as a contemporary ideal? At these points Shakespeare's interest in the Troy saga touches Chapman's interest in translating *The Iliad*. The "soule" of Chapman's translation of Achilles provides an aesthetic and ideational foil for *Troilus and Cressida*, and though Shakespeare's broader examination of heroism cannot be argued simply as a concentrated attack on *Iliads*, nevertheless Chapman does not escape the hit.[32] Clearly Shakespeare had no inclination to translate bloody, ego-centered heroism into an ideal for contemporary nobility. Chapman sees in Achilles a flame of virtue that radiates outward to inform his honorable action; Shakespeare's more general, yet more pointed, insight into heroic passion, honor, pride, and decorum discovers a sick and destructive egomania. *Troilus and Cressida* is what Shakespeare sees in the sham heroism of Troy, and he distorts his medieval and epic sources according to his insight.

One thing that Shakespeare most certainly perceived in the legends of Troy, incorporating it into his play as a dramatic principle, was that the heroes were time-servers. What has been going on all these years? How could it go on so long? The systematic undercutting of plot and language, of action and idealism, and the resulting emphases on vain design, empty verbiage, and ceremonial gesture suggest an answer.[33] The heroic world of Troy exists in the subjunctive mood of "propositions," "hopes," "supposes," "unbodied figures of thought," "surmises," "assumptions," "opinions," "reputes," and "imputations" (1. 3. 1–30, 333–47). The subjunctive mood not only accommodates the sense of paralysis that hangs over the unfinished business but also suggests that the warriors' heroic conceptions of themselves are unreal. In different ways and to different degrees the heroes have all created heroic myths in their own images. Like poet-actors they construct their fiction of love and war and move through the heroic setting largely outside of time and immune to reality.[34] Cressida might speak for them: wooing and beseeching create an idealized world beyond the taint of time or fact; but things won are done, the curtain drawn is an illusion destroyed. The heroes are poets living their own fiction, players living their own illusion. Ulysses and Troilus are bent on consummation and—unwittingly—bent on the destruction of the illusion.

The war must continue because the heroes' creation of love and war in their own heroic images is accompanied by a compulsive belief in the twin fictions. The broad vista of the heroic world is stocked with self-congratulatory symbols of heroism—trumpets, heraldry, armor, *débats*, bombast, enemies, rivals, lovers, pledges, vows. Achilles' remarks about beauty, set in a context defining honor as "Opinion" and arguing the necessity of communicating virtue to others, may serve as a gloss on the heroic narcissism in the play:

ACHIL.: ... nor doth the eye itself,
That most pure spirit of sense, behold itself,
Not going from itself; but eye to eye opposed,
Salutes each other with each other's form;
For speculation turns not to itself,
Till it hath travell'd and is [mirror'd] there
Where it may see itself.

[3. 3. 105–11]

One sees oneself in the enemy and so puffs up the opponent as a self-tribute, or one sees in the enemy a worthy target for an acquisitive ego and so vaunts and threatens. The strange ogling between Hector and Achilles and the ridiculous verbiage of "noblest, hateful love" that passes as chivalric decorum are reflections of a sick egomania. The heroic world has become the proud warriors' glass, trumpet, chronicle; and the twin fictions of love and war are conceived of as congratulatory expressions of heroic identity.

At the center of the fiction is Helen. Both camps must idolize her or lose their heroic quarrel.

HECT.:   Hector's opinion
Is this in way of truth; yet ne'er the less,
My spritely brethren, I propend to you
In resolution to keep Helen still,
For 'tis a cause that hath no mean dependance
Upon our joint and several dignities.
TRO.: Why, there you touch'd the life of our design! ...
She is a theme of honor and renown,
A spur to valiant and magnanimous deeds,
Whose present courage may beat down our foes,
And fame in time to come canonize us.

[2. 2. 188–202]

Hector reneges on truth, natural law, rationality, and reality as a matter of survival. The "life of our design," in Troilus's phrase, is precisely the "joint and several dignities," the subjunctive world of surmise, the heroic fiction built up around Helen and the war. Hector is compelled to believe the fiction, for the life of his heroic identity and that of the entire heroic myth they are creating and living is at stake. Though a moralist might condemn his volte-face as a self-betrayal, in a heroic culture that holds "honor far more precious-dear than life" (5. 3. 28), it would be a worse self-betrayal *not* to believe the fiction. For all the clear-eyed perception of the waste Helen has caused, the real destruction in terms of lives is less fearful than the destruction of the heroic illusion. For the world to remain a proving ground for the heroic spirit, to remain a culture reflecting heroic ideals, then moral and political orthodoxies, supported by reason, truth, judgment, and religion, must be summarily dismissed as alien or irrelevant value systems.

Troilus's interpretive commentary on Hector's volte-face reveals the heroic fiction in the process of creation. Helen is a symbol, but like Cressida, or the idealized woman of Hector's challenge, or the enemy puffed up in worth, she is a projection of the heroic ego. The idolatry bestowed on the fictive "gods" is inescapably a self-idolatry, a supreme pride that is the root cause of the war, the paralysis, the empty talk, the half-hearted resolve, and the time-serving that thwart meaningful action.[35] Though the forms of self-idolatry are protean and its practitioners are legion, Achilles—significantly—is its principal exemplar.

Buoyed by the obeisance of his peers, Achilles creates in his own mind a god of such proportion that no service can be commensurate with the deity's worth.

> ULYSS.:   Possess'd he is with greatness,
> And speaks not to himself but with a pride
> That quarrels at self-breath. Imagin'd worth
> Holds in his blood such swoll'n and hot discourse
> That 'twixt his mental and his active parts
> Kingdom'd Achilles in commotion rages,
> And batters down himself.
>
>   [2. 3. 170–76]

The fiction has taken over the fiction-maker. The second, alien identity that possesses Achilles is a heroic image so overprized that no word or deed is worthy of the god in residence. Achilles' self-idolatry, it may be argued, is Shakespeare's mocking retort to Chapman's version of virtuous isolation and self-assumed moral authority. Equally important, Achilles' infatuation with heroic image, militating against rational, purposeful social action and loosing a furious, self-destructive rage upon the microcosm, suggests in epitome the process by which an entire heroic civilization has turned inward upon its own passionate, delusive conceits of grandeur and will eventually be destroyed by the very fiction it has self-consciously fostered.

The Greeks know that Achilles' egomania must be burst and the disease evacuated. Ulysses will be the physician (3. 3. 44–49). Agamemnon had stressed that self-worth must be evaluated by objective standards of performance and merit reflected in the judgment of others. Ulysses, however, is an extraordinary temporizer who trades not in absolute cures but in behavior modification. His remedy will not deflate Achilles' self-idolatry, but will redirect the service from an internal to an external god.

Ulysses' task is made easier by Achilles' predisposition toward the concept of honor. Achilles' "honor" is external tribute only, subject to Fortune and Opinion:

> A C H I L . : And not a man, for being simply man,
> Hath any honor, but honor for those honors
> That are without him, as place, riches, and favor—
> Prizes of accident as oft as merit.
>
> [3. 3. 80–83]

Ulysses soon makes the logical deduction: no man is master of anything unless it is reflected by others' praise. Honor must be defined and bestowed by others. This, of course, is a distortion of the Aristotelian concept of honor and a notion precisely opposite to that of Chapman's Achilles. The concepts of integrity, of honor as the shadow of inward virtue, and of action proceeding from reason in accord with natural law are strikingly absent. To specify the nature of the contrast further, one might note that Chapman's Achilles would have endorsed Guillaume DuVair's definition of honor: "Indeede true honour is the glittering & beaming brightnes of a good and vertuous action, which rebounds from our consciences vnto the sight of them with whom we liue, and so by a reflection of our selues, brings vs a testimonie from others of the good opinion which they haue of vs. . . . Now this good dooth wholly depend on vs."[36] But rather than honor coming from inner virtue, or virtue being applauded by one's own conscience, or noble actions being rewarded in the performance of them,[37] the definition Achilles and Ulysses advance fits DuVair's notion of "ambition for honor," according to which some seek not after the virtuous essence of honor but "embrace a shadowe in stead of a bodie, and hasten the rest of our minds vpon the opinion of the vulgar sort of people . . . to serue the humours and passions of other men, and are compelled to displease our selues to please them which doe behold vs: so that our affections are hanged vpon the eyes of other men."[38]

Two telling similes fill out the implications of the quest for false honor:

> U LY S S . :   . . . no man is the lord of any thing,
> Though in and of him there be much consisting,
> Till he communicate his parts to others;
> Nor doth he of himself know them for aught,
> Till he behold them formed in th' applause
> Where th' are extended; who like an arch reverb'rate
> The voice again, or like a gate of steel,
> Fronting the sun, receives and renders back
> His figure and his heat.
>
> [3. 3. 115–23]

Having taken away the rational, moral essence of honor from the doer, Ulysses implies that the "communication" of parts need only be loud or flamboyant; for "th' applause" is all, and in fact the bestower of honor makes no rational, moral judgment either.[39] The "opinion of the vulgar sort of people," like stone or steel, simply echoes the voice and reflects the heat of the doer.

Ulysses convinces Achilles to pursue this grimly parodic notion of honor as if it were a commendable principle of heroic behavior. The appetite for honor, seconded by will, put into action by brute, amoral power, will garner the approbation of the blockish multitude. Achilles' murder of Hector follows precisely from the implications of this dialogue. The Myrmidons' cry that "Achilles hath the mighty Hector slain!" (5. 8. 14) will be "echoed" as a heroic fact, not recognized as a despicable lie, by the blockish multitude in the Greek camp and among future generations of readers. It also follows that the notion of time may be defined according to the process of communication Ulysses has outlined. The echo dies soon after the shout, and unless one shone continually like the sun (and it sets each night), the light and heat would die when the combustion died. The present is all one can hope for, and so Achilles must enter the acquisitive, diurnal, competitive race for honor or be trampled. This he is now willing to do.

The dialogue with Ulysses concluded, Achilles shifts his reverential gaze outside from himself, momentarily waking to the competition with Ajax and expressing the need for self-reflection from without in a gush of narcissism:

ACHIL.:   I have a woman's longing,
An appetite that I am sick withal,
To see great Hector in his weeds of peace,
To talk with him, and to behold his visage,
Even to my full of view.

[3. 3. 237–41]

Love and hate for enemy and ally—when the world is a glass for ego, the terms are interchangeable. Only the worst kind of cynicism or a strikingly naive miscalculation could have motivated Ulysses to loose Achilles' self-idolatry on the external world.

The inset that closes the scene is masterful burlesque. Ajax's heroic introspection recalls Achilles' earlier "possession" and, located here, fills out the portrait of a Janus-faced ego. Self-conceit is reflected from without, the thesis of the Ulysses-Achilles dialogue, or from within, from one's own valuation. Ajax is lost in himself, his ego projecting a heroic vision of the encounter with Hector in the theater of the mind. Like Achilles' pride earlier, Ajax's pride has removed him from the community of men and the language of discourse; his godlike excellence has set him above his peers, and only the language of heroic action can fully express his essence. And so the pageant is played out, with Thersites (playing Ajax) distracted from reality and living in the promise of the future encounter; for one who "wears his tongue in 's arms" (3. 3. 270), the "hum's" and "ha's" seem the proud warrior's gestic language and perhaps should be accompanied by massive swipes of the sword. Shakespeare will treat the self-possession syndrome seriously when he turns to *Coriolanus* later in his career, but for now the heroic introspection passes as burlesque.

Taken together, the portraits of Achilles and Ajax in act 3, scene 3, provide a dissection of Homer's warrior hero. When stripped of the legendary aura or of Chapman's interpretive apology and cut to the core, Greek heroism at Troy reveals a sick and savage egomania. "Savage," we recall, is the term Hector uses when he defends his "vice of mercy" against Troilus's charge of "Fool's play" (5. 3. 31–49), and it is a broad term that distinguishes Greek from Trojan. The Trojan heroic ideal is a flash-forward to the martial ideal of English history;[40] Hector is a chivalric warrior-lover, Troilus a chivalric lover-warrior. Next to Achilles and Ajax, the civilized Trojans are bound to seem more appealing to audience and reader. Their code of behavior is a life style in the full sense of the

41

phrase; the courtiers are equally at home in the salon and on the battle-field. Chivalry bridges the gap between the ego and its projection into action; it is a ready-made channel of communication, a behavioral code into which both lover and warrior may project their heroic identities. And yet, though an attractive mechanism because it shapes and mirrors individual ideals, Trojan chivalry is little more than a dreamer's fiction or a player's role.[41] There is little to indicate that Shakespeare's criticism of Trojan self-idolatry is less sharp than that of the Greeks. In fact, as with the case of Ulysses, the criticism may be more pointed simply because Hector and Troilus cannot be reduced to the level of burlesque. Hector sees the truth early and will not face it; Troilus sees the truth late and will not face it. What distinguishes them primarily is that Hector is often able to realize his chivalric ideals through symbolic action; for Troilus, this will not do.

Hector's distinctive characteristic as a warrior is that he is proud and courteous at the same time. Appetitive passion for honor will spur him to the field and shame will fire him with heroic wrath, but as often as not these passions are sublimated into a chivalric code of behavior that mea-sures and reflects Hector's ideal conception of self. The "translation" of appetitive passion into heroic image is evident in the challenge to maiden battle and in the subsequent exchange of accolades with Ajax and the Greeks, but nowhere more painfully evident than in Hector's "vice of mercy." Superficially the "vice" seems the attribute of a humane sensi-bility (4. 5. 105–6, 183–91); one knows from the Trojan council, how-ever, that the behavior is not motivated by moral principle or humane considerations, but by a selfish compulsion to gain glory and to realize a heroic conception of self. Aeneas asserts that what looks like Hector's pride is really courtesy (4. 5. 81–82); but, weighed well, Hector's chiv-alry manifests a fatal pride. "Fool's play," Troilus calls it, and he is right. Hector's dream of war as a symbolic, chivalric enterprise is burst by a shock of tragic reality even at the hero's most courteous moment.

Hector had been urged to stay out of the fray, Cassandra implying that his entry into the battle would be tantamount to suicide and betrayal of Troy (5. 3. 89–90). But the hero stood resolute; honor, integrity, and the life of his heroic identity were at stake. Then, as earlier in the Trojan council, it would have been a worse betrayal of self and country if he had burst the illusion, even though the voices of reason discerned that the illusion was a façade for death and destruction. When Hector takes to the field in act 5, he mows down the Greeks with grim alacrity: "Here, there, and every where, he leaves and takes, / Dexterity so obeying appetite / That what he will he does . . ." (5. 5. 26–28). Shakespeare deliberately avoids an idealization of Hector's "vice of mercy" in these lines. Appetite commands the will both to kill and let live, to "leave and take" from the grim feast of war. Just so, in the next scene, when Hector stands over a helpless Achilles and will not press the advantage, the "vice of mercy" manifests only a superficial nobility. "I do disdain thy *courtesy, proud* Troyan," says Achilles (5. 6. 14; my emphasis), and—unwittingly, one suspects—he speaks to the point. What seems like courtesy is really pride. For Hector to kill Achilles under these circumstances would be a death blow to his heroic identity, a fatal betrayal of the honorable chivalric code in the idealistic extremes of which he has fashioned his conception of self. To kill Achilles would be to "kill" his heroic image (and to bring the curtain down on the heroic stage as well); but to release Achilles would not only preserve but enhance his heroic conception of self.

It is a deeply disturbing and perhaps a consummate irony in the play that Hector's magnificent nonaction is thus a manifestation of acquisitive pride, but such is the case. Unmercifully at this point, Shakespeare has Hector charge off symbol-chasing, passionately hunting the shining armor and superficial glitter in which he has dressed his heroic identity. The courteous incident with Achilles and the proud incident with the "goodly mark" are juxtaposed because they are complementary expressions of an acquisitive ego. Both are reintroduced in Hector's final scene when he is betrayed by the reality of death beneath honor's glittering façade.[42]

When Hector remarks the "putrified core" beneath the "goodly armor" (5. 8. 1–4), it would be reassuring to know that he achieves self-recognition in his final moments: that he finally understands that his own honorable code is only skin deep and that he has been living a fiction and playing a role. But Shakespeare is not inclined to press for Hector's *anagnorisis*. When the hero disarms, one cannot be certain whether it is a conscious symbolic gesture or a thoughtless tactical mistake. In either case—whether a conscious renunciation of the heroic illusion and thus a symbolic suicide ending the fictive "life" of heroism, or a suicidally naive testimony of faith in the code of fair play with which he identifies his heroic image—his life, real and fictive, is done. His body is brutalized, and if the editorial suggestion that he *"hangs his shield behind him"* (5. 8. 4 S.D.) is accepted, the shield stands not as a relic of godlike heroism, but as a symbol of the hollow heroic code that he has consciously fostered and idolized. Hector is the pathetic victim of a self-fiction that is ultimately vulnerable to the reality he chose to idealize in his own case and foolishly ignore in those around him.

Unlike his older brother, Troilus is unable to sublimate passion. It is not enough for him to bask in the self-congratulatory symbols he creates. Troilus's imaginative idealizations, born of the senses and nurtured with affections, have the boomerang effect of heightening the affections' appetite. The interplay of appetite and imagination creates a precipitous urgency driving the will toward action, event, consummation. It is only a slight exaggeration (and tautology) to say that for Troilus every act is a consummate act; what is done is done, what is not done must be done. Proof, tasting (testing), fact, event crown passion's quest; the symbol is a spur to glorious consummation in love and war. Unlike Hector, he is not content to fulfill the role of chivalric lover-warrior; the "pearl" is found in Cressida's bed. For Troilus symbols have meaning not in and of themselves, but only insofar as they spur results. Symbolic meaning is contingent on reality.

But Troilus is by no means a simple pragmatist. As much or more so than the others, his subjective mode of evaluation leads him to idolize Cressida and Helen, the objects of his amatory and martial quests, and so, by reflection, to enhance his own conception of self as heroic lover and heroic warrior. The problem is, however, that the real Cressida and the real Helen give the lie to his idealized vision of them, thus threatening his own heroic image. In response to this threat, Troilus simply enshrines his heroic idealism as inviolate authority for all that he does, and the spin-off of this self-deification is the unlikely doctrine of nonconvertible value: a decision made cannot be undone, what was right cannot be wrong, the ideal cannot be devalued by reality. Troilus's idealism may have been engendered by his passions, but it soon takes on a life of its own. He hangs onto his idealism as if he were hanging onto his identity, and such is the case.[43] To deny the value of the symbols he idealizes would be to deny the value of the heroic passions that created them and so burst the illusion of the heroic identity.

One thing that is clear in the web of illogicality is that Troilus does not believe in the embodiment of his ideals so much as in his own idealism. The symbols are important to Troilus not for themselves but because he has projected himself into them. As Cressida and Helen are symbols reflecting his own identity as heroic lover and warrior, he is their zealous apologist; yet he is also a clear-eyed skeptic about the value of both

44

women in and of themselves. He knows that Helen is not worth the fight (1. 1. 192–94), that she is a whore (1. 2. 174–81), and that time mocks achievement; and he fears that Cressida will not stay true (4. 4. 60–94) and that fortune devours love (4. 5. 293–94). But he refuses to consider that his idealism is as transitory as its embodiments and that his heroic conception of self, subject to time and reality, will suffer a devaluation similar to that of the symbols reflecting it. A Trojan partisan might pass off Troilus's protestations of truth and simplicity as an aspiration for excellence, the more innocent and attractive for their sincerity and na- iveté; but Troilus protests too much, and when salted with his own skepticism about the women he idolizes, the protestations seem more like willful self-deception, his pursuit of excellence more like a quest for heroic canonization (see 2. 2. 202).

The preservation of Troilus's idealism and the heroic identity it sup- ports is clearly at odds with his belief that symbolic meaning is contingent on reality. The conflict tears him apart at the crisis of the love plot.[44] Revealingly, the crisis comes not at the exchange of Cressida for Antenor; Troilus accepts it fatalistically and cashes in on the opportunity for a heroic au revoir with a typical outpouring of idealism for which the sleeve stands as symbol. When Cressida delivers herself and the token of Troilus's idealism to Diomedes in act 5, however, the heroic lover is split in two. At first Troilus would "swagger" out of existence the testimony of eyes and ears in favor of the idealistic image of Cressida he bears in his heart, but reality's claim for allegiance is equally strong: the event crowns all (2. 2. 118–20). Diomedes' Cressida stretches "rule in unity" to its limits, the reality of Cressida existing incompatibly alongside Troilus's idealization of Cressida. Troilus is caught in the web of his own contra- dictory beliefs; the escape is as predictably desperate as it is illogical. He will preserve his heroic identity in spite of reality; he rejects reality in fa- vor of his idealism, rejects the "two traded pilots" of eyes and ears (2. 2. 61–65) in favor of autonomous will and pure subjectivism. It is not Cressida he will fight for, but his love for Cressida—not the objective embodiment of his idealism, but the idealism itself. She is false, but he must be true—to himself and to his heroic image. The "life" and value of the sleeve as symbol of Troilus's heroic image is more "precious dear" than Troilus's real self. "I come to lose my arm, or win my sleeve" (5. 3. 96) is a grotesque rendition of the central issue.

Troilus never does regain the sleeve, nor would it matter if he did. Once enshrined as inviolate authority, willful passion provides more symbols than he can cope with. Will generates passion, passion generates appetite, and the now deluded instruments of willful passion, the eyes and ears, seize on symbol after symbol. The sleeve is forgotten for the horse, the horse for the revenge of Aeneas's capture, Aeneas for the revenge of Hector—the evaluations and actions becoming a discontinuous series of momentary passions and transitory enactments written on the sands of time, each desperate act bent toward a consummation that consummates nothing. Troilus senses (5. 10. 7–9), but never fully acknowledges, that death is the only consummation amidst the chaos within and without. His final exit promises a fatalistic rush toward destruction.[45] Like those of the other heroes—Achilles, Ajax, and Hector—Troilus's sick heroic psyche reflects, as microcosm the macrocosm, the impending annihilation of a sick heroic civilization.

TWO VERSIONS OF HEROISM

The *Iliads* and *Troilus and Cressida* anticipate the distinctive emphases Chapman and Shakespeare will bring to their heroic tragedies. The Senecan pessimism of the *Iliads* and the sharp individuation of hero from society on ethical grounds look forward to the ethical emphasis, the titanic individualism, and the social and situational conflicts of Chapman's heroic tragedies. *Troilus and Cressida* brings to the fore the interrelationship of martial and amatory ideals, the tendency to demythologize legendary titans whom tradition and "translation" have made larger than life, the stress on heroic delusion, and in general the emphasis on psychological conflict in Shakespeare's heroic tragedies. Perhaps more important for us, however, are the precise points of disagreement about the soldier's psyche, the epic genre, and the heroic tradition.

In Chapman's mind the heroic spirit is similar to Homeric *areté*; it is a *libido excellendi*,[46] an inherent aspiration for excellence. This aspiration, whether expressed as the "high exploite" of martial prowess or the "high exploite" of unshakable integrity and virtuous restraint, is an extraordinary quality, an attribute distinguishing the hero from ordinary men. Even when Bussy and Byron respond to a perplexing situation with actions unworthy of their idealism, the idealistic aspiration itself, the "godlike pursute of Eternitie," remains heroic, praiseworthy, excellent, astonishing. Shakespeare, on the other hand, defines the heroic spirit more narrowly. In *Troilus and Cressida*, he displays a simple yet acute insight into the genesis of heroic aspiration: the martial appetite for honor and the erotic appetite for love are psychologically indistinguishable. The heroic psyche translates Helen and Cressida into symbols of virile prowess, and the egocentric aspiration to possess the quest symbols is a radical form of self-idolatry. The martial and amatory idealism of "the matter of Troy" thus cloaks a base, appetitive passion which idolators of the heroic tradition and the self-idolizing heroes themselves have "translated" into an idealistic aspiration for excellence. In general, then, while Chapman would apologize for the heroic spirit, indeed translate the heroic passion for honor and individual excellence into something rich and rare, Shakespeare would devaluate the heroic passion, deflating the pretensions to honor and excellence that gild a destructive egomania.

Nothing is more impressive in *Troilus and Cressida* than the systematic deflation of the language and gestures of epic idealism. Although Chapman will also use epic evocations to place the hero's idealism and his real achievements in ironic juxtaposition, in Chapman's dramas the actions dictated by the heroic spirit are tragic because they are acted out in a social situation uncongenial to heroic individualism. The hero's attempts to accommodate his idealism to a nonheroic environment may have the *ironic* effect of displacing the pursuit of eternity into unworthy actions, but they have the *tragic* effect of bringing his heroic individualism into direct conflict with society's values and norms of behavior. In the broad sense in which the heroes are social misfits, their tragic conflicts are situational. In *Troilus and Cressida*, Shakespeare's *ironic* emphasis falls on the reality that bursts heroic pretensions, while his *tragic* emphasis falls on the unreality of the heroic idealism itself. Shakespeare portrays Achilles and Ajax ironically, but he gives Hector and Troilus a tragic emphasis. Like Hotspur, both Trojan worthies are self-fated by delusive visions of grandeur. By choosing to live their personal epic myths as ideal warrior-lover and ideal lover-warrior, Hector and Troilus doom themselves; as they deliberately implicate society in their heroic fiction, they doom Trojan civilization as well.

Shakespeare's tragic emphasis on the heroes' false conceptions of self is conveyed by metaphors taken from the theater and poetics. Both suggest that the heroic images are fictions, that the heroes are creating self-conceits and playing roles untrue to their real selves. In Shakespeare's heroic tragedies, theatrical metaphors and evocations of heroic literature and legend are similarly used to anticipate or annotate the heroes' delusions of grandeur. At these moments, no matter what are the heroes' perceptions of self, the audience recognizes a tragic discrepancy between the human being and his heroic image. That alien identity must be cast aside before the grandeur of the heroes' human nature may be manifested. Although there are also ironic discrepancies in Chapman's heroic tragedies, the difference is this: Bussy's and Byron's heroic stances and language of heroic idealism are perceived by the audience as true expressions of self, as manifestations of the essential character. Even at moments of ironic deflation, epic evocations nevertheless convey the grandeur of the heroic spirit and its aspiration for excellence which, in a different situation, we recognize, would be not only astounding but admirable and exemplary. Tragedy does not negate the grandeur of heroic aspiration.

Finally, these different approaches to the soldier's tragic characterization suggest different conceptions of heroic tragedy. The reason *Troilus and Cressida* defies generic classification as comedy, tragedy, comical satire, and the like is that its energies are reactionary. It is a negative response to epic. Genre implies an affirmative stance in relation to the world; it defines reality by placing boundaries on it, affirming a vision of reality and the implicit values attendant on that vision.[47] In this respect *Troilus and Cressida* is a negative vision of the heroic genre in search of an affirmative countergenre. But as Shakespeare's insight into "the matter of Troy" affirms nothing, so comic, tragic, satiric beginnings in the play are abandoned or subverted, leaving a work of pure, self-contained irony, an "emptying out" of the heroic genre, as Colie would say.[48] In Shakespeare's heroic tragedies, tragedy itself becomes the assertive countergenre to epic, affirming its own claims of human limitation, yet human value, against delusive attempts at heroic myth-making. Heroism is reevaluated, redefined, and the new values filling up the empty heroic genre change it into something rich and strange. The ability of Othello to recognize his heroic pretensions as foolish, of Coriolanus to follow the promptings of his heart despite the derisive laughter of the gods, and of Antony and Cleopatra to embrace their blind love folly and die in testimony to its value—ironically, an acknowledgment of frailty, limitation, and folly predicates true human heroism and, as death is squarely confronted and accepted, true tragic grandeur.

Chapman also uses epic and tragedy as countergenres, but they are merely juxtaposed from beginning to end. Both genres stake a claim to truth and reality, and neither claim is denied in favor of that of the countergenre. The soldier's evocations of heroic grandeur are placed in sharp, often strident, contrast to the real world of social consensus; and though the epic evocations are perceived by the audience as expressions of the true self, of the essential character, tragedy's insistence on the failure of the heroic quest, on misguided aspiration, or on the limitations of the titanic heroism as an effective agent of social reformation is equally compelling. Chapman's conception of tragic grandeur measures the distance between normative behavior and heroic behavior. If tragedy speaks for social consensus in defining the overreacher's aspiration for excellence as abnormal and unacceptable, the heroic genre speaks for the grandeur of that aspiration. Like that of Essex in the dedication to the *Iliads*, the "godlike pursute of Eternitie" may be doomed to tragedy, but the heroic aspiration itself is never denied, and the grandeur of the epic vision of reality remains.

3

SHAKESPEARE'S *OTHELLO:*

SELF-BETRAYAL AND SELF-REVENGE

In one respect, Othello is unique among the tragic soldiers I shall discuss, for whereas the others violate principles of public responsibility and societal standards of conduct by following a course of excessive individualism, the heroic myth Othello unmetaphors into actual chosen behavior is that of dutiful servant of society. Although initially it may seem paradoxical that this racial and cultural alien should conform his heroic image to the values of Christian Venice, precisely because he is an alien, Othello is anxious about his place in Venetian society. This anxiety has led to a habitual pattern of behavior according to which individual desires are firmly governed by an excessively social consciousness.[1] As Othello would ground his "reputation," "good name," and "honor" on the opinion of Venetian social consensus,[2] individual ideals of martial heroism are enlisted in the service of state, and the private affairs of the heart are subordinated to the "cause" of propriety, morality, justice, and civic duty. Moments before the murder of Desdemona, Othello's heroic conception of self becomes that of God's surrogate on earth: "This sorrow's heavenly, / It strikes where it doth love" (5. 2. 21–22). Like the heavenly Governor, Othello would be a loving yet preeminently just administrator of the social and moral order.

But Othello, we know, is pathetically deluded. The self-styled minister of justice has become in truth a social monster. When Iago "proves" that Othello's love ideals have been betrayed by Desdemona and that his martial ideals have been made ridiculous by his own shameful deviancy from them, the Moor launches a frantic, passionate campaign to plume up his masculine ego. No matter the extent to which the heroic psyche translates the campaign into a self-congratulatory heroic myth,

the course of revenge is barbarously selfish. Othello's decorous pretension to social service cannot obscure the real "cause" of anarchic individualism; like those of the warriors at Troy, his heroic conception of self
gilds a destructive martial egomania.

Othello's tragedy is the more painful and pathetic because the former
love ideals continually break through the false conception of self he has
adopted. But they no sooner emerge than they are enlisted in the service
of the public persona. Remembrances of "humble love" rise in opposition to the Pontic currents of heroic resolution, but only to be gathered
up, to be perverted into fuel for the "cause," and so to speed Othello
on the tragic course with that much more forceful resolve. In the final
moments of the tragedy, Othello reaffirms the truth and value of Desdemona's love, but though this is done wisely it is done too late. Heroic
image and the fool in its service have won the day.

THE GENTLEMAN-SOLDIER

Critics searching for presentiments of Othello's fatal weakness tend to
attenuate the extraordinary dramatic force of his initial appearance on
stage. Shakespeare allows Iago to play upon Venetian and Elizabethan
racial and cultural biases, evoking in the audience's imagination a stereotypical Moor, an ugly black alien and a passionate sexual beast. But once
the hero steps on stage in flesh and blood, imaginative expectations are
exploded in such a way that the audience is likely chagrined by its tendency to think in stereotypes and, by way of apology, likely disposed to
enhance the Moor's manifest nobility. Othello is no bogeyman, no passionate monster, but a figure of aloof composure; the brief, decisive
assertions convey immense power and a decorous self-assurance that
belittle Iago's concerns and Brabantio's nervous preparations. The whirl-
wind of confusion and excitement in the first scene revolves around a
"wheeling stranger" of unshakable stability:

> OTH.:   Let him do his spite;
> My services which I have done the signiory
> Shall out-tongue his complaints. 'Tis yet to know—
> Which, when I know that boasting is an honor,
> I shall [provulgate]—I fetch my life and being
> From men of royal siege, and my demerits

> May speak, unbonneted, to as proud a fortune
> As this that I have reach'd; for know, Iago,
> But that I love the gentle Desdemona,
> I would not my unhoused free condition
> Put into circumscription and confine
> For the sea's worth.
>
> [1. 2. 17–28]

The first-person emphasis and striking use of the passive voice (see also 1. 2. 30–32, 47) have suggested to some a fatal egomania,[3] but in this context the quiet, measured assertions of Othello's initial apologia are certainly not boasts. Words are deeds for Othello; unschooled in the "soft phrase of peace" (1. 3. 82), the soldier must rely on his services to speak for him. Much as a commander might approach an impending battle, Othello has weighed the power of Brabantio against the strength of his own social service and heretofore unknown royal lineage; he is confident that he can meet Brabantio and Venetian social mores on their own ground and emerge from the confrontation victorious.

Regardless of the impression made by Othello's storied biography, the old soldier surveys a limited vista of experience from a predictably narrow point of view. He responds to crises with a martial mentality honed and reinforced by successful passages through dangers spanning a lifetime. Enemy strengths and motivations—whether Brabantio's or the Turk's—must be understood and measured before a strategy of action is determined; doubts must be erased before a course of action is decided on and executed with confident resolution. One perhaps senses the soldier's wariness, perhaps the strategic calculation, certainly the confident resolution in Othello's response to Brabantio's threat; but the analogy of society as a battlefield is serviceable only to the extent that one recognizes Othello's stance as the defensive posture of a racial and cultural alien fighting for social acceptance. If he can survive Brabantio's attack, the marriage will crown his social quest.

In this important respect, Othello's love for Desdemona should be distinguished from the dreamy idealism of Shakespeare's Trojans, particularly from Troilus's "narcissistic hunger for an absolute romantic dedication."[4] However bold and dangerous the elopement and secret marriage, Othello's quest is for social acceptance, for entrance into the domestic circumscriptions of love and social intercourse. If the amatory venture is successful, he will fulfill his desire of entering what Michael

Long has aptly termed Venice's "courtesy-culture."[5] In the early scenes of the play, the social consciousness governing his behavior is manifest. He speaks for rationality and decorum when confronting Brabantio's heated accusations; he speaks with deference in the Venetian council; and when the brawl erupts on Cyprus he appeals to Venice's religious values and social principles of propriety and order. Moreover, Othello seems anxious to demonstrate that he loves like a Venetian gentleman-soldier. His pledge against lethargy and domestication, his acceptance of immediate departure "with all [his] heart," his assignment of Desdemona "with such things else of quality and respect / As doth import [him]," his soldier's farewell—all suggest the extent to which Othello's public persona as dutiful servant of state governs his life. Indeed, in many ways Othello not only speaks for but epitomizes Venice's masculine "courtesy-culture," his status in which he prizes and, even as it is now being threatened by Brabantio, he is confident of retaining and enriching.

This does not necessarily imply, however, that Othello's motives for the elopement and marriage are deceitful or opportunistic.[6] While it is true that the marriage is inseparable from the proud social fortune Othello now reaches, the love is genuine, and the lover's faith is as strong as the soldier's self-assurance. Othello knows that he is risking arraignment and perhaps imprisonment ("circumscription and confine") on behalf of Desdemona, and yet he will accept the hazard, being confident of vindication and certain of his love's value. He will also accept the long-term strictures the relationship will impose on his "unhoused free condition," for though the old soldier of fortune values the freedom of his romantic past beyond the "sea's worth," he values Desdemona's love more. If Othello appears in act 1 to conceive of Desdemona's role in his life as that of submissive domestic helpmate, the conception does not minimize his love for her so much as it suggests that in his mind the public identity as soldier-servant of Venice must in this time of crisis be separated from the private identity as loving husband. Such a conception will ensure society's high estimation of him (1. 3. 274).

Desdemona's transcendent love, on the other hand, leaps over pedestrian fears about how social consensus esteems her. Infatuated with the romantic hero and the romantic world evoked by Othello's improbable seduction speech, Desdemona plunges into the elopement and marriage with heroic resolve. She will follow the Moor to the wars with a similar resolve:

D E S .: That I [did] love the Moor to live with him,
My downright violence, and storm of fortunes,
May trumpet to the world. My heart's subdu'd
Even to the very quality of my lord.
I saw Othello's visage in his mind,
And to his honors and his valiant parts
Did I my soul and fortunes consecrate.
So that, dear lords, if I be left behind,
A moth of peace, and he go to the war,
The rites for why I love him are bereft me,
And I a heavy interim shall support
By his dear absence. Let me go with him.

[1. 3. 248–59]

Desdemona is the true heroic lover of act 1.[7] She has consecrated herself to the soldier and his occupation; her love for Othello is bound to his honor, valor, and warrior nobility. The "rites" for which she pleads are to be fulfilled in the ceremony of war as well as in the marriage bed, for Desdemona's heroic love does not distinguish soldier from husband, Othello's public world from his private world.[8] In effect, what she now trumpets to the Venetian council is a resolve to give up her identity for Othello's; putting family, society, and culture behind her, "in spite of nature, / Of years, of country, credit, every thing" (1. 3. 96–97), Desdemona would enter a storybook world of heroic romance. Ironically, for his part, Othello would just as soon put the "unhoused" warrior behind him, anchoring his life in Desdemona's love and subjugating his individual prowess to the service of Venice.

These different perceptions of their love and partial misapprehensions about their love are never brought to conscious, articulate understanding. The fatal pattern of noncommunication that begins here will continue until Iago becomes interpretive spokesman for Desdemona and shrewd respondent for Othello. But until that moment, to be free and bounteous to her mind, the loving husband will deny Desdemona nothing rather than assert firmly that friendship for Cassio must not enter the public man's decisions. Desdemona, rather than scoring Othello for unspeakable behavior, will acquiesce to the commands of her ideal warrior with silent, dutiful alacrity. At the end of act 4, husband and wife are drawn irretrievably apart. Desdemona retreats from her romantic ideal to a submissive feminine stance of self-sacrifice and resignation and then to the childlike innocence of her father's household; Othello reverts fully from the husbandly ideal of self-giving to a coldly impersonal stance that is—for all its pretensions to civic duty and social justice—passionately egocentric.

The fortunate storm at the beginning of act 2 brings to triumphant conclusion the war plot and love plot generated in the dark night of Venice. Providence rewards Desdemona's heroic love and Othello's dutiful service without further test. The trumpets herald a new drama. The arrival on the neutral ground of the island outpost is a formal presentation scene, and the atmosphere is initially comic. The players are announced with deliberate ceremony—first the courtier Cassio, then the idealized heroine Desdemona, the blunt soldier Iago, and finally the lover-hero Othello.[9] They have stepped onto a fresh stage and entered a new world. The beneficent storm has displaced the lovers from the anticipated milieu of heroic romance and heroic social service; the peace of Venus's island will serve as incongruous backdrop for a more insidious kind of warfare.

The illusion of a new drama is unmistakable. Cassio's hyperbolic language introduces a spirit of courtship and affectation; Iago's blunt tavern talk provides comic counterpoint to the courtier's mode. Desdemona stands at the center of both affected and base tonalities, bantering nervously (as she tells us) while her husband struggles for survival at sea, but playfully enough (as we perceive) to belie the threat of tragedy. She had arrived on Cyprus as a triumphant Venus *anadyomene*,[10] having weathered the storm in Venice and the symbolic test at sea so that she might realize her heroic love ideal of a perfectly harmonious relationship with her soldier. But the heroic milieu has become Venice revisited; her trumpet of heroic resolve has become an instrument tuned for piazza or parlor. The entrance of Mars, however, conveys the real surprise.

Othello is unmanned by Desdemona's escape from the storm, by her presence before him, by the relief and contentment he feels within. For a moment he is oblivious to the compunctions of social decorum; the rampant hyperbole and flow of emotion are not only out of fashion but out of character, marking indeed a significant turn in character. The martial mentality, the soldier's reserve and resolution, and the primary allegiance to the rites of war in the service of state have been displaced by the selfless idealism and passionate hyperbole of a romantic sonneteer about to fulfill the rites of love.

Love now dominates Othello; in a benign sense Desdemona is the captain's captain. "O my fair warrior" (2. 1. 182), says the Moor, and notwithstanding the ominous presentiments of amatory strife the sonnet trope may evoke in the audience's mind,[11] the phrase in context marks the close of a stormy love quest, signaling completion, fulfillment, hence contentment. Brabantio has been circumvented, the Turkish threat removed, the dangerous voyage negotiated. Fortune's beneficent storm has provided the romantic lovers a comic catastrophe, and in the pacific aftermath Othello gives his martial identity to Desdemona fully and beautifully as a pledge to the Cypriot world of love ahead of them. With peace assured and his soldiership behind him, Mars disarms himself.

Othello's contentment also derives from the completion of his social quest, as the recovery of his public persona and appeal to social decorum perhaps indicate: "O my sweet, / I prattle out of fashion" (2. 1. 205–6). Married to Desdemona and military governor of Cyprus, Othello's place in the Venetian "courtesy-culture" is secure. Once a guarded yet self-assured soldier in the threatening social and military contexts of act 1, Othello is now, with gates open and guard down, not only a self-liberated lover on Venus's island but a de facto symbol of Venice and its social and cultural ideals. He has never so much worn his heart on his sleeve as at this moment, and he never will again.

Iago's tragedy begins to take shape with this presentation scene. Cassio's courtliness, Desdemona's silent love and expressive sociability, the Moor's emotional tranquillity and selfless vulnerability—the cast of characters and pacific atmosphere are ideally suited for the worldly confidant to "read" Cassio's extravagance, for the rhetorician to "speak" for Desdemona, for the logician to redefine the Moor's emotions, for the improvisatory dramatist to direct, and the cynical ironist to interpret, his fiction. Iago's deceit gives him the upper hand on this battlefield, and though it is not pertinent to this study to determine why the diabolical artist must seek revenge to plume up his will, the tactics he employs in his grim warfare are essential.

Iago's first scheme with Roderigo results in Cassio's disgrace and dismissal from the lieutenancy. The drunken brawl disrupts the night of peace and night of love, in both respects a night of full, joyous consum-

mation. An unexpected, external discord breaks in upon the Moor's
contentment (2. 1. 196–98). His anger is justified, predictable:

> OTH.: Are we turn'd Turks, and to ourselves do that
> Which heaven hath forbid the Ottomites?
> For Christian shame, put by this barbarous brawl.
>
> [2. 3. 170–72]

Here and throughout the impromptu inquiry one is aware of the public
persona, the spokesman for Venetian social and cultural ideals. But the
governor's exaggeration allows that more than the disruption of sacred
peace and social order is on his mind. Another Christian ceremony has
been disturbed, and Iago presses the point:

> IAGO: I do not know. Friends all, but now, even now;
> In quarter, and in terms like bride and groom
> Devesting them for bed; and then, but now . . .
>
> [2. 3. 179–81]

Even now, the new husband must leave the wedding chamber to play the
old soldier. The public office and private life are set at odds by Cassio's
brawl; at the moment of consummate peace and contentment, Othello's
thrice-driven bed of down has become a steel couch. Anger threatens to
break through the commander's composure:

> OTH.:   Now by heaven,
> My blood begins my safer guides to rule,
> And passion, having my best judgment collied,
> Assays to lead the way. ['Zounds,] if I stir . . .
>
> [2. 3. 204–7]

Othello's composure was one of his salient martial characteristics; the
audience had seen a remarkable display of it in act 1, and both Lodovico
and Iago will later recall Othello's awesome Stoic calm in the midst of
turmoils far more grave than the aftermath of a tavern brawl. The present
show of passion, one suspects, attends his new identity as heroic lover,
and even now the lover's passion threatens to wield the soldier's weapon.
The love for Desdemona, far from "seeling" the "speculative and offic'd
instruments" with dullness (1. 3. 270–71), fires them toward speedy
resolution so that the disruption may be smoothed over and the contentment survive. He pins the Ancient with a threat and an absolute "Iago,

who began it?" But the answer Iago delivers—verbose, euphemistic, indirect—forces Othello to imagine and think the worst in order to satisfy what is becoming a compulsive drive toward resolution.

At the moment of decision, Othello thinks he is separating his personal affection from his public duty, the love for Cassio from an objective standard of judgment, in his mind once again assuming the stance of act 1, where the lover's private affairs were subordinated to the soldier's concerns with the Turkish threat. The audience knows better:

> OTH.:   I know, Iago,
> Thy honesty and love doth mince this matter,
> Making it light to Cassio. Cassio, I love thee,
> But never more be officer of mine.
>
> *Enter* DESDEMONA *attended.*
>
> Look if my gentle love be not rais'd up!
> I'll make thee an example.
>
> [2. 3. 246–51]

One of Shakespeare's more brilliant symbolic entrances places Desdemona precisely between the decision and its rationale, as if to emphasize what one already suspects: Othello's love for Desdemona has been a part of the decision-making process all along. The lover's passion belies the pose of objective, military governor. The judgment against Cassio is too hasty and too absolute ("never more"), evidencing the anger and frustration of the husband who has been summoned unexpectedly from his wedding chamber and who wants to return as quickly as possible. But the damage is done; the contentment has not survived the interruption (2. 3. 257–58). As it had done in act 1 but was no longer expected to do on Venus's island, the soldier's life has frustrated the husband's harmonious rites of love.

It is, of course, a critical exaggeration to claim that the brawl has returned Cyprus to a war footing, but the illusion is one that Shakespeare cultivates as attendant atmosphere for the temptation scene that follows. In act 3, scene 2, we see Othello as military governor, dispatching letters of state and inspecting the island's fortifications. In addition to the patent irony of the moment—the danger lies within the walls, and the husband, not the soldier, is in jeopardy—the brief scene reveals Othello's present stance of wary soldier and dutiful governor. The time is not ripe for Desdemona's witty assault on the public official on behalf of Cassio; the time is ripe for Iago's assault on the defenseless husband.

Desdemona's insistence on Cassio's reprieve and her argument that in matters of slight import public policy ought to yield to personal affection invite a dialogue on personal integrity, public responsibility, and indeed the extent to which Desdemona's love ideal of entering fully into Othello's world is viable. But the dialogue does not occur, for Othello wants most of all to smooth things over, to avoid discord, even this innocent variety of her "downright violence," and to reestablish the harmony and tranquillity that are the expressive context for his love. War—both the reality and the amatory metaphor for disruption, discord, and "battle" between the sexes—must be kept out of the love relationship; the husband must sail clear of the soldier's concerns. Now that Desdemona's and Othello's different perceptions of the love relationship have been recollected, Iago takes over.

Although nothing annoys Othello's "free and open nature" more than indirection and innuendo, Iago's initial success in baiting the Moor into "thinking" the worst[12] is attributable to the fact that Iago's insinuations threaten to stir up discord in the feelings of harmonious love, and Othello is therefore more anxious to get at the truth and effect a quick solution. And so, with Iago's explicit reference to "jealousy" and "cuckold," Othello's earlier composure and self-confidence return. He is not one to suffer on the rack of suspicion: "No! to be once in doubt / Is [once] to be resolv'd" (3. 3. 179–80). This much one knows already from the handling of Cassio's brawl. A firm grasp of the situation preceding a decisive response is the soldier's way, and although Othello would insist that the "business of [his] soul" should be kept apart from his public persona, the brawl scene ought to make one wary of the conjunction of heart and hand, of the lover's passion and the military governor's decisiveness. Furthermore—and this "furthermore" is fatal[13]—Desdemona's virtues are manifest for anyone with eyes to see. The lover stakes his faith in Desdemona on his own ability to judge external "shows," and yet, ominously, the decision-making process and the promise of decisiveness recall not the husband's faith but the governor's impartial weighing of evidence and the soldier's confident resolve:

> OTH.:   No, Iago,
> I'll see before I doubt; when I doubt, prove;
> And on the proof, there is no more but this—
> Away at once with love or jealousy!
>
> [3. 3. 189–92]

See—doubt—prove—decide. Not only will Othello fight on Iago's ground, but he has unwittingly revealed his plan of battle. Iago now begins in earnest.

The first trick, of course, is to undermine the way Othello sees and replace it with another mode of vision. Iago wisely attacks the Moor's inexperience in Venetian society. The telling point is that the Venetian manners are "shows," like the Turkish "pageants" of act 1, scene 3, and that a credulous husband does not know how to see through such duplicity. "Only a soldier could do this," Iago might have continued, "and, like it or not, the soldier's wary mentality should never be separated from the husband's faithful love." Othello's faith in himself as a lover, in his ability to see correctly, and his faith in Desdemona are momentarily shattered. The issue of this shock is the resonant pledge to Iago: "I am bound to thee for ever" (3. 3. 213). The parodic marriage pledge announced both the betrayal of self to Iago's thinking and the betrayal of his wife; it is introduced at this moment because the faithful, loving husband has momentarily disappeared from Othello's personality and from the marriage relationship.[14]

With Othello's confidence as a lover shaken and his faith in Desdemona shaken, the alienation and paranoia that attend jealousy set in, exacerbated in Othello's case because there are so many racial and cultural obstacles to the love to worry about. The Moor's reaction to the anxiety is projected into the reflexive assertiveness of a new marital stance: "Fear not my government" (3. 3. 256). There is no longer any danger that he will outsport discretion in his domestic affairs. Othello has learned that the love relationship should be understood if not as a literal battle of the sexes requiring a martial mentality, then perhaps as a challenge to good governance requiring the wary possessiveness of Brabantio in act 1. The once private domain of love is now inextricably and, in this case, disastrously related to one's public occupation.

The reaction has been extraordinary, but Othello is not yet settled in his new vision of the "worst." The love continues to tie Desdemona to his heartstrings, and one glimpse of her reawakens the former faith:

OTH.: Look where she comes:

Enter DESDEMONA *and* EMILIA.

If she be false, [O then] heaven [mocks] itself!
I'll not believe't.

[3. 3. 277–79]

Suspicion and faith, and the martial and amatory modes of vision that support them, war within Othello. After the handkerchief has been lost and Emilia has secretly given it to Iago, Othello returns to the stage visibly racked by doubt. The poisonous conceit has taken root in Othello's mind, and a visible apprehension of the infidelity begins to bloom: "stol'n hours of lust"; "Cassio's kisses on her lips"; "general camp,/ Pioners and all, had tasted her sweet body." Doubt has driven him to think and imagine the worst; as earlier in Cassio's brawl and earlier in this scene, the reaction is exaggerated and his decision absolute:

> OTH.:   O now, for ever
> Farewell the tranquil mind! farewell content!

For the moment Othello has forgotten about proof. The lover's tranquillity and contentment are forever lost, and the telling heroic evocation that follows suggests that the soldier's ideals are also lost:

> Farewell the plumed troops and the big wars
> That makes ambition virtue! O, farewell!
> Farewell the neighing steed and the shrill trump,
> The spirit-stirring drum, th' ear-piercing fife,
> The royal banner, and all quality,
> Pride, pomp, and circumstance of glorious war!
> And O you mortal engines, whose rude throats
> Th' immortal Jove's dread clamors counterfeit,
> Farewell! Othello's occupation's gone.
>
> [3. 3. 347–57]

Predictably, the cuckoldry strikes at the heart of Othello's manhood; the soldier's virility does not survive the husband's humiliation. In Othello's case, however, the cuckold's predictable anxiety is intensified by an intellectual conviction. Belatedly he has come to realize that amatory and martial identities and ideals are inseparable; and so now, incongruously, the loss of the harmonious, private rites of love means a farewell to the boisterous, public ceremony of war. The soldier's reputation has been blasted together with the husband's love, not only by Desdemona's betrayal but by his own folly. By playing the naive lover when he ought to have been wary, Othello believes that he has kissed away the soldier's dignity, honor, and social estimation. Othello's farewell to his occupation is thus a farewell to his heroic conception of self.

Othello's recovery and his demand for proof (see—doubt—prove—

decide) begins the third part of the temptation process. But because his imagination has all but made the final decision, from now on he will be easy game for Iago. The demand for "ocular proof" is risible; Othello, of course, no longer sees the way he once did, and increasingly Iago is able to flaunt his superiority with grotesque humor. The absurdly sensual description of Cassio's dream and the unlikely coup de grace of Cassio's wiping his beard with Othello's handkerchief fix the ocular proof in Othello's mind. He banishes love from his heart, just as he had promised, and pledges himself to jealousy and bloody revenge.

> O T H .: Now do I see 'tis true. Look here, Iago,
> All my fond love thus do I blow to heaven.
> 'Tis gone.
> Arise, black vengeance, from the hollow hell!
> Yield up, O love, thy crown and hearted throne
> To tyrannous hate! Swell, bosom, with thy fraught,
> For 'tis of aspics' tongues!

Othello would become a passionate, diabolical creature of hatred much like the stock Moor of literary and stage traditions, but he cannot maintain such an uncharacteristic stance. The "fond love" will not blow away so easily, and the croaking for revenge will not translate into effective action unless it is buttressed by the noble principle of martial honor. Iago knows this:

> I A G O :   Yet be content.
> O T H .: O blood, blood, blood!
> I A G O : Patience, I say; your mind [perhaps] may change.

If Iago's master word "content" negatively reinforces the lover's feelings of discord, the clever tease of "patience" and weak-kneed vacillation would lure the soldier's resolution into the service of passion. That is, the evidence is in, the enemy is discovered, and patience and vacillation are now out of the question; it is time for the military governor to take resolute action.

> O T H .: Never, Iago. Like to the Pontic Sea,
> Whose icy current and compulsive course
> Nev'r [feels] retiring ebb, but keeps due on
> To the Propontic and the Hellespont,
> Even so my bloody thoughts, with violent pace,

Shall nev'r look back, nev'r ebb to humble love,
Till that a capable and wide revenge
Swallow them up. [*He kneels.*] Now by yond marble heaven,
In the due reverence of a sacred vow
I here engage my words.

[3. 3. 444–62]

Othello responds to Iago's tease with a formal epic simile stressing martial decisiveness. Pure passion ("O blood, blood, blood!") is transformed into impersonal, deliberative resolve, the cause of revenge into a kind of holy crusade sanctified by vows to heaven.[15] "Never, Iago . . . Nev'r . . . nev'r . . . nev'r"—just as at the moment of decision after the tavern brawl, Othello needs to assert, and wants desperately for Iago to believe, that despite his truancy from sound martial government, he remains a servant of honor who will not be swayed by personal bias. The Mars who disarmed himself by following the course of "fond" and "humble" love will redeem the folly and humiliation by doing the difficult, cold, but honorable thing. Love will not abdicate its hearted throne to hate, but it will to honor.

Othello has come into conflict with himself and with his former martial and amatory idealism. He has turned Turk, pledging a bloody, barbarous revenge against the two Venetians he loves above all others. The revenge action is thus a grim parody of Othello's earlier service to Christian Venice. Moreover, Othello's love ideals have similarly ducked "as low / As hell's from heaven" (2. 1. 190–91), not simply because he has exchanged his "fair warrior" for the "fair devil" beside him, but because his assumptions and priorities have been turned upside down. Othello had earlier wanted to keep domestic affairs in pacific isolation apart from public responsibilities and to separate his private identity as husband from his public persona as soldier. He has heard more since. With reputation blasted and occupation gone, he has come to understand that love is very much a public matter requiring wary governance. And so, to regain his lost honor and social estimation, he will handle the husband's domestic problem from the stance of the impersonal, dutiful military governor.

What is especially pathetic about Othello's role of revenger is the pretense to nobility, honor, and justice.[16] The revenge shall be cruel and bloody, but Othello accepts the role with righteous indignation and moral outrage. Jealous passion motivates him, but Othello's heroic incantation soon transforms the cause into one of sacred honor. The discrepancy between what is real and what is cosmetic pretension, between a real self and a delusive conception of self, ought to recall Shakespeare's critique of the heroic psyche in *Troilus and Cressida*. For at this pivotal turn in character, the soldier has embraced the delusive heroic image; once he acts upon it, like Hotspur, Hector, and Troilus, he shall doom himself to tragedy.

The painful fourth act illustrates the nature of Othello's heroic delusion. Iago, of course, is not really the Moor's lieutenant in the enterprise; Othello is Iago's pawn. The once powerful figure falls into an obsessive trance while Iago jokes openly and triumphantly about the cuckold's headache. Later, Othello will play the dupe in Iago's crude farce, reading into Cassio's laughter and the exchange of the handkerchief the sordid fiction he has accepted as real. One can discern in Othello's imaginative fiction and the private code expressing it ("Goats and monkeys") Iago's cynical vision of the world. At the same time that Othello's own speech has become a vehicle for his inner vision, however, he perceives that Desdemona's language and action are "shows," veiling true intentions and hidden activity. Expecting the worst, Othello now relies on a wary martial mentality that views domestic affairs with cynical irony; he prides himself in being a shrewd observer of "enemy" deceit. No one but Iago can understand what has happened to him:

> L O D .: Is this the noble Moor whom our full Senate
> Call all in all sufficient? Is this the nature
> Whom passion could not shake? whose solid virtue
> The shot of accident nor dart of chance
> Could neither graze nor pierce?
>
> [4. 1. 264–68]

That's he that was Othello. The Venice of act 1 returns with Lodovico's heroic evocation so that the audience might measure the hero's lapse from a former individual and social idealism and might mark the extent to which Othello's tragic progression in character has brought him into conflict with self.

Lodovico rhetorically questions the genesis of Othello's strange impatience and passion. Othello himself will soon suggest whence they come:

> O T H .:   Had it pleas'd heaven
> To try me with affliction, had they rain'd

All kind of sores and shames on my bare head,
Steep'd me in poverty to the very lips,
Given to captivity me and my utmost hopes,
I should have found in some place of my soul
A drop of patience; but, alas, to make me
The fixed figure for the time of scorn
To point his slow [unmoving] finger at!
Yet could I bear that too, well, very well;
But there, where I have garner'd up my heart,
Where either I must live or bear no life;
The fountain from the which my current runs
Or else dries up: to be discarded thence!
Or keep it as a cestern for foul toads
To knot and gender in! Turn thy complexion there,
Patience, thou young and rose-lipp'd cherubin—
Ay, here look grim as hell!

[4. 2. 47–64]

The compulsive course of revenge is not generated from a "Pontic Sea" of hate, after all, but rather from the "fountain from the which [Othello's] current runs." It would have been better if the fountain of love did dry up, but it remains, defiled at its source, and the stronger its pulse the more forceful the motive for revenge. In this pathetic sense Othello does love "too well." The old soldier had devoted the harvest of his heart to Desdemona; he had staked his life and fortune upon the woman who was beyond the "sea's worth." The remembrance of his great love magnifies the enormity of Desdemona's betrayal of his faith; and in much the same way the remembrance of Desdemona's seeming goodness and virtue intensifies the horror of her deceit and hypocrisy:

> OTH.: Ay, let her rot, and perish, and be damn'd tonight, for she
> shall not live. No, my heart is turn'd to stone; I strike it, and it
> hurts my hand. O, the world hath not a sweeter creature! she
> might lie by an emperor's side and command him tasks. . . . Hang
> her, I do but say what she is. So delicate with her needle! an
> admirable musician! Oh, she will sing the savageness out of a
> bear. Of so high and plenteous wit and invention! . . . I will chop
> her into messes. Cuckold me!

[4. 1. 181–200]

Again and again the reality of love still throned in Othello's heart threatens to overwhelm the resolute will, but Iago is there to transform the lover's faith into the soldier's cynical vision. Desdemona's manifestations of virtue thus strengthen the evidence of consummate deceit and hypocrisy; her virtues are turned to a pitch, adding fuel to the Moor's outrage.

Secondarily, Iago continually reminds Othello that the course of "humble love" is the course of humiliating retreat for the heroic soldier. The disgrace of becoming a "fixed figure for the time of scorn / To point his slow [unmoving] finger at" may not be Othello's primary motive for revenge, but it is nevertheless crucial. Othello can talk about being discarded from his life's sustenance, but the vision following that romantic pronouncement is one of the cuckolded husband, the object of scorn and ridicule, the keeper of a cistern fouled by copulating toads. It is that unspeakable *shame* that turns patience's complexion "grim as hell."

The handkerchief stands as symbol for both the blasted love and the blasted reputation. Othello's exotic handkerchief had been a token of the romantic identity to which Desdemona had pledged her love and which he would place in her circumscription and confine. Othello's first gift to the woman he would wed seems to have been the symbolic equivalent of a wedding ring in his mind, and it was also a personal, sentimental, endearing token of a private love isolated from the soldier's public business. To imagine Cassio's wiping his beard with it, then to see the symbol on the streets in the possession of Cassio's prostitute, and this following hard upon Cassio's mocking "triumph," is to see feelingly the public scorn, the ridicule, and the shame attending the loss of love.

The love relationship cannot survive Othello's vision. "Cassio"—"handkerchief," "Cassio"—"handkerchief": Othello and Desdemona now move in different worlds, and by the end of act 4 the racial and cultural separation is complete. He has become a cruel Moor, waging his new kind of "holy war" tainted with the diabolism Brabantio had suspected in act 1. For her part, Desdemona retreats from the ideal of "fair warrior" into the feminine world of sentiment and childhood reminiscence; she has become very much like the little girl Othello first wooed at Brabantio's table. The stage is set for the terrifying love scene of act 5.

THE HEROIC FOOL

Othello's entrance at the beginning of the final scene marks a startling, yet perhaps predictable, change in tone and perception of self. At his exit in the previous scene, he had departed to do the deed while steeping himself in bloody thoughts:

> O T H . : Minion, your dear lies dead,
> And your unblest fate hies. Strumpet, I come.
> [Forth]of my heart those charms, thine eyes, are blotted;
> Thy bed, lust-stain'd, shall with lust's blood be spotted.
>
> *Exit Othello.*
>
> [5. 1. 33–36]

Just as at the end of the temptation scene, Othello would exorcise thoughts of love and invoke hatred, moral outrage, and a rough concept of eye-for-eye justice so that he might wrap himself in the role of bloody revenger; but now, as then, the noble Moor cannot maintain such a stance or act upon it. Once again the conventional croaking for revenge gives way to a formal evocation of heroic image. If earlier he had exalted his selfish motive for revenge with an epic simile and then blessed it with a sacred oath, now Othello invokes the atmosphere of sacrificial ceremony:

> O T H . : It is the cause, it is the cause, my soul;
> Let me not name it to you, you chaste stars,
> It is the cause. Yet I'll not shed her blood,
> Nor scar that whiter skin of hers than snow,
> And smooth as monumental alablaster.
> Yet she must die, else she'll betray more men.
> Put out the light, and then put out the light. . . .
>
> [5. 2. 1–7]

Through an extraordinary act of self-incantation, the passionate revenger transfigures himself into a minister of justice. Needless to say, the self-delusion is colossal.[17] Othello would believe that Desdemona is being sacrificed for the "cause" of morality, religion, and justice; but in fact these values are projections of the heroic psyche's myth of grandeur, elements of the heroic fiction in which Othello conceives of himself as just and dutiful servant of society. In truth, Desdemona is being sacrificed to the selfish cause of Othello's heroic image; the "sacred" ceremony

Othello projects into reality reflects precisely the heroic self-idolatry Shakespeare had criticized so sharply in *Troilus and Cressida*.

Othello needs the incantatory language not only to gird himself with martial resolution and to gild a jealous murder with decorous pretensions to moral righteousness and social duty, but also to charm to sleep the loving husband now entering his wedding chamber. Like the Duke in the Venetian council scene of act 1 (1. 3. 66–70), like the stance Othello himself tried to assume in the brawl scene and promised to assume at the end of the temptation scene and at the exit moments before, the social servant would once again separate his public office of impartial government from the business of the soul, hoping that his "gentle love be not rais'd up" (2. 3. 250), both literally and metaphorically. And yet, by evoking the tranquillity and peace that was the expressive context of that love, Othello creates precisely the opposite effect. As if a reflexive response to the calm and innocence of Desdemona's peaceful sleep, Othello's heart and humanity rise up against his false conception of self, asserting their instinctive, forceful claim to reality against the perverse heroic myth he has self-consciously fostered. The gentle, abiding love threatens the honorable resolve:

OTH.:   [*Kisses her.*]
   O balmy breath, that dost almost persuade
   Justice to break her sword! One more, one more.
   Be thus when thou art dead, and I will kill thee
   And love thee after. One more, and that's the last.

                                                         [5. 2. 16–19]

The kiss of peace and contentment recalls the arrival on Cyprus. From that moment of loving concord the diabolical logic governing the Cypriot stage has brought the husband and warrior to discord in the brawl, to outright opposition in the temptation scene, to the perversion of both immediately after, and now to this pathetic impasse where love and honor must come to the impossible compromise of killing her and loving her after. The impersonal honor of the military governor and the affectionate love of the husband in his wedding chamber force upon Othello a further psychological accommodation, symbolized in the evocation of a new role, that of a penitential and sacrificial priest whose sorrow is "heavenly." Like God, Othello must punish the sinful creature he loves; he will mercifully confess her to save her soul, but sacrifice her for the cause of justice and for his own honorable integrity. But Desdemona awakes, and her protestations of innocence bring on the discord, again heightening the enormity of her betrayal, worsening her steadfast hypocrisy, and feeding the violence of his reaction to both. Ironically, for all his pretensions as honorable soldier and dutiful minister of justice, Othello finally murders Desdemona *in propria persona*: as a base, selfish, passionately jealous husband.

Othello had predicted the "chaos" that comes over him at Desdemona's death. The psychological discord is overwhelming:

> O T H .: My wife, my wife! what wife? I have no wife.
> O insupportable! O heavy hour!
> Methinks it should be now a huge eclipse
> Of sun and moon, and that th' affrighted globe
> Did yawn at alteration.
>
> [5. 2. 97–101]

The identity as husband is gone forever, and Desdemona's momentary revival and assertion of innocence soon deprive him of his public personae of executioner and priest. He has lost all in the chaos:

> E M I L .: O, who hath done this deed?
> D E S .: Nobody; I myself. Farewell!
> Commend me to my kind lord, O, farewell!   [*Dies.*]
>
> [5. 2. 123–25]

"Nobody"—the murder has been a psychic suicide for Othello. The "kind lord" exists in Desdemona's vision of her former husband; the present murdering creature is something beyond description. The creature now seizes the opportunity that Desdemona's selfless love has provided him to evade responsibility for her execution, to deny even the honorable pretense of justice's minister (5. 2. 126–28). Neither loving husband, nor priest, nor honorable soldier, nor minister of justice, nor even passionate murderer—Othello has become at his worst moment a deceitful worm or, as Emilia will soon say, "a blacker devil" (5. 2. 131).

Nevertheless, Othello is not yet willing to face the truth about himself. He cannot achieve self-knowledge without first undergoing a cathartic process of disillusionment. This painful process, retracing the steps of his psychic descent—from assurance of Desdemona's infidelity, to doubt, to the truth about the handkerchief—strips the heroic ego of its delusive conception of self. The handkerchief affirms the reality of Desdemona's love, giving the lie to the quest for honor and social esteem, and

Othello reacts impulsively to his guilt. In the ensuing scuffle, Gratiano seizes Othello's sword, and when passion clears, allowing self-evaluation, Othello understands the implications of being "nobody." The loss of the sword, a symbolic disarming, suggests a true "farewell" to Othello's occupation, for in addition to his wife he has lost everything he killed her for: valor, reputation, honor—in short, his heroic conception of self.

The lost sword and the heroic image it symbolizes for Othello cannot be regained. "Moor, she was chaste; she lov'd thee, cruel Moor" (5. 2. 249)—Emilia's dying indictment confronts Othello with a massive sense of alienation, both from Venetian society and from self. For a moment, Othello reacts desperately, reflexively, clinging to the delusion that the second sword and the evocation of his exotic past will restore at least part of his heroic image. But the truth must be faced; he recognizes the self-deceit in the warrior's pose, the emptiness of the self-dramatization, the absurdity of the self-puffing and self-cheering.[18] He could never revert to his "unhoused free condition." Desdemona was his true harbor, and at journey's end his thoughts turn to her, to his own guilt, and to the punishment that awaits him at the final judgment.

The resignation of the second sword and of any further claim to martial grandeur distances Othello from himself and his fatal mistake: "That's he that was Othello; here I am" (5. 2. 284). The claim of "honorable murderer" (5. 2. 294), a final pathetic plea for social esteem, the last infirmity of the Moor's noble mind, precedes the moment of true self-knowledge. "O, fool, fool, fool" (5. 2. 323)—Othello finally faces the murder and the murderer squarely. Though he could never be the dispassionate minister of justice with Desdemona, he will now pass objective judgment on the heroic fool.

Othello's final speech spans the drama, recalling briefly the former service to Venice, which had been celebrated in act 1, and passing on to describe the nature of the "rash and most unfortunate man" he has put behind him. The first lines convey a subtle claim for self-sufficiency; Othello stops the ministers of justice in their tracks with a commanding "soft you" and follows with the assurance of understatement ("a word or two"). He knows his course; he will handle the problem quietly, decisively, honorably.

> OTH.: Set you down this;
> And say besides, that in Aleppo once,
> Where a malignant and a turban'd Turk

Beat a Venetian and traduc'd the state,
I took by th' throat the circumcised dog,
And smote him—thus.   [*He stabs himself.*]

                                                        [5. 2. 351–56]

The final anecdote about the "turban'd Turk" recalls in low key Othello's former loyalty to Venetian values. Yet he knows that the servant of Venice has turned Turk and traduced those loyalties. The former hero who had betrayed himself in resolving to murder Desdemona now executes himself to affirm the honor and justice he had perverted. Once cleansed of the false heroic image, the pathetic warrior may again dedicate himself to love. Othello falls on the bed that holds his bride's dead body, redeeming with a final kiss of concord the marital vows he had profaned. The public warrior and private lover can find only in self-slaughter a partial measure of redemption.

"GREAT OF HEART"

Othello reveals all of the characteristics that distinguish Shakespeare's approach to heroic tragedy: the turns in character marked by thematic emphases and epic evocations, the illusion of a character coming into conflict with himself, the delusive conception of self precipitating the fatal action, the interplay of martial and amatory ideals, the use of tragedy as an affirmative countergenre to epic. When considered together, these Shakespearean emphases in *Othello* constitute a broad critical perspective against which Chapman's *Bussy D'Ambois* might be compared with point and profit.

Othello's selfish compulsion to create his own heroic myth is little different from that demonstrated by Shakespeare's Trojans in *Troilus and Cressida*. Just as in that earlier acerbic commentary on the making of heroic fiction, the soldier-hero of *Othello* adopts a delusive heroic image that not only legitimatizes a condemnable course of action but recommends it to him as a point of honor. The pivotal turn in Othello's character reveals this heroic delusion in the process of creation. At the end of act 3, scene 3, we recall, Othello pledges himself to jealousy and revenge with a conventional invocation to passion; but soon, at Iago's prompting, the croaking for revenge is transmuted into a sonorous epic simile ("Like to the Pontic Sea"), and the motive for revenge is translated into that of sacred duty. Othello's concern for heroic image compels him to dress a base, passionate, personal action as a noble, legitimate, social enterprise. This way the heroic myth of dutiful servant of society will survive, and the "cause" of morality, honor, order, and justice will be served. Chapman's Achilles apologized for what appeared to be selfish, antisocial behavior by arguing that his personal motivation was in fact consonant with virtue's general law; but in *Troilus and Cressida* and now in *Othello*, Shakespeare forbids that facile translation of acquisitive ego-centric behavior into justifiable social action. Rather, Shakespeare would respond that the heroic ego, spinning a self-congratulatory myth of grandeur, fates the soldier not only to a delusive conception of self and vision of reality but also, as the heroic myth is projected into the social world, to a destructive, antisocial, tragic course of action.

An important element in Othello's false heroic image—and one that anticipates the heroic characterization in *Antony and Cleopatra* and *Coriolanus*—is its unnaturalness. Othello is convinced that in order to regain his lost reputation he must punish Desdemona's infidelity with decisive, impersonal, martial resolution. To this end he launches an inhuman campaign to erase from his consciousness all feelings and thoughts of love, instincts and promptings of the heart, "faith" in Desdemona's fidelity and virtue—in short, all the naive characteristics of the "fond love" responsible for his public disgrace.[19] Othello would exorcise human weakness from his psyche so that once again he might be "possess'd . . . with greatness." It is as if Othello the soldier declared war on Othello the lover, for the Moor's heartstrings are tied to Desdemona, and much of his energy and resolve is bent against his own heart and humanity. Othello's heroic crusade is a crime against human nature, his own as well as Desdemona's.

Othello's conflict with self and the thematic dichotomies that describe it—soldier versus lover, honorable crusade versus natural behavior, heroic image versus human being—point at a fundamental opposition in the play between epic and tragedy. According to Shakespeare's conception of heroic tragedy, the genre of tragedy, by appropriating values from other literary and dramatic "kinds"—sonnet, pastoral, comedy, romance—functions as a countergenre to epic, proffering to the soldier a vision of reality wholly different from his heroic assumptions. The soldier's conflict with self might be described, then, as a conflict between countergenres—between two antithetical sets of assumptions, systems of evaluation, and visions of reality. Typically, even as the soldier's fatal decision in favor of heroic myth-making precipitates the destructive action, at the end he is allowed to achieve self-knowledge, to renounce his delusive conception of self, and to affirm tragedy's antiheroic values.

In *Othello*, tragedy's affirmative response to epic is suggested by the punishment of the deluded fool and the subsequent testimony to the value of Desdemona's love. If the "bloody period" (5. 2. 357) marks the renunciation of heroic image, the final period is a kiss:

> o t h . : I kiss'd thee ere I kill'd thee. No way but this,
>   Killing myself, to die upon a kiss.   [*Falls on the bed and*] *dies.*
> c a s . : This did I fear, but thought he had no weapon;
>   For he was great of heart.
>
>   [5. 2. 358–61]

With the swords signifying Othello's public persona forever lost, a dagger or some other personal or domestic weapon becomes the lover's instrument of liberation—not from a hostile world or malevolent fate, but from himself, from the enemy within. Othello falls on the marriage bed alongside the bride whom he himself has killed, and death becomes a kind of consummation. With this painfully mutant version of a love-death, Othello deliberately recalls his earlier inadequacies and failings in order to correct them; he would die as he could not live, as a heroic lover willing to stake his life on Desdemona's faith and willing to end his life in affirmation of her value.

Of primary importance at this moment, however, is the evocation of the sonnet genre, the literary "kind" in which Othello's amatory idealism has been couched throughout the play, as Colie has shown. When Othello entered the wedding chamber to carry out the murder, the pathetic kisses and subtle adaptations of sonnet conventions stressed that feelings of love were to be sacrificed to the honorable "cause" of heroic image.[20] But now, at the end, Othello would reverse that priority; by putting the heroic soldier behind him and dedicating himself anew to the harmonious rites of love, Othello would revert to the ideals of the exuberant sonneteer when he first arrived on Cyprus. The end of that journey had seen the triumph of love over the potentially divisive obstacles of Brabantio, the Turk, and the storm, and in tribute to the prospect of peace on Venus's island Mars had disarmed himself, sharing his identity with Desdemona ("O my fair warrior!") so that he might enter into a fully harmonious relationship with her. But Othello's psychological storm has since shattered the harmony, and the soldier has since taken up arms against love, setting out on a destructive, antiamatory quest for heroic image. Now, at this "journey's end," the punishment Othello exacts on himself will affirm the amatory ideals the heroic fool has profaned. The pathetic sonneteer shall literally give up his martial identity in testimony to Desdemona's worth, literally donate his life to love, literally die with a kiss. By his suicide, a heroic act of self-transcendence, Othello would make the sonnet-lover worthy of the beloved and thus earn the moment when he gives himself—body and soul—to Desdemona by dying with a kiss.

In his final moment the lover attempts to be as high-minded as the soldier has been base-minded. Othello renounces the calculating mentality and egocentric pursuit of honor associated with his heroic conception of self in favor of love's ideal of resolute faith and selfless service. For this new conception of self and for the amatory values to which it testifies, the genre of tragedy must now speak. Othello is "great of heart," as Cassio says, but this final greatness is predicated on Othello's ability to deal with his heroic folly decisively and to embrace death as a bridegroom, reaffirming the transcendent value of the love that he has once again enthroned in his heart.

4

BUSSY D'AMBOIS AND

THE QUEST FOR VIRTUE

The term "heroic tragedy" seems especially appropriate to Chapman's *Bussy D'Ambois*, for it reflects accurately both the moral ambiguity of the soldier-hero's behavior and the nature of his tragic conflict with society. Bussy's attempt to unmetaphor an epic conception of self leads to astonishing yet morally reprehensible actions that are incompatible with society's standards of acceptable behavior. Although Chapman's heroic tragedy is set in France in the 1570s and purports to be a historical biography, Bussy's conflict with society appears to be influenced by Essex's tragedy at the turn of the century in England, and Bussy's astonishing behavior is directly related to the heroic *areté* of Homer's Achilles. Like Essex—the hero to whom Chapman dedicated his 1598 *Iliads*—Bussy is a "contemporary Achilles," a hero of epic prowess who is tragically displaced in a nonheroic milieu.

Since 1598, however, apparently owing to Essex's tragic blunder and subsequent execution as well as to Chapman's careful review of the second half of *The Iliad*, there has occurred a significant change in Chapman's conception of both Essex and Achilles. Although the depiction of the dispirited court and devious social milieu in *Bussy D'Ambois* would appear to suggest that Chapman's attitude toward Bussy's social dislocation is sympathetic, even as it was toward Essex's in 1598, the moral ambiguity of Bussy's behavior confirms that Chapman is no longer able to extol "ancient virtue" without qualification. In this respect, *Bussy D'Ambois* documents Chapman's painful reassessment of Essex and the Achillean heroism that the translator of *Iliads* had celebrated in 1598 with partisan naiveté.

Although Chapman's new understanding of Achilles' heroism had already crystallized at the time of *Bussy D'Ambois*, it was not formally announced until 1611, when the full translation of *Iliads* appeared,[1] and not formally clarified in relation to *Odysses* until the publication of the complete translation of Homer (ca. 1616):

> And that your Lordship may in his Face take view of his Mind, the first word of his *Iliads* is μῆνιν, wrath; the first word of his *Odysses*, ἄνδρα, Man—contracting in either word his each worke's Proposition. In one, Predominant Perturbation; in the other, over-ruling Wisedome; in one, the Bodie's fervour and fashion of outward Fortitude to all possible height of Heroicall Action; in the other, the Mind's inward, constant and unconquerd Empire, unbroken, unalterd with any most insolent and tyrannous infliction.[2]

These modes of heroism have often been contrasted according to ethical value judgments; that is, Ulysses' "Stoic" virtue is a positive ideal and Achilles' "Predominant Perturbation"—usually understood to connote unbridled passion and anarchic individualism—is a negative exemplum. But Chapman's supposed disenchantment with Achilles—once he has knelt at Ulysses' shrine—has been exaggerated, if not misunderstood.

The *Iliads* of 1598 had been a false start for Chapman. Interestingly, the epic quality exemplified by Achilles is not heroic wrath, not "Predominant Perturbation," but precisely "over-ruling Wisedome." In the crucial moments relating to Achilles' isolation, his exemplary heroism proceeds from the "Mind's inward, constant and unconquerd Empire" which, though sorely tested by Agamemnon, remains "unbroken, unalterd with any most insolent and tyrannous infliction." In retrospect, Chapman came to realize that Homer's emphasis in *The Iliad* is not on the wise "Stoic" hero of the early books but on the ireful, outward hero of the later books. And although Chapman also realized that Achilles' incendiary passion might lead occasionally to irrational, immoral behavior, the translator's change in perception does not produce a change in sympathy. Achilles' dominant mode of heroism may be different, but the hero of the 1598 *Iliads* remains the hero of the full translation in 1611.[3] There is simply no evidence to the contrary.

In the 1611 edition, Chapman is willing to acknowledge Achilles' momentary excesses and local storms (the marginal gloss of "Achilles againe in furie"—*CH* 1:30), but this does not amount to a general condemnation. The passions are tempered, the anger is subsequently defended as just, and the isolation remains a virtuous retreat. Moreover, the vision of glorying over the ruin of friends and foes alike is defended in 1611 as a "frolike and delightsome humour" (*CH* 1:346), his weeping on the shores as "teares of manlinesse and magnanimitie" (*CH* 1:44), and even the abuse of Hector's corpse, though repeatedly lamented as an "unworthy deed," gains the translator's sympathetic understanding (see *CH* 1:449). But more telling evidence that Achilles remains Chapman's exemplary hero resides in the fact that the translator repeatedly—systematically—exalts Achilles' heroic wrath. If the 1598 *Iliads* extols "over-ruling Wisedome," the second half of the *Iliads*, published in 1611, celebrates "Predominant Perturbation," heroic passion, heroic spirit, Homer's *areté*, de Sponde's *virtus*—by any name the martial pursuit of excellence that issues in "outward Fortitude to all possible height of Heroicall Action."

Throughout *The Iliad* and especially in the last twelve books, Homer continually stresses that moments of extraordinary martial excellence are divinely induced. Homer's Olympians, we know, are continually "rousing," "helping," "protecting," "confounding" the mortal heroes. But, significantly, in Chapman's interpretive translation, the gods "inspire," "animate," "disanimate," "impel the spirit of" the mortal heroes. These expansions and interpretive colorings are not only frequent but uniform.[4] Chapman's warriors are filled with a divine *inflatus*, a heroic furor. They are "possess'd," not with a delusive, unnatural heroic image, as Shakespeare would have it, but with a divine spirit of "greatness."

One must recall, moreover, that Chapman translated the second half of *The Iliad* in 1611, when he had entered the so-called "Stoic period" of his career.[5] If he really intended to place Achillean heroism in pejorative contrast to Ulyssean heroism, he might easily have underplayed these moments of divine assistance, using such terms as "fiery wrath," "hot fury," "passions enkindled," "excessive anger's sting," and the like, either to condemn "Predominant Perturbation" outright or to demystify the epic by confining the interpretation to a mortal dimension. He might have followed, in other words, Shakespeare's tactic of demythologizing "the matter of Troy." But Chapman did not do this to "sacred" Homer, insisting instead that something divine impels the heroic spirit, that high "Heroicall Action" exhibits the stuff of divinity. Though their heroism is of a different order from that of the mind's empire governed by divine reason, the warriors of *The Iliad* are also godlike.

Chapman would contend that Achilles' outward fortitude of 1611 and inward fortitude of 1598, his "Predominant Perturbation" and "overruling Wisedome," are complementary, constituent components of the Homeric epic ideal. The heroic passion (*virtus*) that fires Achilles' astonishing martial exploits is divinely inspired, but nevertheless needs the bridle of reason to transform it into "just wrath" in the first half of the *Iliads* and, later, to bring it into conformity with Jove's will, when, as with the abuse of Hector's corpse, the heroic passion becomes an excessive blind passion. The "over-ruling Wisedome" (virtue), exemplified best by Ulysses, is also godlike, but is ineffectual, vain, and lifeless without the animation of heroic spirit; the first portrayal of the dispirited hero on Calypso's island, which we shall glance at at the end of Chapter 6, makes the point emphatically. The man whose divine attributes of heroic spirit and godlike reason are properly proportioned and fully complementary is a "complete man"—the term used in the Friar's valediction to Bussy.

Chapman's new understanding of Achilles' heroism and of Homer's grand epic scheme, announced in 1611 and articulated in 1616, is of central concern to *Bussy D'Ambois*. The pattern of Achilles' epic progress is replicated by Bussy's tragic progress: both heroes leave the isolation of a "Stoic" retirement in order to adopt an active, outward mode of heroism that is astonishing if sometimes condemnable; at the end, both heroes, magnanimously and perhaps repentantly, bring themselves into conformity with Jove's will, confirming their statue as "complete men." But the differences between epic hero and tragic hero are these: first, even more so than Achilles in the 1598 *Iliads*, Bussy is displaced into a nonheroic milieu where the assertion of epic *virtus* precipitates tragic entanglement; and second, while Achilles struggles to keep spirit and reason in proper proportion and thus preserve heroic *virtus* and rational virtue as integral, complementary ideals, Bussy struggles simply to make them complementary. Initially in *Bussy D'Ambois* the ideals of "Predominant Perturbation" and "over-ruling Wisedome" are made to seem antithetical; hence, the tragic hero must set out on a quest to attain the same exemplary stature that the epic hero strives to maintain.

In *Bussy D'Ambois*, the Homeric epic ideals are placed in a tragic context and viewed from a tragic perspective. With a pessimism that seems responsive to Essex's social dislocation, Chapman suggests that the assertion of heroic *virtus* in a base-spirited society leads inevitably to tragedy. With a moral ambivalence perhaps reflecting Chapman's new attitude toward Essex's "ancient virtue," the dramatist suggests that the Achillean hero's quest for true virtue must be a difficult experiential struggle, for heroic passion is inherently incompatible with rational moral virtue. Nevertheless, despite Chapman's pessimism, despite the fact that Bussy is initially deficient in moral virtue and is doomed to tragedy, his quest to achieve an exemplary epic stature is successful. The Friar's celebration of the "complete man" verifies the heroic genre's claim to grandeur in the face of death. Heroic man is able to transcend his tragic world even as Bussy D'Ambois triumphs at the end of a tragic quest for virtue, even as Chapman himself succeeds in reconstructing a heroic idealism that the tragedy of Essex had momentarily shattered.

THE HEROIC SERVANT OF VIRTUE

The tragedy opens upon a Stoic Bussy in solitude and in poverty. His philosophical reflections serve doubly as a choric commentary on the "state of things" and as an apology for his own life. With Stoic themes and vocabulary he castigates the public world. The true values of reason, need, and virtue[6]—the values with which he implicitly associates himself —have been subverted in a world under Fortune's sway. Men have made monsters of themselves, gigantic colossuses of outward forms, ignorant and empty of inner worth and human dignity. The great men who sail the "glassy Glory and the gulfs of State" (1. 1. 29) have yet to learn that only humble virtue can lead them to their final destination, crown their individual quests, provide them with the means to true self-sufficiency.

Bussy has withdrawn to a "green retreat" and "obscure abode" where, solitary and impoverished and contemplative, he appears to be a speaking emblem for the Stoic life of retirement.[7] But the portrait of Bussy is unsettling, and so is the depiction of Stoic idealism. His poetry betrays the lure of potential greatness while formally decrying it;[8] the rich, confident, assertive ships at sea undergo a lifetime of challenge on their heroic voyage, in opposition to which the humble fisherman and the haven of virtue can offer only a quiet, brief denouement. True Stoic retirement was a heroic enterprise in its own way, an active life of the mind in search of self-knowledge, self-reformation, and universal truths that would benefit the citizens of the world.[9] Bussy's retirement, on the other hand, appears to be no more than a final "haven," a place of solace to which he has fled to lick his wounds. The life is sterile, the virtue untested. The pessimism of "Man is a torch borne in the wind; a dream / But of a shadow, summ'd with all his substance" (1. 1. 18–19) saps the rhetoric of any conviction in the same way that the symbolic stage direction, *Procumbit*, saps the man of any spirit. Monsieur's language—"sloth," "lean Darkness," "Turn'd to earth," "Death"—is only slightly exaggerated.

Bussy's apologia creates two related impressions. The first is that Stoic idealism properly belongs to the *ars moriendi* tradition; it does not equip Bussy for life, providing no meaningful purpose, direction, or relation to a course of action. The second impression is that Bussy's philosophy is spawned of misfortune; his rhetoric of virtuous retirement disguises the grudge of a man who would rather be out on the heroic seas. Only in retrospect will the structural irony of the soliloquy, with these two related impressions, become clear. Bussy has predicted his own tragic progress: the admonition against a life of greatness and the affirmation of humble virtue at journey's end will become meaningful to him only after tragic failure on the heroic seas has delivered him to true virtue, reason, and self-knowledge. Though neither he nor the audience realizes it at the moment, his tragic career will be a quest for the kind of virtue that, rehearsed here, will eventually enable him to die well.

Monsieur rekindles the torch. True, he tempts Bussy with a life of "greatness," but the temptation carries with it the metaphorical associations of light, purpose, direction, hope, resurrection. At Monsieur's politic chiding, Bussy seizes the opportunity to enter the public world, and with perfectly admirable motives he sets out to reform the "enchanted glass" of court:

> B U S S . : I am for honest actions, not for great:
>   If I may bring up a new fashion,
>   And rise in Court with virtue, speed his plough.
>
> [1. 1. 124–26]

Bussy sees no disjunction between his personal ideals and the public persona of Herculean reformer he adopts for the active life.[10] He will accept Fortune's banquet, don her gifts, and venture her rise and fall (1. 1. 136–39), for they are matters of indifference to the man of Stoic virtue. Bussy's implicit assumption that he has already attained virtue (or perhaps that his virtue is inherent) distinguishes him from the men of greatness decried in the opening soliloquy; virtue will not only guide him to his harbor, but direct him out of port and throughout his journey on the gulfs of state. One soon learns, however, that Bussy's inherent virtue is the rude stuff of epic *virtus*, not moral virtue. Once at court the hero's campaign for virtue's sake does not survive long.

Early on in the Guise quarrel Bussy's spirit breaks through the court-ier's disguise adopted to carry out his primary role as scourge of vice. He confronts the Guise with immense pride and courage and with relent-less energy. Monsieur knows his protégé; his summary description is a prophecy of the duel scene and of the tragedy as a whole.

> M O N S . : [*aside*] His great heart will not down, 'tis like the sea
> That partly by his own internal heat,
> Partly the stars' daily and nightly motion,
> Ardour and light, and partly of the place
> The divers frames, and chiefly by the Moon,
> Bristled with surges, never will be won
> (No, not when th' hearts of all those powers are burst)
> To make retreat into his settled home,
> Till he be crown'd with his own quiet foam.
>
> [1. 2. 138–46]

The sea image is carefully chosen to convey the enormous natural com-pulsion driving Bussy's spirit on the "gulfs of State." Psychological neces-sity (his internal heat and the stars' influence) joins with external circum-stance to push Bussy on a relentless course toward self-fulfillment.[11] Bussy is not Fortune's slave, but neither is he virtue's servant; he is rather an awesome child of nature whose zealous defense of his own pride and bosom integrity signals a primary allegiance to the heroic edicts of his "great heart."

At the pivotal turn in Othello's character, the Moor adopts a public persona that subordinates his heart, humanity, and feelings of love to the social "cause" of morality and justice. Othello desires to regain his dig-nity and esteem through a heroic course of revenge, to have society honor him and think well of him once again; his heroic image as dutiful servant of society places him in direct conflict with himself, specifically with the love and amatory idealism enthroned in his heart. Othello's cold, imper-sonal martial resolution is "Like to the Pontic Sea" because it is so inhuman and unnatural. Chapman's Bussy, on the other hand, is like to the sea in the respect that from his "great heart" flow awesome but wholly natural emotions. And, unlike Othello, Bussy does not act with the pretext of defending justice, morality, and order. No matter Bussy's original intention, his public role soon becomes an extension of self, a means to self-fulfillment, a vehicle for the expression of individual excellence. If Othello's unnatural heroic image, reflecting the values of Venetian social consensus (or so he thought), brings him into conflict with self, Bussy's course of heroic individualism, dictated by his "great heart," brings him into pointed conflict with society.

The assertion of heroic spirit in the active life alienates Bussy from society's standards of acceptable behavior. Bussy's increasingly idiosyncratic definitions of honor,[12] accompanying a pattern of increasingly individualistic behavior, emphasize what is unique in Bussy's nature and what is inappropriate, alien, and anachronistic about his conception of society as a proving ground for heroic *virtus*. Bussy is a misfit at court and in contemporary French society; the cultural milieu congenial to his conception of self is the "shame culture" of the heroic age. The description of the duel makes the point emphatically:

> N U N . : As Hector, 'twixt the hosts of Greece and Troy
> (When Paris and the Spartan King should end
> The nine years' war) held up his brazen lance
> For signal, that both hosts should cease from arms,
> And hear him speak: so Barrisor (advis'd). . . .
> D'Ambois (that like a laurel put in fire,
> Sparkled and spit) did much much more than scorn,
> That his wrong should incense him so like chaff,
> To go so soon out; and like lighted paper,
> Approve his spirit at once both fire and ashes:
> So drew they lots, and in them Fates appointed,
> That Barrisor should fight with fiery D'Ambois;
> Pyrrhot with Melynell; with Brisac L'Anou:
> And then like flame and powder they commix'd,
> So spritely, that I wish'd they had been spirits. . . .

> [2. 1. 54–78]

Chapman builds up the duel to "all possible height of Heroicall Action." From the moment when the *nuntius* asks that heavenly *aither* inspire him to relate a tale of godlike spirit, the passage sparkles with fire imagery. The psychological context of the imagery is the association of the element of fire with Mars, with choler, and with the passion of anger.[13] But in its grandeur the imagery is associated with the Olympian fire of Zeus the Conqueror, as Hesiod's *Theogony* depicts him (lines 617–719), with the godlike spirit of Homer's epic warriors, and with Achilles' heroic wrath in particular. This crucial epic evocation testifies that Bussy's spirit, like that of Achilles with whom he is implicitly associated, is fueled by Olympian fire, not by the earthly counterfeit. Like Achilles, Bussy is possessed with a divine spirit of greatness, a divine *inflatus*; the martial exploit at the duel is astonishingly heroic.

One is aware, however, that the fire imagery accompanying the heroes of *The Iliad* conveys not only the grandeur but the danger of such a divine gift.[14] Achilles' short, blazing career is the prime example, but even Hector, though a mortal, is allowed the "frail blaze of excellence" before death, the "lightning" symbolic of a short but heroic life (*CH* 1. 17. 174–78). Bussy and the warriors, indifferent to life and death, stand resolute "Like bonfires of contributory wood" (2. 1. 44), the fire imagery befitting the quality of heroic spirit the warriors exhibit and simultaneously foreshadowing the funeral pyres, its inevitable result. The self-destructive nature of Bussy's heroic compulsion had been implicit in Monsieur's image of the sea driving toward the shore and crowning itself in quiet foam. Later, in the choric prelude to the death scene, he predicts, with imagery drawn from the duel scene, what happens to the awesome children of nature in the course of life's journey:

> M O N S . : Right as in ships of war, whole lasts of powder
> Are laid (men think) to make them last, and guard them:
> When a disorder'd spark that powder taking,
> Blows up with sudden violence and horror
> Ships that kept empty, had sail'd long with terror.
>
> [5. 3. 21–25]

In context, Monsieur suggests that Bussy has been equipped by an irrational or perverse Nature; but this same volatile, fiery spirit is nevertheless the condition of the brief but glorious grandeur characteristic of epic heroism in *The Iliad*.

It is essential to Chapman's *idea* of the heroic tragedy and to his ambivalent conception of Bussy that he validate the grandeur of the heroic spirit in the duel, even as it has led to an action inappropriate to the social milieu and even as the ideal of heroic individualism has come into pointed conflict with the epic social ideal of Herculean reformation. By any rational or moral standard of judgment, of course, it is difficult to justify Bussy's wrath in the duel scene, especially as it follows hard upon the pledge of virtuous reformation. Chapman the translator would have attempted the justification for Achilles in 1598; but, significantly, Chapman the dramatist, apparently older and wiser after the Essex tragedy, makes no effort at all for Bussy in 1604. Indeed, by flaunting the flimsy pretexts of the duel and by stressing that Bussy's astonishing *virtus* is an amoral, irrational compulsion, Chapman seems deliberately to have set out to elicit an ambivalent response from the audience. Extreme expressions of Bussy's astonishing *virtus* and defective moral virtue emerge immediately after the *nuntius* concludes his report. The "manly slaughter" according to the code of individual honor is the "wilful murder" according to the law of society.[15]

Chapman's insistence that Bussy's heroic spirit is wholly natural necessitates that he direct the reassessment of ancient virtue toward Nature herself, specifically toward the concept of "Man in his native noblesse." Bussy's contention that natural man is superior to law (2. 1. 193–204)—a contention King Henry will later defend when he argues that man would still be living in a state of nature, in a golden age world, instead of in Fortune's domain had all men, like Bussy, preserved Nature in her prime—is balanced by Monsieur's cynical version of Bussy's selfish, irrational brutality; but neither the romantic "soft" primitivism nor the cynical "hard" primitivism will stand up to careful scrutiny. Rather, Chapman's and our own ambivalent attitude toward a creature of natural *virtus* who is manifestly deficient in rational virtue is most closely analogous with Seneca's conception of primitive man:

> But no matter how excellent and guileless was the life of the men of that age, they were not wise men; for that title is reserved for the highest achievement. Still, I would not deny that they were men of lofty spirit and—if I may use the phrase—fresh from the gods. For there is no doubt that the world produced a better progeny before it was yet worn out. However, not all were endowed with mental faculties of highest perfection, corresponding to their native powers, which in all were more sturdy than ours and more fitted for toil. *For nature does not bestow virtue; it is an art to become good.* . . . It was by reason of their ignorance of things that men of those days were innocent; and it makes a great deal of difference whether one wills not to sin or has not the knowledge of sin. Justice was unknown to them, unknown prudence, unknown also self-control and bravery; but their rude life possessed certain qualities akin to all these virtues. *Virtue is not vouchsafed to a soul unless that soul has been trained and taught, and by unremitting practice brought to*

perfection. For the attainment of this boon, not in the possession of it, were we born; and even in the best of men, before you *refine them by instruction*, there is but the stuff of virtue, not virtue itself.[16]

In granting the lofty spirit and natural superiority of native noblesse while at the same time pointing out its deficiency in rational moral virtue, Seneca casts light on Chapman's own ambivalent response to a child of the gods like Bussy. However splendid the display of natural *virtus* in the duel, Bussy's native noblesse, if left ungoverned, presents the frightening prospect of titanic individualism set apart from morality and above society's sanctions. Hercules' titanic labors were fueled with moral energy; but in the absence of disciplined rational virtue Bussy's reformation promises something akin to a Lucretian survival of the fittest, as the duel and its solitary survivor might suggest.

Chapman's tragedy would be less perplexing and Bussy himself less ambiguous if King Henry's assumption about a golden age of native noblesse were correct, or if Bussy exhibited the true native noblesse which Strozza defines in *The Gentleman Usher* (5. 4. 56–62), or if Bussy were a throwback to the Christian golden age. If Bussy were allowed to step out of the shadows of the prologue as a pristine Adam, then of course one might blame his corruption and death wholly on a degenerate society.[17] But Bussy, like Essex after 1601, cannot be considered simply a heroic victim. In recognizing the limitations as well as the grandeur of Bussy's natural *virtus* and his own complicity in his demise, one confronts the dramatic dilemma Chapman has posed.

Bussy's initial recognition of a world turned morally corrupt ended in a dispirited collapse (*Procumbit*); so, too, the king is a good enough man to perceive the corruption of his court, but he is weak-kneed, lily-livered. At the same time, though, the strength and spirit of an active scourge call upon qualities of "greatness" that are antithetical to a capacity for "goodness." Nature has rough-hewn even the best of her creatures, and in the world of *Bussy D'Ambois* there appears to be no divinity to shape their end. Seneca had said that natural *virtus* possessed the stuff of virtue, but that it was an art to become good. Who is to teach the art? Can the nurture stick on Bussy's nature? What chance is there for maturation without a "disorder'd spark" setting off a premature explosion? Does not Nature, in fact, run a course toward self-destruction? Bussy's career at court suggests Chapman's pessimism concerning the cultivation of virtue.

In what is initially a moral theater of disguise and discovery, Bussy will play the role of courtier in order to search out vice and, by purging it, to reform the enchanted glass of court. But Bussy's nature does not allow the compromise that role-playing requires of his personal idealism. The spark is struck long before he can fulfill his mission as minister of virtue, and the flame is not extinguished until the duel is concluded. No longer a "sudden" courtier in defense of virtue, Bussy is translated from within, by his own spirit, into a heroic courtier who will not brook the slightest challenge to his personal honor and integrity. The pattern is much the same in the tryst scene. Bussy simply arrives in Tamyra's chamber with the Friar, and one might initially presume that he is there in the role of court lover in order to discover vice. By the end of the scene, however, he is not discovering Tamyra's humour but feeding it. He enters immediately and fully into her service as heroic lover. No matter the context—that Tamyra is weak, that love is adultery, that policy and intrigue speed his plow—Bussy will "fare well." An inconsequential quarrel has led to a heroic duel, an adulterous tryst into the heroic cause of chivalric service.[18] "Too much blood and too little brain . . . wars and lechery," Thersites might have said. And Shakespeare might have said that Bussy's quest for honor and quest for love are both generated by base appetitive passion.

The Shakespearean point of view is voiced by Monsieur in the "flyting" episode:

> MONS.:   I think thee then a man,
> That dares as much as a wild horse or tiger;
> As headstrong and as bloody; and to feed
> The ravenous wolf of thy most Cannibal valour
> (Rather than not employ it), thou would'st turn
> Hackster to any whore . . .
> And murder market folks; quarrel with sheep,
> And run as mad as Ajax; serve a butcher,
> Do anything but killing of the King:
> That in thy valour th' art like other naturals,
> That have strange gifts in nature, but no soul
> Diffus'd quite through to make them of a piece,
> But stop at humours that are more absurd,

Childish and villainous than that hackster, whore,
Slave, cut-throat, tinker's bitch, compar'd before.

[3. 2. 336–53]

Except for the contextual specification of "but killing of the King," Seneca might have said much the same about the bloody primitives and "the matter of Troy" recounted by Homer, Virgil, and Ovid; and Shakespeare did say it in *Troilus and Cressida*. But, however blind is Bussy to moral and ethical standards of conduct, his natural gifts do not "stop at humours" and are not basely appetitive.

Bussy is motivated by heroic *areté*. Unlike Othello, unlike Shakespeare's Achilles and Ajax especially, Bussy shows no acquisitive passion for external honors, for gaining social esteem or social status. The duel is selfish only to the extent that a personal ideal is at issue; otherwise, one might contend that the indifference to life and death and devotion to a heroic principle of behavior are astonishingly selfless. And, unlike Troilus, Bussy is not driven into the love affair by sexual passion (at least there is no emphasis on the point); as with the duel scene, the dramatist stresses Bussy's heroic reaction rather than the degrading context leading to the liaison (see 3. 1. 33–41). Like the heroic duel, the heroic service becomes an objective enactment of Bussy's aspiration for excellence.

A more telling indictment one might transport from *Troilus and Cressida* and *Othello* to weigh against Bussy is that Chapman's hero, like Shakespeare's warriors, has become a deluded heroic myth-maker. After all, Bussy creates a personal epic myth out of a quarrel and an adulterous affair, and throughout the play he identifies his heroic conception of self with Achilles, Hercules, Jove himself. The ironic discrepancy between the reality of the situation and Bussy's delusions of grandeur seems as great as that in *Troilus and Cressida* or that at the end of the temptation scene in *Othello*. Nevertheless, Bussy's heroic image is neither delusive nor unnatural. The description in the duel and several choric passages verify the grandeur of his heroic spirit; he is indeed a throwback to the epic heroes of the past, a "contemporary Achilles" of extraordinary gifts. Bussy's true delusion resides in the assumption that his heroic conception of self can be unmetaphored into actual behavior in a degenerate society. Shakespeare had created a congenial cultural milieu for the warriors of Troy, as if intending to stress that in no situation can an acquisitive martial passion be exemplary; Chapman would respond that the situation is crucial and that Bussy's tragedy in large measure follows from his social dislocation. Had Bussy begun his career at court as Jove's eagle, the alliance of Henry's rationality and Bussy's spirit might have proved to be an exemplary, advantageous relationship for France. But by act 3 Bussy's "headless" actions have entangled him in a tragic situation, and the Guise and Monsieur, soon to be joined by Montsurry, are determined to pull the titan down.

Bussy's vulnerability in society increases in direct proportion to his participation in society and dissociation from heroic individualism. By entering into Tamyra's service, by linking his fate with hers, Bussy resigns his freedom to the sublunar world of mutability and passion:

> B U S S . : So women, that (of all things made of nothing)
> Are the most perfect images of the Moon
> (Or still-unwean'd sweet Moon-calves with white faces),
> Not only are patterns of change to men:
> But as the tender Moonshine of their beauties
> Clears or is cloudy, make men glad or sad.
>
> [4. 1. 15–20]

Monsieur had earlier associated Tamyra with the moon (3. 2. 202), and later in the scene he will liken her transformation to that of Cynthia, the chaste goddess of the moon who fashions cuckold's horns from her own divine fabric (4. 4. 117–21). But Bussy is oblivious to the threatening implication of the remark quoted above, unaware that by pledging his idealism to a symbol of feminine mutability he has subjected himself to Fortune's mutable world and to the passion and policy governing it. Blind to the fact that he is vulnerable to the treachery of others, Bussy is also blind to his own limitations:

> B U S S . : None can be always one: our Griefs and Joys
> Hold several sceptres in us, and have times
> For their predominance. . . .
> And therefore, Princely mistress, in all wars
> Against these base foes that insult on weakness,
> And still fight hous'd behind the shield of Nature,
> Of tyrannous law, treachery, or beastly need,
> Your servant cannot help; authority here
> Goes with corruption.
>
> [4. 1. 25–39]

No matter the guise of corrupt passion, whether forces of nature or psychological tyrants or beastly impulses, they have won ascendancy in man's degenerate world because reason and virtue do not have authority. Bussy's philosophical canon reflects on the limitations of his own "headless" nature as well as others'; but he continues to assume, as he has from the start, that he is in possession of the virtue which in reality can be obtained only after a long experiential quest. He continues to be oblivious to the degrading context of his heroism, unaware that the role he is playing in the corrupt world has been transformed from minister of virtue to servant of adultery, just as he was blind to the self-parody when he described the corrupt citizens who must be purged from the commonwealth.[19]

Having made the initial compromise to enter the fallen world, Bussy has not only been entangled by it but increasingly has become a representative citizen of it. He has been corrupted by society, but the defective nature of his heroic spirit, inspiring a blind heroic idealism, has itself been an accomplice in that corruption. Stoic doctrine and Renaissance humanism do not distinguish the law of nature from right reason, and neither does Chapman's pessimistic vision. Nature has no law, reason no power of governance. The age is rife with natural degeneracy, and the process of degeneration was inherent in man in his native noblesse. From the beginning an imperfect and purposeless Nature has been sliding toward chaos.[20]

Bussy's vulnerability to the corrupting influences of a degenerate society is predicated on the absence of true rational virtue to guide his extraordinary natural gifts.

> MONS.: If thou outlive me, as I know thou must,
> Or else hath Nature no proportion'd end
> To her great labours: she hath breath'd a spirit
> Into thy entrails, of effect to swell
> Into another great Augustus Caesar:
> Organs, and faculties fitted to her greatness:
> And should that perish like a common spirit,
> Nature's a Courtier and regards no merit.

[4. 1. 95–102]

Bussy's heroic spirit will not swell "of effect" into the ideal embodiment of Rome's golden age, for Nature unaided can promise no more than it can provide (3. 1. 104–5), and Nature's ungoverned powers predict their own disintegration. The more fully man is equipped, the sooner he will meet destruction. Man must mend Nature, must undergo the difficult experiential process of "soul-making" in order to shape his own proportioned end. Bussy no sooner begins that process than he is caught up in a degenerate world of policy and intrigue, a milieu in which the assertion of undisciplined natural *virtus* effects tragic entanglement.

To succeed in Fortune's mutable domain, inherent merit needs the guidance of policy. What was evident when Bussy first accepted the Friar's politic counsel in approaching Tamyra is later flaunted when the revenge plot is set in motion. Bussy's heroic bluster (4. 2. 9–17), his natural response to the attack against Tamyra's honor, seems a pathetic appeal to a countergenre; his vision of reality is ineffectual, if not irrelevant, in the face of the enemy's secret machinations. At this moment the supernatural is called on to assist the natural. In the burlesque scene that follows, however, Behemoth and his troops are found to be equally helpless (4. 2. 58–60).[21] The demons are themselves caught up in the intrigue, and the ranks split to cross-purposes (4. 2. 73–75). In the end the Prince of Darkness can speak only darkly, and his advice is pointed: "Meanwhile be wise, / And let [Bussy] curb his rage with *policy*" (4. 2. 137–38; my emphasis). Behemoth had entered the degenerate world with the promise of "deepest truth, and secrets never seen" (4. 2. 50); but once he has sized up the situation and salvaged dignity by shifting the blame to his tardy summons and by uttering some dark oracles, he advocates policy and sneaks away. Even the supernatural must throw in the towel.

Bussy's heroic evocations now become politic bombast, but he remains oblivious to the depraved context into which his "great heart" has sunk. The former heroic passion, recollected in the martial metaphor of the following passage, degenerates grotesquely into an intoxicated cruelty akin to Montsurry's and a politic deviousness akin to Monsieur's:

> B U S S .: I'll soothe his plots: and strew my hate with smiles
> Till all at once the close mines of my heart
> Rise at full date, and rush into his blood:
> I'll bind his arm in silk, and rub his flesh
> To make the vein swell, that his soul may gush
> Into some kennel, where it longs to lie,
> And policy shall be flank'd with policy.
> Yet shall the feeling centre where we meet
> Groan with the weight of my approaching feet:

I'll make th' inspired threshals of his Court
Sweat with the weather of my horrid steps
Before I enter: yet will I appear
Like calm security, before a ruin;
A politician, must like lightning melt
The very marrow, and not print the skin:
His ways must not be seen: the superficies
Of the green centre must not taste his feet,
When hell is plough'd up with his wounding tracts:
And all his harvest reap'd, from hellish facts.

[4. 2. 155–73]

This perverse evocation of Bussy's heroic passion and martial ideals should be contrasted with the epic duel. The grotesque discrepancy between the martial vehicle and the villainous tenor, culminating a pattern of disjunction between Bussy's heroic idealism and his unworthy actions, signals the fall of natural *virtus*. Bussy has now fully resigned the personal epic myth of heroic individualism in favor of a cruel, Machiavellian persona that makes him scarcely distinguishable from his enemies and is—for Bussy—pathetically *unnatural*. The "contemporary Achilles" has put aside his ancient virtue, adopting in its stead something far worse, an antiheroic image, a conception of self as a base politician, one who typifies the very court he had initially pledged to reform. The metamorphosis of man in his prime into Fortune's politic creature is now complete.

THE CROWN OF MORAL VIRTUE

The choric commentary announcing the final scene brings the full context of natural *virtus* into pessimistic perspective.[22] Monsieur's recapitulation of earlier remarks—that Nature bestows gifts from her rich treasury at random and without purpose and that they are not only self-destructive but vulnerable in Fortune's world—is countered by the Guise's suggestion that Nature's end need not be "great," that Nature's decorum cannot be judged by Fortune's worldly standards of success (5. 3. 26–37). The Guise's assumption that Nature must have an ultimate purpose is closer to the truth, but if Monsieur cannot foresee anything beyond the tragic explosion of *virtus*, so, too, the Guise does not understand that man must shape the end Nature has rough-hewn. Bussy will perfect his "headless" nature by embracing reason and virtue, his final moments signifying a true "coronation" in his own quiet foam—to recall Monsieur's sarcasm of act 1. As embodiments of fate, the choric spokesmen articulate the pessimistic perspective of the tragic genre, according to which Bussy's quest will be crowned with death; Bussy himself, however, will deliver the heroic genre's response to tragedy. The final moments of the drama will assert that the boon of heroic grandeur and human dignity can be snatched from the jaws of tragic failure. Something beyond the inner glow of defiance Webster found amidst the ashes, Bussy's heroic defiance of death will be seconded by an equally heroic Christian magnanimity and moral goodness. To achieve self-knowledge amidst the tumbling chaos is small recompense, the Jacobean escape being a distant reflection on the educative process of virtue Seneca and Plato had envisioned,[23] but the final metamorphosis on Chapman's stage nevertheless testifies that in the impenetrably dark world of evil the stars shine still.

The third, authoritative choric voice in act 5 is Friar Camolet's. The holy pander, slave of Fortune and Opinion,[24] advocate of psychological determinism and hypocritical policy, comes to a true knowledge of himself and the world in which he has lived only after death. Destined to roam the earth as a shade seeking contrition for his corrupt life,[25] he no longer wears the hypocritical robes of his former office. He offers the advice of a new ministry, responding to Tamyra's complaint that life ends in grief from the superior vantage gained through death:

> GHOST :   'Tis the just curse of our abus'd creation,
>   Which we must suffer here, and 'scape hereafter:
>   He hath the great mind that submits to all
>   He sees inevitable; he the small
>   That carps at earth, and her foundation-shaker,
>   And rather than himself, will mend his maker.
>
> [5. 3. 69–74]

The grim Stoic *sententia* affirms cosmic justice and human culpability. The man with a "great mind" submits willingly to the inevitable that he might be in harmony with the universal order; rather than complain against heaven, the truly great man mends himself. Unfortunately, the implication of the play is that this process may be effected only by a purgatorial experience after death (like the Friar's) or by a purgatorial experience at death (like Bussy's). To win a head and lose a body is a grim sentence indeed. Nevertheless, a truer choric voice than Monsieur or the Guise, the Friar defines greatness as a quality of the mind, as if predicting the haven of virtue at which Bussy will finally arrive.

In the moments before the climax of the tragedy, Bussy begins a welcome process of ennoblement. He is prepared to cross the politic advice of the supernatural, to cast aside the antiheroic persona of devious politician, and to "fare well" above all else. Bussy's return to his heroic individualism marks the return of former values. The thought of Tamyra rekindles his natural *virtus*, inspiring a heroic evocation typical of Bussy's earlier characterization: "O how it multiplies my blood with spirit, / And makes me apt t' encounter death and hell" (5. 2. 95–96). He will obey the summons of her letter and act heroically, if once again compulsively, against all odds.

Bussy speaks with the bravado of the earlier scenes when he arrives at Tamyra's chamber. The challenge rings with a familiar assurance:

> B U S S . : Murder'd? I know not what that Hebrew means:
>   That word had ne'er been named had all been D'Ambois. . . .
>   Murder'd? Who dares give all the room I see
>   To D'Ambois' reach? or look with any odds
>   His fight i'th'face, upon whose hand sits death. . . .
>   Fate is more strong than arms, and sly than treason,
>   And I at all parts buckled in my Fate.
>
> [5. 3. 76–88]

This is no submission to the inevitable, but an indifference to life and death that recalls the epic duel. Bussy responds to the dangers confronting him with a strident assertion of heroic idealism; he will snatch from the chaos not self-knowledge or a wider vision of cosmic justice but his own personal integrity, freedom, and nobility. Once again he plays the role of Nature's minion, as if determined to spark the glorious but fatal explosion Monsieur had predicted.

The reassertion of natural *virtus* runs counter to the Friar's espousal of humble virtue. Having renounced the policy that had perverted his greatness, Bussy dedicates himself anew to the noble service of a chivalric lover. The Friar's chilling admonition to mend oneself may frighten moral approbation from the audience, but Bussy's titanic heroism wins its admiration and, given the degeneracy of the hostile society, its sympathy. It appears that Chapman will have it both ways, celebrating the grandeur of heroic passion while at the same time insisting on a program of moral reformation. In the two phases of the death scene the dramatist makes his attempt at a final reconciliation of *virtus* and virtue.

Chapman's dark irony places Bussy's greatest challenge at his best moment. Just when he heeds Tamyra's appeal to spare Montsurry and tempers his wrath, the coward fates shoot him in the back, as if to dramatize that "Reward goes backwards." After a brief philosophical excursus, Bussy responds to the mortal wound and to the cosmic injustice with the pessimism of the opening soliloquy: "Nothing is made of nought, of all things made; / Their abstract being a dream but of a shade" (5. 3. 133–34). But the murmur of self-pity soon leads to a heroic complaint against heaven:

> B U S S . : I'll not complain to earth yet, but to heaven,
> And (like a man) look upwards even in death. . . .
> Prop me, true sword, as thou hast ever done:
> The equal thought I bear of life and death,
> Shall make me faint on no side; I am up
> Here like a Roman statue; I will stand
> Till death hath made me marble: O my fame
> Live in despite of murder. . . .
>
> [5. 3. 135–46]

The odds have been stacked too high against Bussy and the depravity around him painted too thick for the audience not to recognize in these lines the glow of a magnificent spirit, the "frail blaze of excellence" that marks the end of a brief but heroic career. This powerful tribute to the heroic ideals of the pagan epic reveals the translator of *The Iliad* at his very best. Bussy stands as a great Roman, not the Augustus Caesar of the golden age whom Monsieur had envisioned, but a Roman of an older "shame culture," propped by his heroic *virtus* and indifferent to life and death. Bussy is once again the active warrior of the epic duel, this time triumphing over death by winning a Herculean fame that will mock Fortune's vicissitudes. Nevertheless, as Monsieur had predicted, the end of Nature in her prime is only a brief, if glorious, flash of lightning—or so it would seem.

The Friar had advised against such complaints in favor of individual moral reformation. Now playing the scriptural role of the humble "fisher of men," the Friar asks Bussy to forgive his murderers, intending to guide the hero to a calm and virtuous repose. Immediately, unexpectedly, Bussy heeds the Friar's admonition, swallowing his defiance of a malevolent fate. The forgiveness is validated by the resignation of his sword, a weighty symbolic gesture that is accompanied—one assumes—by Bussy's slumping to the stage floor, a physical submission that will recall the *Procumbit* of the opening soliloquy. Humble virtue will now guide Bussy into harbor.

When Othello resigns his second sword at journey's end, the gesture signifies a submission to truth and reality. He scorns the false conception of self, acknowledges his guilt, and will soon assess the delusive heroic image as that of a colossal fool. Othello is finally "great of heart" because the human being gives over any further pretense to heroic grandeur, faces his self-deception squarely, and enacts a revenge upon himself in testimony to the social and amatory ideals he has betrayed. Bussy's heroic magnanimity at journey's end is something quite different.

> BUSS.:   I forgive them all;
> And you my Lord, their fautor; for true sign
> Of which unfeign'd remission, take my sword;
> Take it, and only give it motion,
> And it shall find the way to victory
> By his own brightness, and th' inherent valour
> My fight hath still'd into 't, with charms of spirit.
>
> [5. 3. 159–65]

The grandeur of Bussy's heroic *virtus* and the inherent value of his heroic conception of self are not scorned but insisted upon. The resignation of his titanic heroism in favor of a Christian magnanimity at this moment is by no means a renunciation of heroic image; indeed, the latter stance of human compassion is validated precisely by the fact that Bussy gives up so much to assume it.

After the "killing spectacle" of Tamyra breaks his heart, however, Bussy regards himself and his heroic pursuit of virtue from a critical distance, from the rational, moral perspective recommended by the Friar:

> BUSS.: O frail condition of strength, valour, virtue,
> In me like warning fire upon the top
> Of some steep beacon, on a steeper hill;
> Made to express it like a falling star

Silently glanc'd—that like a thunderbolt
Look'd to have stuck, and shook the firmament.
                    He dies.

[5. 3. 188–93]

The *de casibus* sentence stresses the futility of human aspiration and—
inescapably, it would seem—the moral deficiency of Bussy's natural *virtus*. Self-knowledge, reason, and moral virtue come to Bussy only at a
final, tragic recognition, but the emblem he creates from their vantage
may still help others to mend themselves. They may see in the fallen
titan a beacon overlooking the seas he had sailed so confidently, warning against ambition, presumption, and a life of greatness and guiding
them to a haven of virtue. At the end, Bussy displays a "great mind,"
submitting to the inevitable and attempting to "mend himself."

Bussy's assessment of self, however, cannot be the final word, for it
does not reflect the ambivalence one has felt toward the hero throughout
the play and feels for him at the moment of death. We know Bussy was
wrong and welcome the clear-eyed acknowledgment of guilt and failure;
but, given the pessimistic context of the heroic quest and the grandeur of
Bussy's *virtus*, especially in act 5, the final *de casibus* indictment seems
partial, seems indeed an unwarranted and unwelcome affirmation of
Monsieur's pessimistic point of view. The Friar's authoritative, summary
valediction provides a needed corrective to Bussy's self-evaluation:

GHOST : Farewell brave relics of a complete man:
    Look up and see thy spirit made a star,
    Join flames with Hercules: and when thou set'st
    Thy radiant forehead in the firmament,
    Make the vast continent, crack'd with they receipt,
    Spread to a world of fire: and th'aged sky,
    Cheer with new sparks of old humanity.

[5. 3. 268–74]

Bussy's titanic spirit, while glorifying the hero in outfacing death, has
been perfected at the end by moral virtue. The "Predominant Perturbation" displayed in the first half of the death scene has been overruled by
wisdom; Bussy has progressed from the astonishing yet morally deficient
mode of *virtus* to the better mode of virtue. With moral defect made
perfection, with "Predominant Perturbation" now bridled as rational

moral energy, Bussy's purified heroic spirit rises as ethereal fire to join the Hercules of the Stoic-Christian tradition in the starry firmament.

Chapman would contend that the two parts of the death scene are complementary and that the ethical conflict between epic *virtus* and moral virtue has been resolved in the ideal of the "complete man." One must confess, however, that the attempted reconciliation of heretofore antithetical ideals is not convincing. The splendor of Bussy's heroic defiance of death dwarfs the concluding portrait of goodness and, conversely, the moral heroism undercuts, as if to cancel out, the astonishing grandeur of the heroic spirit. And though the ideals are yoked by dramatic expediency together, the ethical conflict between them is never fully resolved.[26] Nevertheless, the Friar's authoritative tribute to the "complete man" *is* aesthetically satisfying. In his final moments the hero's display of compassion and acknowledgment of frailty place him as a member of the human community, enabling the audience to sympathize with Bussy and, given the assurance of his final goodness, liberating the audience to celebrate retrospectively the splendor of the titanic failure. The language of the Friar's epilogue provides the opportunity for such a celebration: "brave relicts," "spirit," "Hercules," "set'st / Thy radiant forehead in the firmament," "new sparks of old humanity"—the grandeur of Bussy's aspiration for excellence is what the Friar's language remembers for the audience and what the audience—assured that *virtus* has been channeled into moral virtue—remembers from the play.

Unfortunately, the "frail blaze of excellence" that speaks for the heroic genre against Chapman's tragic vision does little to alleviate the gloom on the world stage. The cruel irony of Chapman's pessimism suggests that rational, disciplined virtue can be no more than an *ars moriendi* consolation and that its lesson is lost on others who have not yet suffered enough as a necessary preparation for embracing it. Tamyra and Montsurry evidence that the struggle with imperfect virtue continues unrelieved in the fallen world. Implicit in the Friar's epilogue may be the notion that Bussy's flame will ignite a universal conflagration out of which cleansing fires the world will be born anew, but one doubts that Chapman's vision was so optimistic.

CHAPMAN'S "COMPLETE MAN"

In his final moments, Bussy's magnanimous actions and harsh evaluation of his heroic quest would seem to conform to the Shakespearean conception of heroism, according to which the soldier's delusive conception of self must be put aside in order for a true human heroism to emerge. Bussy has been cast "headlong from the sky" (see 1. 1. 130–39); like Essex, an Elizabethan Icarus, like Byron after him, the overreacher had been enraptured by a heroic conception of self, had been "possess'd . . . with greatness," and at the end that heroic image was betrayed by his own humanity, by his real human limitations: "O frail condition of strength, valour, virtue" (5. 3. 188). Bussy was self-fated by delusions of grandeur, the argument might continue, and his greatest moment was his last, when he recognized the pretense and folly of his heroic image and, embracing humble virtue, transformed himself into an emblem warning against the very kind of heroic aspiration that had brought him low. But this apparent similarity between Chapman's Bussy and Shakespeare's tragic soldiers is deceptive. Bussy is not at all like Othello, and the dramatists' conceptions of the soldier's psyche, the heroic genre, and the nature of tragic grandeur are substantially different.

Although in the wake of the Essex tragedy Chapman does acknowledge that Bussy is partly responsible for his own demise and that his behavior is amoral (if not immoral), the dramatist's attitude toward Bussy's tragic dislocation and moral deviancy is far more ambivalent than Shakespeare's might have been toward such a "contemporary Achilles" as Bussy or Essex. Chapman's pessimistic vision of a malevolent fate, seconded by Machiavellian duplicity, suggests that Bussy was as much the victim of a degenerate world as he was self-fated by soaring presumption. And, indeed, in a society where moral standards are at best relative, who is to condemn Bussy's amoral spirit? Unbridled heroic passion would be open to censure in the ideal court of Elizabeth (1. 2. 1–26), but in the French court where reason is perverted into calculating policy or enervated by frailty and inaction, or in the Jacobean court in England, or (thinking of Essex) in the real Elizabethan court at the turn of the century, the amoral compulsion may well be preferred to patent immorality and hypocrisy. ·

Furthermore, Bussy's heroic passion should be distinguished from that of Shakespeare's tragic soldiers. Essex's reprehensible behavior and Achilles' moments of blind wrath in the second half of *The Iliad* intimated to

Chapman that pure heroic passion was a powerful amoral compulsion that might be misdirected toward base objectives or properly guided by reason toward worthy ends; of itself, however, the heroic passion is never base. Nor is it unnatural. At the pivotal turn in Othello's character, we recall, the Moor adopts a heroic conception of self that wars against his natural human instincts; Othello's heroic image, as it turns the soldier against the lover and ultimately leads to a "heroic" murder, perverts Othello's true humanity as surely as it precipitates a crime against nature. Bussy, on the other hand, is too much the "natural." His astonishing spirit is a gift of nature, and though his heroic behavior may be rash and unbridled, it is never unnatural. And neither, therefore, is his heroic image pretentious; if anything, it is too exact a reflection of the inherent aspiration for excellence that dominates his psyche.

But perhaps most important is the fact that Bussy does not renounce his heroic conception of self at death. Rather, he transcends it by progressing to a higher, more admirable mode of heroism. To be sure, in his final moment Bussy embraces the better course of virtue by forgiving his adversaries; but, just as the resignation of the sword is not a renunciation of the heroic image it symbolizes, Bussy's virtuous stance does not deny the grandeur of his initial defiance of death. On the contrary, Chapman would contend that Bussy's "outward Fortitude" is not rejected, but complemented and improved upon by an inner fortitude equally extraordinary, equally heroic, and in this situation morally superior. The heroic defiance of death followed by a virtuous submission to the inevitable and an effort at self-reformation define Bussy as a "complete man"; he has become at the end a fully equipped, fully exemplary hero who unerringly bridles or looses his heroic spirit depending on the situation.

Having defied death and a malevolent fate heroically, Bussy then bridles his titanic spirit, assuming an equally heroic stance in the second part of the death scene. The grandeur of Bussy's acceptance of the inevitable recalls that of Achilles in the 1598 *Iliads* when he resigned himself to Briseis's departure:

> *Shee wept and lookt upon her love; he sigh't and did refuse.*
> *O how his wisdome with his power did mightilie contend—*
> *His love incouraging his power and spirite, that durst descend*
> *As far as Hercules for her, yet wisedome all subdude,*
> *Wherein a high exploite he showd, and sacred fortitude.*
>
> [CH 1. 1. 360–64]

In this passage (which Chapman added to Homer's text) Achilles' "over-ruling Wisedome" subdues his "Predominant Perturbation," his Hercu-lean spirit, that might otherwise have issued in the "high exploite" of "Heroicall Action." But this rational restraint is itself astonishing pre-cisely because the Herculean spirit that reason overrules is so powerful. Achilles' submission to the inevitable thus constitutes a titanic exploit, not of outward fortitude but of inner fortitude. Similarly, although Bussy would seem to humble himself when resigning his heroic *virtus* in favor of rational fortitude, there is nothing "humble" about the moral virtue he displays; rather, the virtue should be understood as a "high exploite," a titanic, Herculean exhibition of moral courage.

Bussy's grandeur, whether exemplified by heroic *virtus* or moral vir-tue, is predicated on extraordinary epic behavior; whether the "high exploite" of outward fortitude or the "high exploite" of inner fortitude, Bussy's actions transcend normative human behavior. Chapman's con-ception of heroism as an extraordinary, transcendent "height" to be attained by fulfilling the heroic ideals of classical and Renaissance epic is thus diametrically opposed to a Shakespearean heroism based on the renunciation of heroic grandeur and the humble acceptance of one's own frail, foolish, errant humanity.

In his final moments, Bussy displays the "learning" which the Guise of *The Revenge of Bussy D'Ambois* proclaims to be "the crown of man, and all his parts" (2. 1. 84) and which he judged to be lacking in Bussy's career at court. That this "learning" should be achieved at the moment of death and that the educative process should be one of tragic suffering and failure indicate the depth of Chapman's pessimism. The hero's great natural gifts, as they drive him inevitably toward conflict with society, are themselves a tragic liability. Indeed, Chapman's vision of Nature as inherently disordered, irrational, and self-destructive in its awesome, ungoverned power veils an apology for both Bussy and Essex. They are not only heroic victims of society, exemplars of ancient virtue who are pathetically dislocated in a degenerate milieu, but they seem to be victims of an irrational Providence as well. In the world of *Bussy D'Ambois*, Nature is as blind and monstrous as Fortune; the more fully the hero is equipped, the sooner he will meet destruction.

Against this pervasive pessimism, which at moments approaches a vi-sion of the world as a tragic theater of the absurd, the heroic genre asserts its luminous claim to reality. Bussy's quest to reform society is a tragic failure, and his final plea for reconciliation between Tamyra and Montsurry is fruitless; but he does achieve an individual triumph that the tragic world cannot darken. At the climax of the tragedy, Bussy's "Predominant Perturbation" is brought into exemplary accommodation with his "over-ruling Wisedome." Although I have suggested the problematical nature of the reconciliation between *virtus* and virtue, the two ideals symbolized by Bussy's starry apotheosis as "complete man" speak with one voice for the heroic countergenre and the hero's ability to transcend his tragic world.

5

THE IMPROBABLE HEROICS

OF *ANTONY AND CLEOPATRA*

Because Shakespeare's *Antony and Cleopatra* is so different from Chapman's *Bussy D'Ambois*, a cursory glance at some of the similarities is likely to be startling. Each contains, for example, a martial hero of extraordinary prowess, Herculean in his grandeur; a passionate woman associated with feminine frailty and lunar mutability, whose maleficent power over her warrior is fatal to him; the moral vacuum in a world in which the hero must assert individual values and justify them by dying for them; the seeming endorsement of an adulterous love relationship; the chivalric coloring of the heroic love; the discrepancy between the mundane love affair and the hyperbolic poetry celebrating it; the victory of Fortune and her Machiavellian favorites; and much more. These similarities are implausibly superficial, of course, and for one to argue in these superficial terms that *Antony and Cleopatra* responds explicitly to *Bussy D'Ambois*—necessitating a fruitless thematic exercise that would leave untouched what is unique and most attractive about Shakespeare's play —would be utter folly. Nevertheless, given these similarities and the plays' dating (*Bussy D'Ambois*, probably written and performed in 1604, was published in 1607; Shakespeare's play is thought to have been written and performed in 1607), the likelihood is that Chapman's play did have a negative influence on *Antony and Cleopatra*, one that enabled Shakespeare to clarify his own conceptions of Herculean heroism, heroic passion, feminine frailty, amatory idealism, and human heroism by distinguishing them from those of Chapman. Initially, these distinctions might be focused on the characterization of Antony and Cleopatra.

When news of Antony's suicide reaches Caesar at Alexandria, Maecenas and Agrippa are allowed a fascinating reflection on Antony's life:

M A E C . :   His taints and honors
   Wag'd equal with him.
[A G R . :]   A rarer spirit never
   Did steer humanity; but you gods will give us
   Some faults to make us men. Caesar is touch'd.
M A E C . : When such a spacious mirror's set before him,
   He must needs see himself.

$$[5. \ 1. \ 30-35]$$

In spite of the gracious tone and the timely evocation of sympathy, this brief eulogy is an inadequate description of the Antony whom the audience has witnessed since the battle of Actium. The Romans, locked into a limited historical perspective for which Caesar is the principal spokesman, reveal a conception of tragedy different from the tragic romance Shakespeare has written for Antony and Cleopatra. In paying tribute to a titan brought low in the *de casibus* tradition of the *Mirror For Magistrates*, they suggest that Antony's rare Roman spirit has been ill-served, perhaps debased, by the "taints" and "faults" earlier associated with the "strumpet's fool." At best, however, this accounts for only half of the tragedy. Antony's passionate love folly, even as it strips him of Roman greatness, has fostered a different kind of heroic spirit and heroic grandeur, a magnanimity and fidelity to the values of the heart that are contrary to Roman nobleness and beyond the range of Roman comprehension.

One may suggest, in fact, that the Romans' commentary is more appropriate to Chapman's Bussy than to Shakespeare's Antony. The "rare spirit" that steers Bussy's human nature toward honor and excellence makes appropriate analogies with Hercules and Achilles. Although "frailty" and a malevolent world of Fortune bring the titan down and Bussy himself pronounces the *de casibus* moral on his tragic career, the hero falls as a falling star, and the splendor of the titanic attempt is what we remember, the astonishing spectacle of man trying to overreach human limitation is what we celebrate. When the Friar announces Bussy's starry apotheosis at the end of Chapman's heroic tragedy, the audience joins in sympathetic tribute to a "rare spirit" indeed. A human grandeur based on human frailty,[1] however, is something quite different.

L E P . :   I must not think there are
   Evils enow to darken all his goodness:

His faults, in him, seem as the spots of heaven,
More fiery by night's blackness.

[1. 4. 10–13]

The willful venality that betrays Antony according to history's record, confirming the Roman judgment of tragic loss, is precisely what generates an improbable defiance of that same world of time and Fortune, calling into question the simplistic *de casibus* perspective that has judged him. The tragic grandeur Antony gains through death will not shake the "round world" as Caesar supposes it should (5. 1. 14–19), will not "crack" the "vast continent" as the Friar expects Bussy's will (5. 3. 271–72); Antony does not die as a glorious triumvir, a titanic shaper and shaker of the empire, but as a lover, a private man testifying to the values of love's world. By persevering in his allegiance to a passionate love vision that blinds him to reality, Antony emerges from the heart of loss with transcendent values that outshine, as if "spots of heaven," the ideals of a mundane, benighted empire.

Bussy's quest on Fortune's seas might be described as an attempt to achieve the titanic stature of Hercules, his mythical prototype. Although the hero's natural *virtus* is Achillean in its heroic furor throughout most of the play, he does not achieve Herculean stature until the heroic passion is transformed by suffering and failure. At the end, when heroic *virtus* has been crowned with exemplary moral virtue, Bussy's "rare spirit" joins that of Hercules in the starry firmament. The absence of a like ethical emphasis in Shakespeare's heroic tragedy is typical, but the immediate point is that Antony must put aside his pretension to heroic image in order to achieve a different quality of grandeur. The Roman ideal of martial excellence, symbolized by Mars, and Antony's own Roman ideal of fame through world dominance, symbolized by Hercules, must be renounced both in word and deed.[2] The mere verbal recantation of act 1, scene 1, is insufficient; but when Mars is ignominiously betrayed by the actions at Actium and when Hercules deserts the chivalric dreamer a few scenes later, then the great heart is purified, and a truly "rare spirit" emerges. Significantly, Mars and Hercules will return to pay tribute to Antony's human heroism, but they do so in incongruous roles and in Egyptian dress. The Mars we witness after Actium is a warrior who celebrates the glory of Venus's enfetterment, fighting in testimony to love's value, and the Hercules, a titan who is redefined by Cleopatra's dream-vision as one who stands up peerless in love's world.

Cleopatra's "taints" and "faults" are similarly the source of her ennoblement. In the last chapter we saw that Tamyra was associated with the moon, both with the symbolic governess of the mutable world whose variations "are patterns of change to men" (4. 1. 18) and also with Cynthia, chaste goddess of the moon who nevertheless fashions cuckold's horns from her own divine fabric (4. 1. 117–21). The latter allusion presses the identification of Tamyra with the lunar principle of self-transformation and, specifically, with the mythological transformation of Diana into Venus.³ Both aspects of the lunar association are damning to Tamyra, the first suggesting that the female's maleficent power over the hero is a debilitating limitation placed upon him, the second stressing her inherent inconstancy and frailty. Shakespeare found in the Egyptian Isis,⁴ the benevolent goddess of the moon, the prototype for Cleopatra's magical transformations, both for her own transformations and for the changes she brings about in her "servant." Initially, though, Cleopatra is distanced from the benevolent Isis. As "terrene moon" she is symbolic governess over the flux of values and debilitating transformations of identity that bring about Antony's defeat and demise. Her power over him appears maleficent; as seductress, she seems the Venus who emasculated Mars and as sorceress, a baleful Circe. The "infinite variety" of her own transformations, moreover, seems an endless arsenal of seductive ploys and deceitful postures in the service of lust. The apotheosis of Cleopatra as *myrionymos* Isis in the final moments of the play, however, signals that she has transcended the frail and maleficent aspects of her Venereal, Circean, and lunar associations. The "infinite variety" of her human nature is ennobled, and that ennoblement validates the benevolent magic of her love as well. For when Cleopatra proves her own nobility, the audience must pay retrospective tribute to the magnanimous lover who resigned his pretense to Roman nobleness in favor of her strong toil of grace. At the end, her "faults" also shine like "spots of heaven."

The lovers' defiance of reality represents the lyric imagination's rejection of the values implicit in history's *de casibus* judgment of them.⁵ Late in the play, as Antony and Cleopatra's lyric projections spill into comedic and romance visions of reality, the audience becomes increasingly aware that they are creating a legend in defiance of their grim antagonists, Caesar and historical fact. In this respect the lovers and the poet are of imagination compact. The story within the history is what motivated Shakespeare to recreate Plutarch's *Lives*, and the poet shares with Antony and Cleopatra their vision of love, its lyric projection, its claim to reality, its human heroism. Caesar, of course, does not share the vision; and yet, at the end of the play he is allowed to intimate a distinction between the historical fact of his victory and the legend of heroic love Antony and Cleopatra have forged from the ashes of their chance:

> CAES.:   High events as these
> Strike those that make them; and their story is
> No less in pity than his glory which
> Brought them to be lamented.
>
> [5. 2. 360–63]

The distinction between the human triumph of the "story" and the *de casibus* verdict of history is crucial, for to the extent that the "story" is celebrated, Caesar, Fortune, and history itself are defied by the lovers and dramatist alike.

THE "STRUMPET'S FOOL"

Shakespeare might easily have written a tragedy for Antony that would make good the choric appraisals of Maecenas, Agrippa, and Caesar, but he chose rather to play against the *de casibus* narrative a story that peeped through the scars of history. This double perspective accounts for the generally ambivalent response of the play's critics to the lovers themselves. Of the critical realists who hold that Shakespeare's play is essentially a *de casibus* history with some romantic (often ironic) overtones, it might be said that common sense is on their side.[6] For no matter the distinction Sidney draws between the historian and the poet, the lovers' story at every point defies what experience defines as real and what art defines as appropriate. In the first instance, the conflict between perspectives centers on that between storybook time and historical time, between the power of the human imagination to construct a private reality and history's "objective" record of public events.

Although we are wont to qualify the great-man theory of history, common sense tells us that the Roman concept of time in *Antony and Cleopatra* is closer to the truth.[7] The present grows out of the past and the future grows out of the present. For the Romans in the play, time is the stuff of politics and history; it revolves like Fortune's wheel, but because its seemingly endless revolutions are predictable, Fortune's minion —the shaper of time, politics, and history—can defeat the past and conquer the future if his present actions are expedient and opportune. As Caesar well knows, history demands its own kind of artistry, the politician's improvisatory ability to shape present events, even as they are pressured by the past, into a historical vision of the future. According to Cleopatra's storybook sense of history, however, politics is subsumed in love, and past love is annihilated by present delight in her "man of men." When Antony is at Alexandria, Cleopatra exhibits a seductress' improvisatory artistry designed to ensure the perpetuity of the present. When Antony is away, Egypt's languid procession of present pleasurable moments simply stops; Cleopatra's "gap of time" is filled with narcotic reminiscences[8] of her former triumphs over Pompey and Caesar, men who, buried in time, are the root causes of Rome's present garboils, but who remain only lovers in Egypt's reminiscent history and now pale in comparison with Antony.

Egypt is governed by Nature and dominated by a comedic vision of reality. Fortune-telling simply has no claim on the Egyptian sense of time. In the comic toast to Cleopatra that begins act 1, scene 2, her libertine girls mock the soothsayer's solemn pronouncements, substituting for his sense of the future their own jokes about royal men, sexuality, and fertility. Isis is invoked, as if one of the girls' bedfellows, to preside over a future full of jokes, daydreams, and playful reveries celebrating love's victory over history's kings; the fickle moon goddess and a sense of time governed by natural cycles of love and fertility are set in direct opposition to the Roman sense of time dominated by politics, history, and opportunism. Common sense tells us, as I say, that the Roman point of view is closer to the truth.

A storybook sense of the improbable informs Shakespeare's characterization as well. Art had its own laws of reality, its appropriate rules of decorum that were supposed to ensure that the artist's creation was *like* truth. But by any decorous standard—not to mention moral and ethical standards—it is absurd to think that a Roman warrior's metamorphosis into a "strumpet's fool" should be the basis for a final heroic grandeur. Yet this is the paradox Shakespeare's story will explain and the audience will be challenged to understand.

On the river Cydnus, Cleopatra as Venus "pursed up" the soldier's heart; she has since subdued Mars in her toil of grace and has presided over his transformation into love's "soldier." As Philo's initial heroic evocation makes clear, Antony's present metamorphosis threatens a complete loss of martial identity; in fact, the condition of his enrollment in the school of love is the denial of all that Rome and its codes of civic duty and martial heroism stand for. Surprisingly, the Mars we are asked to note voluntarily exchanges the battlefield for love's net, countering Philo's vision of martial heroism with an evocation of heroic love. Antony exorcises from his psyche Fulvia, Caesar, and the remembrance of things past, and to validate the sincerity of the psychic transformation he constructs his new world and new value system on the ruins of the former allegiance.

> A N T . : Let Rome in Tiber melt, and the wide arch
> Of the rang'd empire fall! Here is my space,
> Kingdoms are clay; our dungy earth alike
> Feeds beast as man; the nobleness of life
> Is to do thus [*embracing*]—when such a mutual pair
> And such a twain can do't, in which I bind,
> [On] pain of punishment, the world to weet
> We stand up peerless.
>
> [1. 1. 33–40]

At Cleopatra's prompting, the aspirant to love's soldiership constructs the lovers' cosmos in direct opposition to all that the Roman empire lives by: time, space, sensible reality, ideals of heroism and nobility, standards of decorum. His time is present pleasure, his space Cleopatra's arms, his vision of reality the blind love passion that mocks political and martial idealism. The lover's exultant poetry signals a kind of death for the Roman soldier, and this voluntary renunciation of his Roman heroic image validates the assertion of love's value and, above all, of Cleopatra's value.

Antony is not simply beguiled. Implicit in Antony's assertions is that his hyperbolic expression and excessive actions are an appropriate response to the love he feels in his heart and to the woman he celebrates—one might say, to the natural deity he worships. The Cleopatra who sails down the river Cydnus, after all, "o'er-pictur[es] that Venus where we see / The fancy outwork nature" (2. 2. 200–201). Something more than a Venus *armata*,[9] with something above the captivating art of the seductress, she seems a goddess who possesses a magical power over nature. Sensuality may be her medium, but Shakespeare's telling use of personification brings nature to life in response to her presence, indeed makes all of nature her paramour. And yet, it is not Cleopatra's person but the natural magic of her personality that beggars all description.[10] She has a magical gift of decorum:

ANT.:   Fie, wrangling queen!
Whom every thing becomes—to chide, to laugh,
To weep; [whose] every passion fully strives
To make itself [in thee] fair and admir'd!

[1. 1. 48–51]

Whether petty, abrasive, silly, or noble, the sincerity of her raw emotion and the naturalness of her conscious duplicity,[11] the integrity she brings to diversity and the concord to discord suggest the natural magic of human nature.

Antony's love for Cleopatra suggests that in Egypt he is emancipated from the dehumanizing fetters which Roman law and social mores have placed upon him.[12] At the end of the opening dialogue, Antony's suggestion to "wander through the streets and note/The qualities of people" (1. 1. 53–54) is both a pledge of allegiance to the naturalness and humanity of love's world and a celebratory progress of those who stand up peerless in that world. The action is as meaningful from the Egyptian perspective as it is irresponsible and whimsical from that of the Roman presenters. For all this, though, one must admit that Caesar is right. As long as Antony maintains, or attempts to reestablish, his psychological ties to Roman ideals and his political ties to the empire, such actions do not "become him."

The messenger from Caesar is eventually admitted, and with him comes the reflux of Roman time, space, vocabulary, values, reality—an entire psychic reorientation, just as Cleopatra had feared. "I must with haste from hence" (1. 2. 132)—the iambic accents land on duty, expediency, and geographical space.[13] He has been living in a fool's paradise, in a lotus land of dotage, in a state of deathlike oblivion. While he has idled time away, powers "breed" faction, the hated are "grown to strength" and "grown to love," Pompey "creeps apace," winning the hearts of those who have not "thrived," quietness has "grown sick of rest" (1. 3. 44–54). Historical cycles of time have revolved, and the use of fertility imagery associated with Egypt places in causal relationship the wanton state of Antony's psychological garden in Egypt and the unweeded garden in Rome. For Antony to become a good governor in Rome, he must not only seize the moment to act expediently, but he must also govern himself. He must quit Egypt and reject its values.

The vegetation imagery is but one stroke in Shakespeare's full sketch of Antony's dilemma. He cannot stand as triple pillar in Rome and peerless lover in Egypt at the same time. He thinks he can. The first of Antony's attempts to evade the dilemma occurs in the third scene. The martial *and* amatory conception of self Antony assumes is perhaps predictable:

> ANT.:   By the fire
> That quickens Nilus' slime, I go from hence
> Thy soldier, servant, making peace or war
> As thou affects.
>
> [1. 3. 68–71]

While the heroic image as "soldier" would ease the psychological pressure of the "Roman thought" and conform to what Roman consensus esteems noble, the heroic image of "servant" responds to the decorum of love's world. As Cleopatra makes clear, the heroic images are not compatible. The pose of a chivalric lover willing to stand an "honorable trial" (1. 3. 75) in order to prove he can play the Roman soldier-statesman without compromising his love for Cleopatra is met by a "dying fit" and an equally predictable storm of ridicule: "Good now, play one scene / Of excellent dissembling, and let it look / Like perfect honor" (1. 3. 78–80); "How this Herculean Roman does become / The carriage of his chafe" (1. 3. 84–85); "Courteous lord, one word" (1. 3. 86). Antony entertains the notion of extending the lovers' vision into reality where real martial battles are fought for real space, but for Cleopatra at this moment love's soldier is a metaphor, and she would have his love completely and forever. She knows that Antony's Roman eye has translated her natural decorum into deceitful "becomings," and as for the role he assigns her—that of a supernal Roman matron like Octavia—an edge of sarcasm, inevitable after what we have just heard, suggests its impropriety and impossibility:

> CLEO.:   Your honor calls you hence,
> Therefore be deaf to my unpitied folly,
> And all the gods go with you! Upon your sword
> Sit laurel victory, and smooth success
> Be strew'd before your feet!
> ANT.:   Let us go. Come;
> Our separation so abides and flies,
> That thou residing here, goes yet with me;

And I hence fleeting, here remain with thee.
Away!   *Exeunt.*

                                                  [1. 3. 97–105]

Antony's paradoxes will not be realized until several unsuccessful role adjustments have brought the lovers to disaster. Then Antony, as if he were living a fiction, will assert his soldierly service in a final death swoon, and Cleopatra, separated from him, will "die" into a dream-vision that will confirm Antony's heroic conception of self, making good the paradox of abiding love despite physical separation. For the moment, however, the compromise role of soldier-servant seems improbable, the love that transcends time and space seems impossible.

It is true, of course, that Antony does have his moment of "heavenly mingle" and that the mutual faith symbolized by the messengers bridges the physical separation momentarily.[14] But it cannot last. Once in Rome, Antony is no longer her servant. With the marriage to Octavia, a stroke of political opportunism that relegates love to the service of empire, he renounces his Egyptian identity and tries to become for a while an ideal Roman of the Augustan era: discreet, politic, temperate, decorous, but certainly no great-hearted Mars.

Antony loses "heart" in Rome, both as servant of love and—the telling irony—as soldier of Rome. In this sense, he is the empire's fool. Individual derring-do no longer has a place in a world where martial ambition must be tempered by discretion, as Ventidius reminds us (3. 1. 21–27), and where martial spirit is squelched by political propriety, as Enobarbus's role as foil for Antony reminds us (2. 2).[15] The old soldier has become the new politician. Antony cannot reclaim the martial grandeur in Rome as he had thought and as the audience had been led to believe; rather, lover and captain share the same heart, and the inspiration to grandeur for both servant and soldier resides in Egypt.[16] The soothsayer puts it another way: Antony's "Noble, courageous, high unmatchable" (2. 3. 21) spirit exists apart from Caesar and apart from a Rome that rewards temperance and calculation. Worldly success will never be his, but the soothsayer implies that at least in Egypt and with Cleopatra there exists for Antony the possibility of grandeur.

The return of Antony to Egypt is marked by a public celebration signaling a crucial role adjustment in the lovers' relationship. The coronation in the marketplace (3. 6) fulfills his pledge to "piece / Her opulent throne with kingdoms" (1. 5. 45–46), unmetaphoring the rapture of act 1, scene 1, by literally refashioning the empire into love's world. The fact that Cleopatra appears as Isis suggests that Antony has again placed politics in the service of love and dedicated himself anew to Egypt's natural deity. At the same time, however, by extending the love vision into reality, by claiming the geography of the empire as tribute to the psychic expanse of the lovers' passion,[17] Antony formally invites Cleopatra to share his political and martial identity in the Roman world and to stand up peerless according to its values of honor and nobleness. This time it is she who must effect an impossible compromise between love and empire; and if the Isiac identification in the marketplace has not suggested the inappropriateness of Cleopatra's active participation in the world of Fortune and politics, certainly the Roman invectives should ring more ominously than earlier, if only because Antony's donation to love is now real: he has "given his empire / Up to a whore" (3. 6. 66–67), his "potent regiment to a trull" (3. 6. 95). This "bewitchment" must have fatal consequences.

One of the reasons Antony left Rome, we recall, was that Caesar's genius had a magical power over his own, but neither the soothsayer nor Antony reflected on the debilitating power Cleopatra holds over him. At the strategy session before the battle of Actium, Enobarbus does:

> ENO.: Your presence needs must puzzle Antony,
> Take from his heart, take from his brain, from's time,
> What should not then be spar'd.
>
> [3. 7. 10–12]

Unfortunately, Cleopatra will not listen, for she herself has been bewitched by the new political stature Antony has given her. Formally inaugurated into Antony's world, she assumes a martial posture that is accompanied by a strong sense of Roman honor; unlikely as it seems, she has adopted a heroic conception of self. Cleopatra's sharp rebuke of Antony's laxity secures his confidence in her soldiership, triggering in turn an even stronger assertion of manhood from him.[18] He will fight Caesar by sea:

> CLEO.:   By sea, what else?
> CAN.: Why will my lord do so?
> ANT.:   For that he dares us to't.
>
> [3. 7. 28–29]

Judgment and vantage are thrown to the winds, just as Enobarbus had predicted. But Cleopatra's presence has not taken anything from Antony's heart, except perhaps the discretion that should temper it. Buoyed by love, Antony reacts as a soldier-servant; the word "dare," taken from Hotspur's vocabulary, colors the decision with the derring-do of a chivalric knight. Cleopatra has in fact rekindled Antony's great heart and with it the "noble, courageous, high unmatchable" spirit that is doomed to failure.

Reality quickly gives the lie to Cleopatra's heroic image as bold-spirited soldier. Her ignoble retreat from the battle sets in relief the maleficent aspects of her lunar association. Feminine frailty is chiefly responsible for her flight, as she will later claim (2. 11. 55), but one wonders whether her decision to retreat "i' th' midst o' th' fight" also mirrors a priority of values, that is, whether Cleopatra would rather win the battle of the sexes by defeating Octavia and recapturing Antony than succeed in the martial role that the battle of the empire has imposed upon her. She flies as a "cow in [June]," the derogatory allusion to Isis[19] mocking her political and martial pretensions and at the same time marking a retreat to love's world and to her true source of power. Of course, there is no suggestion of thought, much less of calculation, in Antony's decision to follow Cleopatra. The choice between the world of love flying from him and the empire standing a good chance to be won is made in a moment of blind passion. The strumpet has stolen the warrior's heart entirely, and, when the impact of his action strikes home, Antony is disgraced, dishonored, unqualitied, unmanned. In every respect Mars has surrendered command to Cleopatra. The Herculean rage suggests that the shirt of Nessus is already upon him.[20] Good name, fame, and stature in the eyes of the empire are not easily donned or lightly put off; the loss of the Roman heroic image burns him to the quick.

At Actium, Antony and Cleopatra adopt delusive conceptions of self that fate them to tragic loss: hers is a Roman heroic image and his a chivalric image, that of a soldier-servant of love. If Cleopatra's frailty soon betrays her pretension to Roman nobleness, her retreat forces upon Antony, in turn, a fatal choice between martial and amatory conceptions of self. Nevertheless, even with tragedy now assured, Shakespeare allows Antony and Cleopatra to indulge an amatory vision of reality in the face of tragic fact. Immediately following the battle that virtually seals Antony's *de casibus* tragedy, the lovers begin to assert the countergeneric values of comedy and romance in defiance of history, Fortune, and empire, at first moderating the audience's harsh judgment of their folly and finally, I believe, seducing the audience to folly's camp.

A LEGEND OF HEROIC LOVE

Antony had told Octavia earlier that "If I lose mine honor, / I lose myself" (3. 4. 22–23), and that is precisely what has happened. But, ironically, that is the only way he can fully reenter love's world. Antony's initial contempt for Cleopatra the conqueror is met by the sorceress' simple plea for pardon and—miraculously, magically—after a pregnant silence that ushers in an Egyptian thought, the lover reconstructs his vision of worth on the ruins of the empire:

> ANT. : Fall not a tear, I say, one of them rates
> All that is won and lost. Give me a kiss.
> Even this repays me. We sent our schoolmaster,
> Is 'a come back? Love, I am full of lead.
> Some wine, within there, and our viands! Fortune knows
> We scorn her most when most she offers blows.
>
> [3. 11. 69–74]

When Antony fled the battle of Actium, even as vantage appeared to favor him, he broke allegiance with Fortune and empire; now he will defy both with love's values and the heart's reality. Unfortunately, however, this is not the world of *The Merchant of Venice* where one can hazard all for love and win, nor is it the world of *As You Like It* where Nature blesses those who defy Fortune with the foolish values of the heart. And so, this assertion of love's value, like those that follow, is accompanied by an inevitable sense of unreality, if only because the defiance of Fortune must be played out in a world where actions dictated by love and the heart are doomed to failure.

In Fortune's politic world standards of success and standards of grandeur are incompatible. The point is made when the lovers respond to Caesar's scheme to divide them. Cleopatra's selfless pledge of loyalty to Antony—"That head, my lord?"—a foolish response from the perspective of the worldly wise, evokes from Antony a heartfelt response even more grand and foolish. He "dares" Caesar to individual combat, oblivious to the fact that the common sense required of a man who would conquer Fortune and triumph in history's record will scorn the naive romantic lover.

The genesis of Antony's "dare," indeed the source of the personal myth as heroic lover that Antony would now unmetaphor into actual chosen behavior, is crucial to Shakespeare's conception of heroism. Chapman had defined Bussy's heroic love as Achillean heroic passion in the service of Tamyra; but Antony's blind, natural compulsion is the love passion itself. His "great heart [that] will not down" is not the epic warrior's great heart fueled with godlike spirit, but the lover's heart inspired by Cleopatra. Antony will not defy Fortune with heroic values, but with foolish, amatory values associated with comedy and romance. Shakespeare did not allow the warriors at Troy to succeed in their attempt at heroic myth-making because they, like Chapman's Achilles and Bussy, were devoted to an egocentric, destructive "godlike pursute of Eternitie." But Antony will succeed in creating his own legend of heroic love, for the "heroism" Shakespeare celebrates in *Antony and Cleopatra* proceeds not from pretensions to greatness, but from a selfless emotion inspired by love. Shakespeare's "grandeur" has at its source a blind love passion that —as it inspires a great-hearted disregard for discretion and vantage—the worldly wise would account foolish. Lamentably, however, the grandeur is also tragic; for foolish, great-hearted actions, such as that at Actium, are incompatible with success in Fortune's world, and though Antony is blind to reality he compulsively makes a claim on reality, dreaming that he can conquer rather than defy Fortune, that he can regain the empire and, with it, his Roman heroic image.

The unlikelihood that Antony's dream can be projected successfully into a world governed by Fortune and her minion is underscored by Enobarbus immediately after Antony decides to deliver the "dare" to Caesar:

> E N O . : [*Aside.*] Yes, like enough! high-battled Caesar will
> Upstate his happiness, and be stag'd to th' show
> Against a sworder! I see men's judgments are
> A parcel of their fortunes, and things outward
> Do draw the inward quality after them,
> To suffer all alike. That he should dream,
> Knowing all measures, the full Caesar will
> Answer his emptiness! Caesar, thou hast subdu'd
> His judgment too.

And four lines below:

> E N O . : [*Aside*] Mine honesty and I begin to square.
> The loyalty well held to fools does make
> Our faith mere folly; yet he that can endure
> To follow with allegiance a fall'n lord
> Does conquer him that did his master conquer,
> And earns a place i' th' story.
>
> [3. 13. 29–37, 41–46]

Enobarbus's Roman perspective would league fortune with discretion in war and calculation in politics, measuring value according to external standards, be they riches, stature, or power. Antony's "dare" is thus a foolish action dictated by the heart and fit for the stage; in its manifest disregard for reality, it is an action that a dreamer might take. Nevertheless, for the moment a wise fool like Kent, Enobarbus will stand on the loyalty and faith that will earn him a place "i' th' story"—a record of the heart's defiance of Fortune and reality, a true account, but one better suited for the poet than the historian to relate.

Immediately, Enobarbus's Egyptian perspective is put to a severe test. Owing to his present stance as loyal and faithful friend, he was perhaps expecting to hear Cleopatra's foolish, defiant replies to Thidias's overture from Caesar; instead, he hears politic replies (3. 13. 46–62) and hurries off to report her betrayal to Antony. As might be expected, the "dying lion" whips Thidias and tongue-lashes Cleopatra for allowing the servant to kiss her hand, but when the Herculean rage of one who has lost stature not only as soldier but also as lover is improbably transformed into love's fury, Antony exceeds Enobarbus's understanding of what it means to defy Fortune, reality, even death. With Cleopatra's strident pledge of loyalty ringing in his ears, Antony again takes "heart."

> A N T . : I am satisfied. . . .
> Where hast thou been, my heart? Dost thou hear, lady?
> If from the field I shall return once more
> To kiss these lips, I will appear in blood;
> I and my sword will earn our chronicle.
> There's hope in 't yet.
>
> [3. 13. 167–76]

Antony's "chronicle" is something different from Enobarbus's "story" of the heart's defiance of Fortune and from Caesar's objective record of history, though it partakes of both. The high events Antony envisions—inspired by the heart, chivalric in nature—belong to a fictional romance; yet his "hope" of standing up peerless in the world's estimation also presses a claim on historical reality. It is not enough that the "strumpet's fool" has again embraced the deceitful seductress, but blind to the reality of what is required for success in the world of empire and yet at the same time incongruously pledged to greatness in that world's eye, he would create and live a historical fiction, that is, a dream of chivalric grandeur, a personal epic myth, that he thinks can be projected into real history.

> E N O . : Now he'll outstare the lightning: to be furious
> Is to be frighted out of fear, and in that mood
> The dove will peck the estridge; and I see still
> A diminution in our captain's brain
> Restores his heart. When valor [preys on] reason,
> It eats the sword it fights with. I will seek
> Some way to leave him. *Exit.*
>
> [3. 13. 194–200]

Enobarbus cannot dare the blind, irrational foolishness of this "rare spirit."

The restoration of Antony's heart releases the "noble, courageous, high unmatchable" spirit that will snatch grandeur from inevitable failure. Plutarch notes that at Cleopatra's birthday party Antony and his soldiers took a pledge to die together;[21] Shakespeare, however, omits the "Order of Death" incident, stressing instead Antony's individual vow to die valiantly and allowing a communal sense of doom to shroud the atmosphere as if a darkness to set off Antony's light.

> A N T . : To-morrow, soldier,
> By sea and land I'll fight; or I will live,
> Or bathe my dying honor in the blood
> Shall make it live again.
>
> [4. 2. 4–7]

Antony pledges a valorous action that will redeem his honor, but it will be an Egyptian soldier inspired by love that will erase the dishonorable record at Actium. What the Roman has lost because of love the soldier-servant of love will regain. The victory will celebrate the grandeur of the human spirit, much as the fraternal warmth Antony and his loyal followers share at the last supper emphasizes the communal values of the human heart. At this moment, the desertion of Hercules rather than Bacchus (as Plutarch has it)[22] is essential to Shakespeare's "story" and to the quality of heroism he portrays. Historical fame and world dominion according to the Roman conception of greatness are denied Antony; Cleopatra has the soldier's heart, and only in love's world can he stand up peerless. To emphasize the point, Shakespeare now creates a scene in which Eros and Cleopatra squire an Egyptian Mars who has been rejuvenated and transformed by Venus's love and now "goes forth gallantly" (4. 4. 36), as if the hero of a chivalric romance, reflecting both the divinity and the insanity of love.[23]

The desertion of Hercules and Cleopatra's own misgivings create an atmosphere of impending doom, and when love's soldier takes the field against impossible odds, the audience is also reminded of Caesar's historical perspective:

> CAES.: The time of universal peace is near.
> Prove this a prosp'rous day, the three-nook'd world
> Shall bear the olive freely.
>
> [4. 6. 4–6]

Caesar's prediction of what the audience knows is historical fact is used further to offset Antony's improbable victory, which is totally unexpected and, surely in the emphasis given it, largely unhistorical. Plutarch did mention a brief encounter,[24] but Shakespeare raises the miraculous moment to a symbolic prominence equivalent to that of Actium itself. As he will with Cleopatra in act 5, Shakespeare allows Antony the status of a surrogate dramatist who successfully creates a legend in defiance of history and reality. The chivalric language of "gests" and "feats" and the allusion to the "great faery" queen who has "charmed" her servants, recalling Spenser's fiction,[25] are fully in keeping with the romance Antony is living. He greets Cleopatra:

> ANT.:   leap thou, attire and all,
> Through proof of harness to my heart, and there
> Ride on the pants triumphing!
>
> [4. 8. 14–16]

In conquering Antony's heart, Cleopatra has inspired the warrior to conquer Caesar. Past failures to accommodate concerns for love and empire are thus perfected in the ideal relationship of the soldier-servant and his beloved.[26] The "jolly march" through Alexandria, bringing to a close the "St. Martin's day summer"[27] that began with the feast the night before, celebrates all men equally, symbolizing the victory of the human spirit and the human heart. At the same time, however, the lovers' progress is also a martial triumph. The Egyptian Mars has redeemed the honor that the Roman Mars had lost at Actium. For the moment, Alexandria is transformed into the public correlative of love's world, the vision of "new heaven, new earth" and poetic hyperbole gracing the brief victory with apocalyptic reverberations.[28] Never again, not even at death, will Antony approach so near to the realization of his heroic image as soldier-servant of love.

Shakespeare places Enobarbus's death scene after the victory to pay tribute to the Antony who has defied Fortune with the values of the heart. Earlier, Antony's judgment about Enobarbus's desertion had been precisely to the point: "O, my fortunes have / Corrupted honest men!" (4. 5. 16–17). By sending Enobarbus's treasure to him, Antony had written a page in the very "story" of friendship and loyalty a self-serving Enobarbus had betrayed to Fortune. Antony continued "still a Jove" (4. 6. 28–29), and to Enobarbus he was a "mine of bounty." Antony's extraordinary magnanimity, a boundless generosity of spirit,[29] displays the grandeur of one who would just as freely give up the world in testimony to the values of the heart as dominate the world according to the values of the empire. He has been an Egyptian Hercules, and Enobarbus's heart is broken. Now, at the end, no matter how the world's register may record his infamous action, Enobarbus will square his personal accounts. With the Egyptian moon as his witness, the unhistorical character repents his revolt and earns his place in Shakespeare's "story" by dying a lover's death: "O Antony! O Antony!" (4. 9. 23).

It is inevitable that the vision of an Alexandrian world of love Antony has created will not last. The "heavenly mingle" of soldier and servant, the improbable alliance of fiction and reality, is of necessity short-termed; for not only is the love vision being projected into a world that rewards cold, hard realism, but whenever Antony's heart has been inspired by Cleopatra he has pressed a dreamer's claim on reality, and momentary success will only increase the illusion that he can defeat Caesar on Fortune's battlefield. The lovers' victory has rekindled his hope, and with it his concern for empire and for a Herculean Roman stature in the world's register.

SCAR.:   Antony
    Is valiant, and dejected, and by starts
    His fretted fortunes give him hope and fear
    Of what he has, and has not.

                                                    [4. 12. 6–9]

No longer frighted out of fear, "by starts" realistic and blind, concerned
with worldly prospects and a Roman heroic image, but still inspired to
fight "i' th' fire or i' th' air" (4. 10. 3), Antony's psychological state is
reflected in the decision to fight by land and by sea, on both Roman and
Egyptian elements. The land battle never materializes, for the betrayal of
the Egyptian fleet again returns him to the heart of loss:

ANT.: The shirt of Nessus is upon me; teach me,
    Alcides, thou mine ancestor, thy rage.
    Let me lodge Lichas on the horns o' th' moon,
    And with those hands, that grasp'd the heaviest club,
    Subdue my worthiest self.

                                                    [4. 12. 43–47]

A violent disillusionment may have been predictable, but the sense of
Herculean heroism that had colored Antony's "hope" and is now reflected in its deflation shows Antony at his unworthiest. The inappropriateness of the Hercules allusion measures not only the mistaken assumption about Cleopatra's deceit, for which there is no evidence, but
Antony's own delusions of Roman greatness. Of course, there is reason to
believe that had Cleopatra stayed to defend herself Antony would have
found all that was lost recompensed by a single kiss. But this time she
does not stay to weather the storm, retreating instead to the monument
to protect herself against Antony and Caesar alike.

Of all Shakespeare's tragic heroes Antony has the hardest time dying.
The self-evaluations are inadequate, the postures assumed in preparation
for death are unsatisfactory, the suicide is botched, and the final death
scene more than tinged with burlesque. He remains the "strumpet's fool"
to the end. In a moment of demystification following the storm of anger,
Antony compares the insubstantiality of his identity to one of black
vesper's pageants; Cleopatra's betrayal has cut through the dream he was
living, and it is now time for a clear-eyed Roman assessment of self ("She
has robb'd me of my sword"—4. 14. 23) and a Roman solution ("there
is left us / Ourselves to end ourselves"—4. 14. 21–22). But there follows

a second demystification that reveals Antony's Roman clarity as fiction. With word of Cleopatra's death, the Egyptian Mars is also unmanned, and the identity as love's "soldier" is what really matters to Antony: "Unarm, Eros, the long day's task is done,/And we must sleep. . . . O, cleave, my sides! / Heart, once be stronger than thy continent, / Crack thy frail case! . . . No more a soldier" (4. 14. 35–42). Now he can only be a "servant" of love:

> ANT.: Eros!—I come, my queen!—Eros!—Stay for me!
> Where souls do couch on flowers, we'll hand in hand,
> And with our sprightly port make the ghosts gaze.
> Dido and her Aeneas shall want troops,
> And all the haunt be ours. Come, Eros, Eros!
>
> [4. 14. 50–54]

The poetic tribute to love's world and to the lovers themselves envisions the "new heaven, new earth" in the lovers' paradise where he and Cleopatra will stand up peerless. Predictably—in view of Antony's recurrent anxiety about Roman heroic image when inspired by love—there is some backsliding, thoughts about winning honor and avoiding shame. But Cleopatra's "love-death" and Eros's selfless death confirm that the hero's way is the way of love (*heros*—eros).[30]

> ANT.:   My queen and Eros
> Have by their brave instruction got upon me
> A nobleness in record; but I will be
> A bridegroom in my death, and run into't
> As to a lover's bed.
>
> [4. 14. 97–101]

This "nobleness" is defined by love; the "record" is love's legend. Antony is assured that the peerless act in death, as in life, is "to do thus," to embrace Cleopatra. But the suicide fails, and the lover's vision must now confront the fact of Cleopatra's deceitful ploy. Although Antony may now die literally in Cleopatra's arms, the same "space" that will show him a transcendent lover will show him a "strumpet's fool." Story and history, dream and reality, epic myth and fact, will collide at the monument. The audience is likely to expect a summary confrontation centered on betrayal and loss and, no doubt, a summary reconciliation asserting that the values of love are worth all that was lost.

IN PRAISE OF FOLLY

Among the many surprises in the monument scene is Antony's total lack
of reflection on Cleopatra's deceit in reporting her death to him. The fact
is that he simply will not consider it. Though he is physically dying, news
that Cleopatra is still alive has brought to Antony a typical psychic
rejuvenation that once again delivers him into the world of high romance
and fictional history. He has taken "heart," and in a typically blind love
vision he presses an improbable claim on reality: he is and will be the
noble Roman and noble lover at the same time, an identity he never could
maintain in life and can achieve in death only at the risk of a devastating
irony. The noble Roman speaks:

> ANT.:   Peace!
> Not Caesar's valor hath o'erthrown Antony,
> But Antony's hath triumph'd on itself.
> CLEO.: So it should be, that none but Antony
> Should conquer Antony, but woe 'tis so!
>
> [4. 15. 13–17]

The verdict of history, of course, will attribute Antony's overthrow to the
foolish, irresponsible affair with Cleopatra, and as for the claim of victory over himself in death, Cleopatra might better have remained silent,
for the seductress is his conqueror on that score also. But Antony's
reveries seem to have insulated him from reality and so from the ironic
perspective. Now the heroic lover speaks:

> ANT.: I am dying, Egypt, dying; only
> I here importune death awhile, until
> Of many thousand kisses the poor last
> I lay upon thy lips.
> CLEO.:   I dare not, dear—
>
> [4. 15. 18–21]

The stereotypical flavor and histrionic tone of Antony's lines suggest that
he is again writing a romance,[31] and yet before he has begun to warm to
the task of creating the ideal death scene, reality again breaks in, this time
reminding us not of Cleopatra's maleficent power over Antony but of the
frail human nature that is unable to play the ideal heroine in Antony's
heroic romance.

And so it goes. The possibility of a symbolic apotheosis is mocked by the grunts and groans, the funereal dignity by a devastating pun ("A heavy sight"), the mythological accoutrement by "Wishers were ever fools," the magical kiss of life by the acknowledgment that kisses have no such power. Regardless of all, the heroic lover begins again: "I am dying, Egypt, dying. / Give me some wine, and let me speak a little" (4. 15. 41–42), but again Cleopatra interrupts him, now with some railing against Fortune. The dying man's advice to seek honor with safety is inappropriate, the advice to trust Proculeius, dead wrong. Finally, instead of a vision of the lovers' underworld, which would at least be consonant with the high romance he is creating, Antony returns at the end to his role in history, projecting a congratulatory reminiscence of the past that presses an unrealistic, Herculean claim for personal nobility in the world's record:

> A N T . : The miserable change now at my end
> Lament nor sorrow at; but please your thoughts
> In feeding them with those my former fortunes
> Wherein I liv'd, the greatest prince o' th' world,
> The noblest; and do now not basely die,
> Not cowardly put off my helmet to
> My countryman—a Roman by a Roman
> Valiantly vanquish'd.
>
> [4. 15. 51–58]

The attempt to accommodate the roles of noble Roman and heroic lover in a final conception of self appears to be disastrous, creating dissonance, not concord. As for the heroic lover, Cleopatra herself has been largely responsible for invalidating that stance; what she has been in Antony's life and what she does and says at his death prick with devastating reality the histrionic posturing of high romance. As for the noble Roman, Antony's reminiscent history leaps from the early glory of the triumvir to the supposedly Roman suicide, simply erasing from memory the "miserable change" at the end. But perhaps most disturbing to the audience, when Antony claims Roman nobleness and historical greatness, he would appear to be backsliding again; as if flaunting the aesthetic decorum that the play and the audience's sentimental expectations would impose on his final moments, Antony is unwilling to accept a diminution in Roman stature as the price for embracing Cleopatra's frail but miraculous nature. The surrogate dramatist indeed defies Caesar, history, and reality, but apparently only by defying the love "story" Shakespeare has been writing for him. At the end he seems blind to the reality of history and to love's reality as well.

It may seem unfair to judge a dying man so harshly, but unless one is willing to face Antony's colossal foolishness and the sharp ironies that bring his final moment perilously close to burlesque, then the grandeur of Antony's death cannot be reckoned.[32] For Antony's final moments are grand precisely to the extent that the unrealistic, erring, amatory vision of reality is foolish. News that Cleopatra still lived had given Antony "heart," and the hoax that precipitated his suicide attempt is forgiven without a word. Inspired by the love that had always blinded him to tragic fact and responding to her fault with the same generosity of spirit that had closed his eyes to Enobarbus's betrayal earlier, Antony would defy reality with the values of the heart. He lapses into an Egyptian reminiscent vision of history, assuming a peerless Herculean identity as Cleopatra's "man of men" to please her thoughts and to pay tribute to the value of her love. The final posture of "a Roman by a Roman / Valiantly vanquish'd" is the most glorious "lie" of all, for in absolving Cleopatra of any complicity in his death Antony displays a colossal magnanimity.

In his final moments, Antony is true to his characterization. Typically buoyant and blind with love, he would die as he had tried to live since Actium: creating a legend in defiance of history, realizing a personal myth as heroic lover. Such a heroic image Shakespeare allows Antony, for it has little to do with the epic values of individual self-assertion that Chapman and literary tradition would seem to endorse. Rather, Antony's heroism proceeds from a selfless love and from a great-heartedness that is excellent not because it is above the rest of humanity but because it is finally inseparable from the frailty and folly of human nature.

If Antony's myth-making pays tribute to Cleopatra, she in her final moments must validate his improbable dream by making herself worthy of his tribute. The "strumpet" must redeem the "fool" by verifying his insight into her. To do this she will die in tribute to him; she will die as he would, as an honorable Roman, as a heroic lover, conquering Caesar in history's terms and creating a love legend that will withstand the test of reality.

Cleopatra's response to Antony's death is patterned after his response to the false report of her death: the torch is out, all length is torture, and Roman resolution is the word. Her dying fit, recalling his cleaving sides and breaking heart, signals the collapse of love's world as well as her loss of a meaningful identity in life. The symbolic divestiture of her public titles, analogous to the disarming of the soldier earlier, emphasizes the loss of identity.

> CHAR.: Lady!
> IRAS.: Madam!
> CHAR.: O madam, madam, madam!
> IRAS.: Royal Egypt! Empress!
>
> [4. 14. 69–70]

No longer lady, madam, queen, empress—Cleopatra revives as a poor woman who will now forge her nature anew according to the values of the heart; for her this means in the "high Roman fashion," as Antony would wish it. There is never a serious question, one should add, about Cleopatra's intentions in act 5. If there is any backsliding from her tough-minded resolution, Shakespeare does not allow the audience to doubt her for long. The *contemptus mundi* renunciation of the world and a frantic suicide attempt bracket the Proculeius embassy, while the dream of her colossus and the summary rejection of Caesar's policy ("He words me, girls, he words me"—5. 2. 191) bracket the face-to-face confrontation with the "sole sir o' th' world" (5. 2. 120).[33] Cleopatra seems—to me, at any rate—as loyal as a submissive wife, as resolute as a Roman matron.

In Cleopatra's mind, the way of death is the way of love, for in that sleep of death there is the dream reality of an Antony transfigured into the "new heaven, new earth" of love's universe. Cleopatra dreams of an "Emperor Antony," a Herculean soldier and Herculean lover, Roman in his strength and stature, Egyptian in his bounty and delights.[34] In Cleopatra's celebratory vision, Antony is a noble Roman and peerless lover who can dominate and donate the world with equal facility. Pleasing herself with Antony's former fortunes both in the Roman world and in love's world, Cleopatra makes Antony her "space"; he now contains love's world and symbolizes its ideal of human nature.

> CLEO.: Nature wants stuff
> To vie strange forms with fancy; yet t' imagine
> An Antony were nature's piece 'gainst fancy,
> Condemning shadows quite.
>
> [5. 2. 97–100]

Like Antony's improbable dream at the monument, Cleopatra's vision cannot countervail tragic reality any more than fiction can change fact, but it can appeal to a higher reality and to superior values that are no less real for being immaterial and no less verifiable for the foolish actions they inspire. Cleopatra's dream proceeds from a vision of love and nature that one associates with comedy and romance; but though she may be of imagination compact with the poet, her dream would be judged a "lie" by the historian, just as it is by the Roman who shares the historian's vision of reality.[35] In her final moments, Cleopatra will validate the "lie" by renouncing Caesar's paltry world and embracing death in testimony to Antony and the transcendent values of her dream-vision.

The audience's insights into Cleopatra's mind and heart throw into near comic relief the show she puts on for Caesar. The Seleucis episode confirms Caesar's assumption that the weak woman wants life and will contrive to preserve it. What Cleopatra will have, however, is Caesar in her web and Antony riding triumphant in her heart, having inspired the miraculous victory of his soldier-servant. With Caesar hooked and all but netted, with her resolution firmly fixed, Cleopatra's mood and the tone of the play now turn toward comic triumph. The ridicule heaped on Roman puppet shows, cheap rhyme, and poor theater is a pointed indictment of the historical perspective she would defy. The shameful play in which she might see "Some squeaking Cleopatra boy my greatness / I' th' posture of a whore" (5. 2. 220–21) has been, and continues to be, a Roman history play written by Caesar; Shakespeare's Elizabethan audience has been watching something different, and Cleopatra as surrogate dramatist will now complete the "story" by fooling the Machiavellian artist with his simplistic perspective. Renouncing the moon and calling on a marble constancy Caesar would not now expect from her, she will write a noble, dignified love-death "fitting for a princess / Descended of so many royal kings" (5. 2. 326–27). Cleopatra is again for Cydnus—a sentimental touch that reveals her desire to relive a moment of reminiscent history. As Antony had in the monument scene, she dreams of an ideal romantic closure in the tradition of high love tragedy. Like Antony's, however, her fiction is not immune to reality.

Enter the clown, an extempore "stager" whose ironic voice is more suited for the Roman play but is of necessity an incongruous and unwelcome instrument in her own. The folksy prose, the sexual innuendo, the reminders of the deceit and evil to which women are prone, and the emphasis on the finality of death shatter Cleopatra's pretensions and with them her dream-vision. She would prefer, of course, to exorcise the ironic voice of reality as quickly as possible, and yet she cannot get the ambitious fool off the stage. The same personality that often plagued the dramatist's best-laid plans—if Hamlet's vilification is trustworthy—Shakespeare now inflicts upon Cleopatra, as if in cruel jest. But the jest is purposeful, not cruel. The rural fellow is an unpracticed and disrespectful participant in the high art Cleopatra hopes to create, and in this there is a lesson to be learned. In Antony's death scene, we recall, Cleopatra's frail human nature—evidenced in the fearful decision to remain in the monument and in the continuous nervous banter—broke in upon the high art he was fashioning; now the peasant threatens Cleopatra's romantic close with a similar burlesque irony. Human nature, whether in the guise of professional fool or irreverent peasant or weak woman, will not easily be bridled by the artist's dream or by art's decorum. And it should not be. The real threat to Cleopatra is not the clown but her own unwillingness to accept the reality of human nature that he symbolizes and she, in turn, would displace or transcend. Antony's adamant attempt to forget his own shortcomings and to disregard Cleopatra's frailties, substituting for their reality a dream of historical fiction and high romance, resulted in an ironic deflation of his final idealistic posture. And so, it appears, with Cleopatra. By renouncing rather than accepting the moon as her planet, by exorcising rather than embracing the clown, by mending her human nature with high art rather than acknowledging it, Cleopatra threatens her final conception of self with a similar ironic deflation. Fortunately, however, Cleopatra's own human nature will not be bridled by her art.

In the final moments before the suicide, Cleopatra renews the pledge to her artistic vision. The pose of dignified queen and courageous wife—accompanied by a renunciation of her Egyptian identity and her human frailty—would sweep the clown from memory. After the unexpected death-kiss, recalling the "serpent of old Nile," however, the high art gives way to a series of nondeliberative postures: the love-death becomes sexual, the submissive wife a charming but petty female worried about first kisses, the Roman matron a nursing mother, the instruments of death improvisatory props. The "clown" is back, and with Cleopatra's frail and foolish humanity returns the moon, her human nature displaying an infinite variety of divine quality and diversity. In the monument "joyning hard to the temple of Isis,"[36] Cleopatra is again for Cydnus. Assumed and nondeliberative roles merge in the celebration of a human nature whom everything becomes. Like Isis, Cleopatra is an enthroned queen; the bridal vision of "husband, I come" recalls the Egyptian goddess of marriage; the aspic's poison and the liberating kiss bestowed on Iras, a kind of *mos osculi*, reflect on the sacred sorceress' power over life, death, and Fortune; the maternal image celebrates the goddess of the family as well as the larger Isiac identity as a Lucretian Venus, goddess of fertility and first principle of life; Cleopatra is also an Isiac earth goddess like Ceres or Demeter and a virginal "lass unparallel'd" like Isis as Diana.[37] At the end, the infinite variety of artful and natural postures is fixed in a timeless, miraculous stasis. The art that would mend nature has instead merged with it and been blessed by its folly; art has not been transcended but encompassed by a natural artlessness that has its own improbable laws of decorum. In her final moments, Cleopatra displays the self-transforming magic of human nature. As the apotheosis as *myrionymos* Isis is meant to convey, her frail humanity has been miraculously translated: she embodies that Nature which is above the art that would mend nature.

Cleopatra's suicide is enacted as a pledge of loyalty to the colossus of her dreams. She gives herself fully to him, at the end withholding not even the human frailty that her art had initially attempted to mend. Although Cleopatra could never share Antony's martial identity in life, the victory over Caesar's policy and the victory over herself in death has earned that identity with him. The final words spoken of Cleopatra from inside the secret, Charmion's final epitaph, seal Cleopatra's triumph: "Ah, soldier!" (5. 2. 328). To be consistent, one might identify the allusion as that to Isis as Bellona, but the cryptic tribute cannot be adequately parsed. With Antony in her heart to inspire her, Cleopatra has died as he would, as a noble Roman and as a heroic lover, validating Antony's transcendent insight into her.

ANTONY AND CLEOPATRA'S HUMAN HEROISM

As I remarked at the beginning of the chapter, despite several superficial similarities, Shakespeare's *Antony and Cleopatra* seems a world removed from Chapman's *Bussy D'Ambois*. Notwithstanding the geographical scope and scenic largess of an expansive vision that dwarfs Chapman's narrow intrigue at the French court, the fundamental difference between the plays may be focused on the humanizing vision and humane tone of *Antony and Cleopatra*—its naturalistic characterization, its intrepid realism, its frivolous, wry, and poignant humor, its credible expression of impossible dreams. The tragic folly of *Antony and Cleopatra* is human, and so, too, is its conception of heroism and grandeur. But this fundamental difference, I would argue, is precisely what makes the juxtaposition with *Bussy D'Ambois* meaningful.

Perhaps more so than any other great writer in the language, Shakespeare's creative genius was reactionary; indeed, "negative influence" —broadly defined—is virtually synonymous with what is sometimes referred to as Shakespeare's dramatic "inspiration." In the conception as well as the creation of Shakespeare's heroic tragedies, the point of departure is always an assumption, or thesis, or obstacle that his creative imagination will confront and struggle to redefine or transcend. Doubtless there were several points of departure for *Antony and Cleopatra*— perhaps Daniel's *Cleopatra*, Jonson's ideas about dramatizing history in *Sejanus*, a historical account in Plutarch's *Lives*, earlier themes and conceptions from Shakespeare's own canon. *Antony and Cleopatra*, like Shakespeare's other heroic tragedies, is conceived and written in a spirit of creative dialogue: with himself, with sources, with contemporaries. The assumptions about titanic heroism, feminine frailty, and heroic love in *Bussy D'Ambois*, however, would appear to provide the critic, as they did Shakespeare himself, with the single best context for clarifying the dramatist's conception of heroic themes and characterization in *Antony and Cleopatra.*

Chapman's fundamental conception of heroic tragedy—that one transcends a tragic world and a tragic human nature with heroic values— posits a protagonist of extraordinary capacity, a "hero" in the strict epic sense of the word. Chapman's Bussy and Byron possess the quality of greatness associated with Zeus, Hercules, Theseus, Achilles, Alexander, and the rest of the luminaries in the heroic tradition.[38] Although Chapman believed that a "contemporary Achilles," such as Bussy, Byron, or Essex, was destined to be brought low in a devious, antiheroic milieu, the hero was nevertheless able to snatch grandeur from tragic defeat by responding heroically to victimization and failure. Bussy's heroism in the two-part death scene, first as he outfaces death with outward fortitude and then—equally astonishing—as he bridles his heroic passion, displaying moral fortitude, is extraordinary, titanic, worthy of Hercules himself. Significantly, in *Antony and Cleopatra* Shakespeare uses such a conception of Herculean heroism to offset his own ideas about tragic grandeur. Antony must put aside pretensions to Herculean greatness in order for a human heroism to emerge. He becomes, finally, an Egyptian Hercules, not a great-spirited hero who gains fame through martial excellence and world domination, but a great-hearted man who faces squarely his own frailty and folly, forgives others their inadequacies, and dies in tribute not to empire but to love and the values of the heart.

If the Romans cannot comprehend Antony's quality of greatness, they have virtually no idea at all about Cleopatra's final heroism. From their point of view, Cleopatra has been to Antony what Tamyra was to Bussy: a weak woman associated with lunar mutability who brings out what is base in the hero, deflecting the "rare spirit" from his proper course, entangling him in conflict, and ultimately leading him to a tragic demise. The Romans could not possibly understand how anything of value has emerged from Antony's relationship to Cleopatra, much less how Cleopatra at her death has exploded the brittle social and heroic myths on which the notions of Roman empire and greatness are based. The vision of heroism informing Cleopatra, the unlikeliest "soldier"-hero in this book, celebrates the redemptive magic of love and the self-transforming magic of human nature. The values defining Cleopatra's final heroism are thus consonant with those of the festive comedies and anticipate those of the late romances; like Antony's, Cleopatra's heroism is diametrically opposed to epic conceptions of martial excellence and heroic grandeur.

Fundamental to the traditional conception of tragic character is a psychological movement evidencing that there has been some compensation for tragic suffering and loss, that is, some lessons learned, insights achieved, values clarified, a sense of self recovered or fully secured for the first time. In Chapman's heroic tragedies, where there is little internal conflict, little sense of tragic choice, of psychological agon, or of development or progression in character, one is not made aware of a psychological movement toward self-knowledge and a final clarification of values. Chapman's monopathic heroes exhibit their astonishing spirits through heroic action and heroic response, but seldom come into conflict with themselves. Thus, at journey's end, with little in themselves to sort through or clarify, Bussy's and Byron's final insights are limited to *de casibus* acknowledgments of failure to fulfill their titanic aspirations. For Shakespeare, on the other hand, the development of a psychological or spiritual counterplot is essential to the legend of heroic love he creates for Antony and Cleopatra. Caesar's historical victory cannot be denied, but it is beguiled, defied, perhaps scorned by the lovers, the dramatist, and an audience that is privy to the lovers' "story."

In *Antony and Cleopatra*, Shakespeare is engaged in his own version of myth-making, something quite different from the Herculean myth Chapman creates for Bussy. Unlike Bussy's heroic love, in which the soldier marshals his heroic spirit and epic prowess in the service of the lady, the myth of heroic love Shakespeare allows Antony and Cleopatra to unmetaphor into actual chosen behavior partakes of a comedic and romance vision of reality. The grandeur of their love is predicated on the acceptance of human frailty in themselves and in others; its value stems from a reckless disregard for reality that the worldly wise would judge to be foolish. As in *King Lear*, the ultimate price is exacted from those who foolishly embrace the heart's values; but, by doing so, the lovers bring to the ignominious record of history a vision of reality that transforms tragedy into an affirmative countergenre. Love is worth all that is lost and worth the ultimate donation of life itself. As Antony and Cleopatra die in testimony to their "story," comedy and romance join hands with tragedy, bringing affirmative values to bear against history's narrow assessment of success, Rome's pedestrian standards of greatness, the epic genre's inadequate vision of human excellence, and George Chapman's simplistic conception of tragic grandeur.

6

THE CONSPIRACY AND TRAGEDY OF BYRON:

CHAPMAN'S ANATOMY OF THE HEROIC SPIRIT

The final two heroic tragedies I shall discuss, Chapman's *The Conspiracy and Tragedy of Byron* and Shakespeare's *Coriolanus*, are closely related to Daniel's *Philotas* and to the real-life tragedy of the Earl of Essex. Love is not an issue in either play; central to each is a political conflict deriving from the soldier's dislocation in a peacetime society. Byron and Coriolanus are unwilling or unable to accommodate their heroic conceptions of self to the normative modes of behavior that social consensus—rightly or wrongly—expects of them. Both soldiers are social and political misfits, brought into conflict with society by the heroic individualism that sets them apart from and above society. The ancient virtues of martial prowess and epic idealism that define the soldiers as heroes on the battlefield define them as enemies in the forum.

Chapman found in Grimeston's translation of Jean de Serres's French history a perfectly structured *de casibus* biography of Byron, requiring only judicious trimming and dramatic shaping for its presentation on stage. The tragic design and moral perspective announced in Chapman's Prologue is an accurate reflection of his source:

> As when in wealthy Autumn his bright star
> Wash'd in the lofty ocean, thence ariseth,
> Illustrates heaven, and all his other fires
> Out-shines and darkens, so admir'd Byron
> All France exempted from comparison.
> He touch'd heaven with his lance, nor yet was touch'd
> With hellish treachery; his country's love

He yet thirsts, not the fair shades of himself;
Of which empoison'd spring when Policy drinks,
He bursts in growing great, and, rising, sinks:
Which now behold in our conspirator,
And see in his revolt how honour's flood
Ebbs into air, when men are great, not good.

[12–24]

Byron's spectacular fall was nearly as well known among English theater-goers as that of Essex, and Chapman's Prologue promises a predictably straightforward account of it. But the dramatist's *idea* of Byron's tragedy and the audience's response to the hero will be far more complex than the Prologue would indicate. Much as Shakespeare had done in *Antony and Cleopatra*, though to a lesser degree, Chapman uses the cold, hard facts of the historical account to offset his own dramatic conception. And yet, significantly, whereas Shakespeare had marshaled the generic assumptions of comedy and romance to darken the values implicit in Caesar's historical perspective and to advance his own improbable conception of heroism, Chapman has the epic genre speak for Byron, not to overwhelm or deny, but to mitigate the harsh moral censure of history. More clearly than that of either Bussy or Antony, Byron's tragedy is presented as a *de casibus* history of a "rare spirit."

A sharp distinction between the Achillean ideals of the pagan epic and the ethical ideals of Christian humanism is the thematic crux of Byron's social dislocation. The heroic spirit that Byron projects into French society is the epic *virtus* that animates the heroes of antiquity. The tempters "glorify his valour" and attempt to spark his "Roman spirits," and time and again Byron parades members of the heroic pantheon to mirror his conception of self: Hercules, Achilles, Alexander, Pompey.[1] In addition to revealing Byron's colossal delusions of grandeur, these recurrent evocations underscore the conflict between heroic *virtus* and society's moral virtue, between the warrior's ireful passion and King Henry's reason. Especially in *The Conspiracy*, the audience perceives the personal conflict between Byron and Henry as a confrontation of rhetorical styles. Byron's strident claims of grandeur in the epic mode are countered by the king's sober discourse, the poet's enthusiasm by the historian's rationality.[2] Although this stylistic confrontation is typical of all the heroic trage-dies, the discrepancy between the heroic idealism for which the epic style speaks and the factual realism with which tragedy responds is elsewhere sustained at such length and with such devastating irony only in Shakespeare's *Troilus and Cressida*.

Indeed, in nearly all of its important aspects Shakespeare's negative assessment of the martial psyche in *Troilus and Cressida* is replicated in Chapman's portrayal of Byron. He is politically ambitious, and he thinks that by merit he should be king; his pursuit of honor is appetitive, acquisitive, selfish; he puffs himself up by embracing a delusive heroic image, and his devotion to it is a form of self-idolatry; like Hector and Troilus, he is self-fated, that is, his tragedy is determined by the conception of self he adopts; his actions are often base, at times bestial. Chapman's Byron is "possess'd" with the "greatness" of a heroic image, as Shakespeare's Achilles was, and the politic La Fin, the "French Ulysses," is able to prey on the hero's debilitating pride and direct it toward unworthy ends. Nonetheless, for all this, Chapman's purpose is not to debunk epic heroism or to recant the grandeur with which he had earlier graced Bussy's "Predominant Perturbation."[3] Although Chapman would be willing to concede Shakespeare's negative critique of the heroic psyche, admitting that delusions of greatness are crucial to Byron's tragedy and to that of Essex as well, he would still insist on the grandeur of the heroic aspiration for excellence. The same heroic spirit that inspires the beast inspires the titan. Context is crucial.

The normative social and psychological contexts in the *Byron* plays that weigh against the hero and at the same time weigh in favor of the hero are analogous to those of Tasso's *Gerusalemme Liberata*. "Godfrey," says Tasso, "is no other in the Allegory but the Understanding; Rinaldo, who in action is in the second Degree of Honor ... is ... the *irefull Virtue* ... which amongst all the Powers of the Mind is less estranged from the Nobility of the Soul."[4] Heroic *virtus* of the kind Byron exhibits can be justified only in action on behalf of king and country, heroic passion only insofar as it subjects itself to the governance of reason. Like Tasso, however, Chapman endorses martial heroism as the king's right arm and ireful passion as reason's chief instrument. Chapman is no more inclined than Tasso was to accept the Stoic doctrine that reason must reject heroic wrath as it does all the other passions: "The reasonable Part ought not (for herein the Stoics were very much deceived) to exclude the irefull from Actions, nor usurp the offices thereof ... but it ought to make her her Companion and Hand-maid."[5]

In *The Conspiracy and Tragedy of Byron* the inherent worth of Byron's "rare spirit" is never denied. Like Tasso's Rinaldo, who is distinguished from the host of soldiers, representatives of the body, Byron is set apart from and above the petty men of politic whispers who manipulate the hero to advance their own ambitious designs. The audience is always aware that in the proper context Byron's heroic spark of divinity might elevate him to a kind of starry apotheosis that "Illustrates heaven," as it did during France's civil war. Even at his worst moments, moreover, Byron's blind fury may be distinguished from bestiality. The choric voice of La Bosse makes such a distinction:

> LA B.: The heavenly Powers envy what they enjoin;
>   We are commanded t'imitate their natures,
>   In making all our ends eternity,
>   And in that imitation we are plagued,
>   And worse than they esteem'd that have no souls
>   But in their nostrils, and like beasts expire,
>   As they do that are ignorant of arts,
>   By drowning their eternal parts in sense
>   And sensual affectations: while we live
>   Our good parts take away, the more they give.
>   [C. 3. 3. 10–19]

Byron's spirit is never drowned in sense and sensual affectations, though it is "esteem'd" so, indeed described so, by others. From beginning to end, Byron's spirit fires an aspiration for eternity. In *The Conspiracy*, the lofty ideals of Renaissance optimism that Byron strives to realize suggest the splendid natural predilection of the titanic spirit; but when he is most the aspiring idealist he is most the deluded rebel. In *The Tragedy*, at those moments when Byron strives to become pure spirit, pure hero, he appears to be pure beast. The aspiring spirit that makes Byron a transcendent hero on the battlefield makes him an irrational monster and titanic rebel in a society at peace.

Chapman's evaluation of the heroic spirit, the source of the extreme antitheses animating the Prologue, does not deny Shakespeare's appraisal of the martial psyche in *Troilus and Cressida*. But Chapman would reply to Shakespeare that his own conception is a fairer, a more even-handed, and a more accurate appraisal of Byron and Essex. By allowing the heroic genre to assert the potential splendor of Byron's aspiration for excellence without denying *de casibus* tragedy's adverse judgment on Byron's anarchic pride and moral culpability, Chapman would direct the audience's response away from simple moral censure, certainly away from moral ridicule, toward an acknowledgment of pathetic waste and, perhaps, toward a metaphysical complaint. By some quirk in nature the extraordinary gifts that glorified Byron cursed him:

> E P .: We have not any strength but weakens us,
> No greatness but doth crush us into air.
>
> [*T*. 5. 3. 193–94]

BYRON'S FIEND

From the beginning of *The Conspiracy*, Chapman insists that Byron's heroic spirit is both a glory and a curse, a strength and a weakness. The valorous soldier dwarfs the conniving politicians who open the play; and yet, owing to the hero's vainglory, they shall turn his great gifts to unworthy ends. The peculiar nature of Byron's excellent but vulnerable spirit is revealed in the temptation scene at Brussels. Picoté is the tempter. First, he spreads a carpet depicting the history of Catiline in which Byron will find his Roman spirit reflected (C. 1. 2. 17–18). The carpet, symbolic of a kind of *cursus honorum*, thus becomes a visual metaphor for conspiracy and ambition. The "*Loud music*" (S.D.) in which man "may hear the harmony / Of all things moving" (C. 1. 2. 23–24) simultaneously bathes Byron's psyche in cosmic harmony, becoming an aural metaphor for divine aspiration and apotheosis. Alone, the earthly carpet and celestial music are likely to work to cross-purposes: Byron's imagination must equate "conspiration" with "aspiration" if Picoté's ploy is to produce a single effect.

Byron's reaction to the temptation is cast into the first of several generally neo-Platonic contexts that Chapman employs to convey the hero's aspiration for eternity. The context in this first temptation is that of a contemplative rapture induced in large measure by spiritual magic. The emphasis on music in the passage, together with the explicit reference to Apollo (C. 1. 2. 45–49), suggests Chapman's general familiarity with Ficino's system of astrological magic, largely solar, wherein man's spirit (*musica humana*), physiologically motivated by precise tonal impressions (*musica instrumentalis*), vibrates in sympathy with the music of the spheres (*musica mundana*), thus creating an aereal/aural conduit for celestial influence.[6] Byron feels himself in harmony with the universe, and, as microcosm, its container and temple; his blood turns to soul, his flesh dissolves, and his "spirit," freed of the senses, is transported into a heavenly realm:

> B Y R .: What place is this, what air, what region,
>   In which a man may hear the harmony
>   Of all things moving? Hymen marries here
>   Their ends and uses, and makes me his temple.
>   Hath any man been blessed, and yet liv'd?
>   The blood turns in my veins; I stand on change,
>   And shall dissolve in changing; 'tis so full
>   Of pleasure not to be contain'd in flesh.
>
> [*C.* 1. 2. 22–29]

But the audience knows, and indeed Byron himself knows, that a tragic gloss accompanies the rapture. Byron's first words—"What place is this, what air, what region?"—echo those of Hercules when he awoke from his mad nightmare into tragic reality, clearly an inauspicious prologue to a life of aspiration.[7] Hercules' defiant arrow, moreover, was shattered by thunderous retribution (*C.* 1. 2. 41–43), and Semele's aspiration to deity was glorious but fatal (*C.* 1. 2. 37–38). Byron understands the tragic implications of his aspiration, and this clear-eyed fatalism adds to the astonishing character of his spirit:

> B Y R .: To fear a violent good abuseth goodness,
>   'Tis immortality to die aspiring,
>   As if a man were taken quick to heaven;
>   What will not hold perfection, let it burst;
>   What force hath any cannon, not being charg'd,
>   Or being not discharg'd?
>
> [*C.* 1. 2. 30–35]

Byron seems to envision a glorious but fatal explosion of natural *virtus* similar to that Monsieur had predicted for Bussy; but, come what may, he will act nobly and in accord with the dictates of his heroic spirit. In effect, Byron makes the Achillean choice for a short, luminous life of aspiration that is, however tragic, both "high and right."

The irony in Byron's response to the temptation resides in his incongruous assumption that a "godlike pursute of Eternitie" can be enacted through a political conspiracy that is neither "high" nor "right." Byron appears incapable of relating the destructive grandeur of the sun in the Hercules and Semele analogies to the pageant and justice of Henry IV, appears incapable of understanding that a political conspiracy like Catiline's is unlikely to generate or to express true heroic *virtus*. A telling discrepancy between Byron's heroic aspiration and its unworthy enactment is present from the start. The tempters hope to convince Byron that a political conspiracy can be "high and right," but there is reason to believe at the outset that the tempters will not succeed.

After an emblematic inset recounting d'Aumale's punishment for treason and loss of honor alerts the audience and hero to the real consequences of misguided aspiration, Byron adopts a rational, measured voice of orthodox virtue that is in sharp contrast to the exultant language of rapture. If he had been deceived by the temptation, it was a momentary lapse, for he now stands on loyalty to the king (C. 1. 2. 76–85). Nevertheless, Picoté renews the attack, using his sophistic arguments to gloss the music and carpet. The tempter equates loyalty to a degrading servility and a deprivation of natural worth. According to him, Byron must "carve" out his own perfection and find reward in the fulfillment of his own nature; he must be absolute, meaning that he must eliminate any privation of his virtue, any form of servility, any challenge to his preeminence. The tempter accents this philosophy of "royal man" with two similes, both of which nicely link Byron's spirit to its aereal element: first, Byron's "highness" must transcend both bodily humours and earthly corruption in order to claim exclusive possession of the purest air; second, Byron must be like the air itself, which receives the sunlight, becomes the disperser of light, and so usurps the sun's function (C. 1. 2. 103–11). As one had been led to expect, Picoté's pun on "highness" marries Byron's divine yearning to its political enactment, his individual aspiration to the tempters' "conspiration." Byron must not only seek his own perfection by raising his spirit above bodily humours but must also stand alone above an inferior society, an exalted highness which the simile of the sun's usurpation helps to identify as the throne of France.

Byron rejects Picoté's sophistry unequivocally, once again assuming the voice of orthodox virtue (C. 1. 2. 137–64). For the moment, Byron shares the play's normative values and choric voice. He is a "temple" of goodness (T. 5. 3. 205–8), not of sedition—rational enough to see through Picoté's ploy, realistic enough to apply to himself the tragic lesson of d'Aumale. This is the Byron whom we will later encounter in the favored clime of Elizabeth's court and who, after a lapse, will fall to his knees in the climactic scene of *The Conspiracy* to reassert his loyalty to the king. But despite Byron's virtuous resolve, he remains vulnerable to temptation; for immediately following the assertion of virtue the Archduke's compliments and gifts elicit from him a significant resignation of willpower (C. 1. 2. 170–76). A series of "royalty" puns then suggest the "particular objects" now expected of him. Chapman has used the temptation scene to establish the contrary pulls of aspiration and loyalty in the warrior's psyche; enraptured by the dictates of the heroic spirit yet fully aware of moral and social obligations, Byron stands as Hercules at the crossroads.[8] The double departure scene symbolizes the confrontation between social consensus and personal aspiration, between sovereign reason and the fiendish spirit rising in rebellion against it. The private good-bye of the aspiring conspirator wars against the public leave-taking of the dutiful ambassador.

Now that the "fiend" within Byron has surfaced, it is appropriate that La Fin begin to work on him. We learn immediately that he will draw Byron to his will through magic, a complex metaphor on which Chapman pivots the Byron–La Fin relationship. In the king's mind, of course, La Fin's gift of fascination is a kind of black magic, a notion Henry conveys through two related motifs. The first deflates the idea of transcendent spirit by attributing the Duke's ballooning self-conceit to a blind acceptance of flattery's insubstantial breath, a kind of siren's song. The king's language thus wages metaphorical warfare against the aural temptation; that is, the music, the spiritual magic, the promise of a glorious, transcendent aspiration are all empty air. The second of the king's motifs encounters the implication of celestial influence head-on. With the noxious fumes and hellish vapors of flattery, the tempters have created an unhealthy conspiracy that hangs over France and infects Byron's melancholic humour as if a kind of urban pollution.[9] Hence the political conspiracy is identified with the foul psychological vapors generating Byron's delusion. The hero may be temporarily rehabilitated by a sojourn in England's fresh air, but ultimately the more promising cure is the departure of Savoy from France, which will cleanse the air of conspiracy and cleanse Byron of the foul vapors inspired by Savoy's diabolical wit (see C. 5. 2. 264–68).

Byron is also aware of the tempters' black magic, but his recognition comes too late. Not until the trial will he acknowledge that La Fin, rather than inspiring his transcendent spirit, has in fact conjured up his fiend: "Sure he call'd up the devil in my spirits, / And made him to usurp my faculties" (*T*. 5. 4. 91–92). He makes this plea of possession, we recall, as part of his defense, and the judges dismiss it because witchcraft cannot taint an honest mind or a resolute will (*T*. 5. 2. 174, 282–86). The judges are correct, and indeed magic serves Chapman's drama less as a metaphor for witchery than for self-fascination. Black magic describes the process that takes place in Byron's sick psyche, in which the rule of reason and its instrument, the will, has been usurped by the heroic spirit and its instrument, the imagination.[10] Like Shakespeare's Achilles, Byron is "possess'd . . . with greatness," "possess'd," that is, with a heroic conception of self. La Fin's dramatic function as an agent of fascination is thus less important than that as a symbolic embodiment of the "fiend" within Byron. La Fin becomes a mirror image for Byron, the "empoison'd spring" from which Narcissus drinks.

To be sure, La Fin does present himself in the role of magician, attempting to seduce the overreacher to his will by promising extraordinary control over nature and, more relevant, powers far beyond the king's capacity. A man with La Fin's gifts would be the ideal instrument for Byron's conspiratorial designs. But the fact remains that Byron never acknowledges this practical application of magic, and his interests are drawn to La Fin himself, drawn subjectively to La Fin's personality and predicament, and not to his art per se. In Byron's mind, La Fin's plight mirrors his own: the superior person of heroic spirit, of unlimited aspiration and worth, rejected or unappreciated by an ungrateful king. Savoy appears to have anticipated Byron's attraction to La Fin:

> S A V . : You are reported to have skill in magic
>   And the events of things, at which they reach
>   That are in nature apt to overreach;
>   Whom the whole circle of the present time,
>   In present pleasures, fortunes, knowledges,
>   Cannot contain; those men, as broken loose
>   From human limits, in all violent ends
>   Would fain aspire the faculties of fiends;
>   And in such air breathe his unbounded spirits,
>   Which therefore well will fit such conjurations.
>
> [*C*. 2. 1. 39–48]

Although the practical application of magic is not discounted, the thrust of the passage is clear: Byron reaches for superhuman attributes not in a base, ambitious grab for power, but rather in a Faustian quest to fulfill his own superior nature and his transcendent aspiration. Here, I believe, one discerns a second, broadly neo-Platonic context that Chapman employs to highlight Byron's aspiration: that of the *magus*, the divine magician who is the embodiment of Pico della Mirandola's "miraculous man," a participator in the cosmic intellect infused throughout the living world of nature, an ascendent spirit in harmony with celestial influences.[11] These "faculties" Byron identifies with La Fin.

However, just as the carpet depicting Catiline's conspiracy undercut the idealized rapture of the first temptation, surely the real character of La Fin, as the king describes him earlier (C. 1. 1. 112–63), ought to undercut Byron's identification of him with the *magus* ideal. But it does not. For in seeing a transcendent *magus* in what is essentially a mirror image of himself, Byron is measuring his own worth, not La Fin's. Similarly, when Byron takes up La Fin's cause, he subconsciously casts that cause into a heroic vocabulary appropriate not to La Fin's brooding malcontent but to his own Achillean reaction to royal injustice:

> B Y R . : I am put off from this dull shore of [ease]
> Into industrous and high-going seas;
> Where, like Pelides in Scamander's flood,
> Up to the ears in surges I will fight,
> And pluck French Ilion underneath the waves!
>
> [C. 2. 1. 149–53]

This is real magic. Its source is the heroic imagination. Byron seizes on La Fin's suspect political cause and translates it into an epic enterprise to which he shall dedicate his Achillean *areté*. Like Bussy in this respect, like Shakespeare's warriors at Troy, Byron is projecting a heroic conception of self into reality, fabricating an epic myth, transforming unlikely events and an uncongenial milieu into a heroic context so that he might realize his heroic image. But the hero can live this fiction only at grave risk. Though blind to reality, the heroic vision is not immune to it. In effect, Byron will now marshal his epic *virtus* in rebellion against the king; conflict is inevitable, tragedy is likely.

Given Byron's identification with La Fin, moreover, it is not surprising that he not only adopts La Fin's (and Picoté's) philosophy of natural superiority but also goes on to embrace Fortune, policy, and falsehood as the means to advance his cause. The irony is patent. Byron pledges the heroic valor of Achilles to bring down "French Ilion," but he will use the means of wily Ulysses to do it, that is, the same kind of inglorious deceit

La Fin himself, the "French Ulysses" (C. 2. 1. 52), has used to bring down Byron's citadel. Byron has fallen. The "fiend" has usurped his reason and the moral values it supports; the conspirator will usurp his king and the societal values he represents.

The following scene highlights the extent of Byron's fall. Roiseau's description of the onetime chivalric champion of France now engaged in "state adultery" (C. 2. 2. 1–24) is followed by Savoy's encomium to a titanic warrior who has in fact betrayed his heroic idealism. Using the epic style characteristic of Byron's own self-assertion, Savoy celebrates the soldier's valorous deeds in the civil war as a full-blown epic *aristeia*. By his rhetoric the politician hopes to goad the king into a rash rebuttal, which might then be used to inflame Byron. But King Henry remains judicious and cool, responding as the objective historian might to the epic poet. The key issue of the discussion is virtue. Savoy claims that Byron succeeded in the civil wars despite Fortune's opposition, just as Hercules conquered Juno's ill will, but the king asserts in turn that Fortune blessed Byron's heroic exploits. The debate cannot but reflect retrospectively on Byron's fall, for at this moment he is neither Fortune's conqueror nor minion, but her slave. Just as important, the debate establishes the Alexander motif and the Fortune-virtue dialectic which Byron, substituting the *virtus* he has embraced for the virtue he has discarded, will seize on often to argue the individualistic prerogatives of "royal man."[12]

Savoy's epic celebration of Byron's exploits is a deliberate exaggeration of factual reality; placing the epic style in the service of rhetoric, Savoy consciously uses art to mend nature. But when Byron evokes the heroic genre to express his conception of self, such as when he "put off from this dull shore of [ease]," the evocation becomes a metaphor for a vision of reality. In this respect, Byron may be likened to a player acting out his own epic fiction, a dreamer living his own myth of epic grandeur. Such a subjective vision of reality is implicit in Byron's philosophy of moral indifference, which he thinks should buttress the heroic individualism of "royal man":

> B Y R . :　　There is no truth of any good
> To be discern'd on earth: and, by conversion,
> Nought therefore simply bad; but as the stuff
> Prepar'd for arras pictures is no picture
> Till it be form'd, and man hath cast the beams

Of his imaginous fancy through it,
In forming ancient kings and conquerors,
As he conceives they look'd and were attir'd,
Though they were nothing so: so all things here
Have all their price set down from men's conceits,
Which make all terms and actions good or bad,
And are but pliant and well-colour'd threads
Put into feigned images of truth.

[C. 3. 1. 47-59]

The amoral subjectivism at the heart of this skeptical philosophy is used to justify rebellion, for Byron goes on to argue that it is the silliest kind of superstition to serve and honor a king whose royal assumption of truth, virtue, and the right is as fallibly subjective as the next man's. For Byron the world thus becomes a relativistic moral chaos in which each man's conceits create truth. One is reminded of Shakespeare's Troilus in the Trojan council scene, when he spoke in favor of prizing Helen highly and continuing the fight; for Byron's subjectivism is an implicit defense of misprision and idolatry.

In addition, however, the analogy that Byron draws between subjective evaluation and creative art also provides an apt commentary on the nature of his own psychological lapse. The place of reason, the arbiter of good and evil, has been usurped by imaginative conceits, and in Byron's psyche these are "self-conceits" generated by his aspiring spirit. As Byron would liberate the artist's imaginative vision of past history from the historian's false standards of objectivity, so he would subvert the moral and political perspective on the present that social consensus has blindly adopted. Just as man can create out of the stuff of history his own vision of the past, so out of the means at hand the man of epic *virtus* can shape the present and the future in his own heroic image. The point is not lost on La Fin: "You persuade, / As if you could create" (C. 3. 1. 64-65).

The creation of reality in one's own image is inevitably accompanied by the claim to self-creation. The point is emphasized in the following scene (3. 2), when Byron poeticizes (epically) his past service to France, reading his "imaginous fancy" into the stuff of recent history: his patriotism in the civil wars was equal to that of Curtius's patriotism to Rome; his spirit sustained Henry's kingship as the sun sustains purple clouds; he was the soul and motive force of the entire French army; and so on (C. 3. 2. 63-105). While Byron feeds on such fantasies, on the other side of the stage a painter sketches his portrait, clearly a dramatic emblem for what Byron himself has been doing all along. The gigantic figure Byron would carve into the side of a mountain comments on the "monstrous humours" at work in the self-portrait. This statuary passage, a para- phrase from Plutarch,[13] suggests that Byron sees himself as Alexander, the royal man of virtue, the self-created titan who carved out his destiny on the face of the earth. The audience may or may not recall that Alex- ander, true man of virtue, had refused a similar gigantic tribute, but in any event the irony of the comparison with Alexander is patent. A slave of Fortune cannot create his own destiny through absolute virtue; an amoral, politic artist is something different from Plutarch's heroic shaper of history.

The metaphorical emphasis on creative art—weaving, painting, sculp- ture—suggests a third, broadly neo-Platonic context that the dramatist uses to express Byron's aspiration for excellence. As Chapman well knew, the idealistic tradition of Renaissance aesthetics likened the artist's crea- tive powers to God's, setting the poet above the rest of mortal men.[14] The notion of divine furor made the link between God and poet explicit, and in Ficino's theory of creative melancholy—in which the Saturnian *divinus melancholicus* was equated with divine fury—the artist's con- templative imagination was elevated to a godlike vision of reality.[15] It should scarcely need remarking, however, that Byron's "melancholy adust" is not *divinus melancholicus*, his "imaginous fancy" not the con- templative imagination, his possession by a "fiend" not the sacred rap- ture of divine fury. King Henry twice warns against false poetry (see C. 2. 2. 84–85; C. 3. 2. 163–69), and Byron's dubious claim to creative power should be associated with what the king earlier described as false magic and empty aspiration.

Implicit in Byron's comparison of himself to Alexander, man of vir- tue, is an optimistic assumption that heroic man, through rational virtue and strong will, might tame destiny[16] or, to paraphrase the Essex-like hero of Daniel's *Philotas*, might steer Fortune by the compass of his mind (line 169). Byron's well-known exhortation of act 3, scene 3, is a summary expression of this Renaissance tradition of heroic individualism:

> B Y R . : Spite of the stars and all astrology
> I will not lose my head; or if I do
> A hundred thousand heads shall off before. . . .
> I have a will and faculties of choice,

To do, or not to do: and reason why
I do, or not do this: the stars have none;
They know not why they shine, more than this taper,
Nor how they work, nor what: I'll change my course,
I'll piece-meal pull the frame of all my thoughts,
And cast my will into another mould:
And where are all your *Caput Argols* then? . . .
O that mine arms were wings that I might fly,
And pluck out of their hearts my destiny!
I'll wear those golden spurs upon my heels,
And kick at fate; be free, all worthy spirits,
And stretch yourself for greatness and for height,
Untruss your slaveries; you have height enough
Beneath this steep heaven to use all your reaches;
'Tis too far off to let you, or respect you.
Give me a spirit that on this life's rough sea
Loves t'have his sails fill'd with a lusty wind,
Even till his sail-yards tremble, his masts crack,
And his rapt ship run on her side so low
That she drinks water, and her keel plows air.
There is no danger to a man that knows
What life and death is; there's not any law
Exceeds his knowledge; neither is it lawful
That he should stoop to any other law.
He goes before them, and commands them all,
That to himself is a law rational.

[C. 3. 3. 106–45]

It is all there—sovereign shaper of the universe, Protean self-creator, master of destiny, heroic spirit in quest of self-fulfillment, bold pilot on Fortune's seas. But with strange addition. Byron has buckled his will to heroic spirit, thus avoiding the difficult educative process of refining rude passion into rational virtue—a process Chapman is at pains to describe in "The Teares of Peace." The psychological subversion of reason by the unbridled force of spirit, reflected in the political subversion of the king to which Byron has pledged his heroic *virtus*, makes this ringing proclamation of freedom a rattling of the chains. Like Milton's Satan—another false artist, *magus*, creator of self, and master of destiny—the man of will and unbridled spirit lashes out at an alleged

145

cosmic injustice in lieu of confronting himself, of acknowledging the
"law rational" he has perverted and the hierarchical order he has con-
spired against. Psychological and social contexts define Byron's vision
of heroic freedom as a blind enthrallment to heroic spirit.

Byron's famous heroic evocation responds to La Bosse's prediction of
his *de casibus* fate. Ironically, the heroic spirit's aspiration for freedom
and excellence seals Byron's ignoble destiny; his great strength is his
fatal weakness. This man who aspires to stellar heroism, to mastery
over other stars, indeed to the status of sun king, is crossed by that very
aspiration. Chapman twice compares Byron to Sirius, the brightest star
in the heavens (see Prologue, 12–17; T. 3. 1. 143–50); in addition to
evoking Sirius's traditional association with a malignant influence (see
Iliads 5. 5–8; 22. 23–30), the two Sirian allusions also imply a political
context that places Byron's grandeur in ironic perspective. Sirius's helia-
cal rising, though glorious in and of itself, outshining and dimming the
other heavenly fires, ultimately ushers in the rising sun, the greater light.
Like Lucifer in this respect, Byron would divorce himself from the
political context that sanctioned his former exploits as preeminent servant of the king and usurp the role of the sun king. Much like the
morning star of *Isaiah* 14:12–14, Byron is doomed:

> E P . : Farewell for ever! So have I discern'd
> An exhalation that would be a star
> Fall, when the sun forsook it, in a sink.
>
> [*T.* 4. 2. 291–93]

The sun king has been rising steadily during the course of *The Conspiracy and Tragedy of Byron*; once settled in his "sun of height" (*T.* 5.
1. 138), he must cast out of the heavens the ambitious spirit who has
made a treasonous claim to kingship.

In England, in act 4 of *The Conspiracy*, Chapman establishes beyond
doubt the normative values by which the audience is to judge Byron's
delusive conception of self. What remains of a badly censored text
suggests that the English climate and the virtuous influence of Elizabeth
and her court bring Byron to his senses. He once again becomes an
eloquent spokesman for orthodoxy, placing in proper perspective the
relationships of king and subject, of regal understanding and ireful
passion. Once back in France, however, Byron's fiend reasserts itself.
The king and his rebellious subject confront each other once again. At
issue is command of the citadel of Bourg, which Henry believes is

unwise to place in Byron's control and Byron believes he merits. The warrior faces his king with absolute confidence, for he is certain that France cannot survive without him. Byron is lost in self-conceit, making the shock of the king's refusal to grant him control of Bourg all the more devastating to him. The insult pricks at his integrity and draws a roar of self-delusion. Byron's strident, hysterical self-glorification leaves no doubt that he truly believes what he is saying. He is no conscious hypocrite; he is totally *possessed* by the delusion of grandeur. The king's laughter at the blind, hysterical rage goads Byron's "mighty spirit" into drawing his sword, but the king's departure precludes violence.

Slighted, humiliated, self-deluded, furious, Byron confronts Henry at the moment of climax. The king blames Byron's distemper on the insubstantial whispers of flattery, asks him to pledge his loyalty anew, to light the inward fire of wisdom, to repent and be at peace with himself. The measured tones of Henry's rational discourse dominate the scene and win the day. Byron kneels before the king, a dramatic emblem of the normative values in the play. The gesture of humility and subjection and the pledge of loyalty and obedience, recalling the reconciliation of Rinaldo and Godfrey in Book 16 of Tasso's *Gerusalemme Liberata*, bring Byron a final, healthy peace of mind, bring him "sanity" in both English and Latinate senses.

> H E N .: O Innocence, the sacred amulet
> Gainst all the poisons of infirmity,
> Of all misfortune, injury, and death,
> That makes a man in tune still in himself,
> Free from the hell to be his own accuser,
> Ever in quiet, endless joy enjoying,
> No strife nor no sedition in his powers,
> No motion in his will against his reason. . . .
>
> [C. 5. 2. 85–92]

Byron's spirit has been calmed, his imagination cleared, his inner harmony now in tune with king and society—"'Tis music to mine ears," says Henry (C. 5. 2. 107). The star has been washed anew and rises again "by absolute merit" (C. 5. 2. 110).

Byron had been possessed with a heroic image; but for the moment he has tamed the fiend. The bent knee, the quiet tones of rational discourse, the subjection of spirit to reason and of servant to sovereign indicate that Byron has returned from the enchanting, visionary world of personal epic myth. He is eagerly accepted back into the social and political order because Henry IV knows what the dramatist knows: that unlike Shakespeare's soldiers and lovers at Troy, men whose heroic idealism was a cosmetic expression of an appetitive sexual passion and an acquisitive passion for honor, and unlike Othello, whose selfish concern with heroic image had translated a "cause" of jealous passion into something like that of sacred duty, Byron's heroic passion is of itself a pure aspiration for excellence. The godlike pursuit of eternity may be misdirected toward unworthy ends, leading to satanic pride and anarchic ambition, but if provided an appropriate context for its enactment, the heroic spirit can validate the lofty individual ideals of Renaissance optimism with which the dramatist has graced it and, in doing so, benefit society immensely. Context is crucial. Henry IV, assured that reason governs the microcosm and king governs the macrocosm, confident that psychological and social contexts have been reestablished so that the potential defects of heroic spirit and heroic soldier will be made perfection, welcomes his repentant Duke back into the fold as preeminent servant and handmaid of the king.

THE BESTIAL TITAN

The exposition of *The Tragedy* announces Byron's relapse. The king is amazed that the warrior who rose in dignity and status from colonel to lieutenant general of France would justify his newly rekindled treason with a claim of royal ingratitude, that the "complete man" at the end of *The Conspiracy* would again betray himself:

> HEN.: The Spaniards . . . found him still
> As an unmatch'd Achilles in the wars,
> So a most wise Ulysses to their words,
> Stopping his ears at their enchanted sounds;
> And plain he told them that although his blood,
> Being mov'd, by nature were a very fire
> And boil'd in apprehension of a wrong,
> Yet should his mind hold such a sceptre there
> As would contain it from all act and thought
> Of treachery or ingratitude to his prince.[17]

Byron has again upset these social and psychological hierarchies. But because Byron's relapse precedes the action, obviating the need for another temptation sequence, dramatic emphasis will shift from a psychological examination of transcendent spirit in *The Conspiracy* to a social study of unbridled *virtus* in *The Tragedy*. Individual aspiration will now be examined primarily as political ambition.

In *The Tragedy*, Byron and the "fiend" are one and the same. The hero's initial pose is that of a titan standing apart from king and country, self-charmed, self-deluded. In the more overtly social context of *The Tragedy*, the dramatist describes Byron's exhalations of spirit as a gathering of storm clouds threatening France with anarchy; the king, like Zeus, will have to disperse the clouds with awesome pyrotechnics. Behind this metaphorical emphasis looms the myth of the gigantomachy and its political lesson: "elle consâcre le triomphe de la Loi sur les mées au moment de la fondation, période dangereuse pour les hommes et pour les dieux, parce qu'elle marque la transition entre le chaos et l'harmonie."[18] In the formal legal ceremonies of acts 4 and 5, Chapman will celebrate the triumph of law over lawlessness, but the political import and allusive reverberations of the myth are present from the outset.

One encounters the titan in act 1, scene 3, a scene Chapman designed to parallel the self-apotheosis of *The Conspiracy* (1. 2). In the first drama, Byron's growing egotism inspired a vision of reality according to which he was his own king, his own law, the master of his own destiny; now the egocentric vision has brought him to an arrogant self-deification. The satanic titan would be God, the supreme artist-magician-creator:

> B Y R . : We must reform and have a new creation
> Of state and government, and on our Chaos
> Will I sit brooding up another world.
> I, who through all the dangers that can siege
> The life of man have forc'd my glorious way
> To the repairing of my country's ruins,
> Will ruin it again to re-advance it.
>
> [*T.* 1. 2. 29–35]

In Byron's mind the world has gone awry; a sensual peace has inverted the standards of virtue. France must return to its former glory, and Byron shall be its deliverer and creator.

Byron conceives of virtue as heroic *virtus*, believing himself to be its sole exemplar. In *The Conspiracy*, the habitual transposition of political ideas into martial vocabulary, the compulsive cataloging of military triumphs, and the comparisons to mythical and historical warrior-heroes had defined Byron's heroic conception of self. In conjunction with a growing egotism and increasing reliance on "imaginous fancy," the soldier gazed into the world and saw reflected there his heroic image. Here at the beginning of *The Tragedy*, Byron arrogantly conceives virtue, France, everything, in his image: the world's decline reflects his own decline; an enervating peace has overturned virtue in general as his own *virtus* has been degraded in particular; valor and fame have been replaced by cowardice and infamy. One must infer that Byron would revert to an era of war where *virtus* might be asserted in heroic deeds, for according to his myopic vision true virtue and freedom must be shown in defiance, true individualism must be armed. Indeed, the reformation that Byron envisions, as if following Hesiod's chronology, would return France's iron age not to a golden age but to the heroic age of Thebes and Troy.[19]

Chapman counters Byron's concept of *virtus* and vision of reform early in the play, leaving no chance for the audience to be led astray by the soldier's poetic raptures. An emblematic inset is placed at the beginning of the drama in which Henry prays over the infant dauphin. In tone and detail the king's description of the present turmoil owes much to Ovid's description of the iron age of war and self-love when justice fled the earth (*Metamorphoses*, 1. 127 ff.); he then prophesies that the dauphin, sword in hand, shall usher in an era of peace and virtue, of Apollo's harmony and Astrea's justice—an implicit allusion to Virgil's "messianic" eclogue and to the Augustan golden age. Against these normative ideals, Byron's present espousal of individual valor in war and his vision of destroying France to save it appear barbaric. His ambitious rebellion, when considered against the principle of lawful succession symbolized by the dauphin, becomes "gross and giantly," to borrow Elizabeth's precise word usage (C. 4. 1. 143).

The myth of the gigantomachy and the attendant motif of a political reform that will usher in an Apollonian golden age of peace and virtue should weigh heavily in the audience's perception of Byron's impious rebellion. But this mythic dimension of the play can also be confusing to the careless spectator or reader, for Byron, convinced of his own "royal" nature, not only claims for himself the prerogatives of kingship but also sees himself in the roles of Zeus and Apollo in the pending conflict. Gilding the reality of his impious rebellion with the idealism of virtuous intentions, Byron becomes a spokesman for the orthodox values that in reality he has set out to subvert, at one point claiming that he, as "royal man," by a kind of natural religious right, ought to replace the impious king as God's vice-regent on earth (*T*. 3. 1. 1–48), that his "harmonious finger" (*T*. 1. 2. 92) will calm the chaos, return virtue, religion, harmony to France, usher in a golden age analogous to that of Augustus. The irony is unmistakable. Byron assumes the very roles that the king himself must play when dealing with Byron's anarchic individualism, thus calling the audience's attention to a startling discrepancy between one Byron who is lost in idealistic dreams and visionary raptures and another Byron whose feet tread the earth of France, as if walking the carpet of ambition.

The audience's response to a hero who is both moral idealist and reprobate villain is difficult to describe. In the terminology of this study, Chapman has stretched "heroic tragedy" to its limits; on the one hand, one encounters the epic idealism of heroic exploit and virtuous reform, and on the other, the tragic reality of condemnable rebellion. To explain away the discrepancy as a huge irony seems simplistic, for this tends to reduce the tragic hero to a thick-skulled, if not ridiculous, pawn in Chapman's moral design.[20] Ridicule of Byron's moral obtuseness may be part of the response to him but certainly not all of it. To apologize for Byron or to acknowledge the pathos of Byron's delusion, even as one's sympathy may necessitate a final appeal to a kind of psychological determinism, is an equally likely but equally partial response.[21] Byron's heroic passion, the stuff of *virtus*, may be a powerful compulsion, but as the judges know (and we know), the delusion is willful. The audience's response to Byron, as it was to Bussy, is likely to be truly ambivalent, for each of the countergenres stakes an irrefutable claim to reality. Even as Byron has pledged allegiance to conspiracy and rebellion, the heroic idealism that sets him apart from and above the ambitious politicians is manifest. He believes his course is high and right, and the astonishing commitment to self-integrity and the heroic resolution, even as these exemplary qualities are directed toward unworthy ends, tend to mitigate one's sense of an immoral, antisocial titanism. The audience recognizes that the same heroic passion that now seems no better than satanic ambition was, and might become again, a commendable, "godlike pursute of Eternitie." For this reason, one's final response, I suggest, is likely to be that of pathetic waste, knowing that Byron's heroic idealism, tragically misdirected, might in a different context have won the approbation usually bestowed on an exemplary epic hero.

There is remarkably little action in *The Conspiracy*, even less in *The Tragedy*: the announcement of Byron's treason, its substantiation, the recall of the soldier to court, his haughty protestations of innocence, the trial, the sentence to imprisonment and death, Byron's reactions to both. It is appropriate, nevertheless, that the mainspring of the tragic action, such as it is, is La Fin's betrayal of Byron. In *The Tragedy*, as in *The Conspiracy*, La Fin continues to function as a symbolic embodiment of the "fiend" within Byron. La Fin's breach of loyalty to the hero, launching the political plot in the drama's foreground, is simultaneously a dramatic metaphor for self-temptation and self-betrayal in Byron's psychodrama. The hero's growing megalomania, fed by heroic image and justified by an absolute equation of inner worth and outer estate, leads Byron deeper and deeper into a web of delusion. Even as Byron bristles that his valor for France has gone unrewarded, his rage drives him further into his ego to justify himself. The insult of being requested to return to court when an enemy attack on the frontiers seems imminent appears to be the last straw. The insult pricks his honor and, together with the gnawing sense of royal ingratitude for past service, sets off a psychic chain reaction: the hurt feeds the sense of injustice, the injustice conjures up the visions of past glory, the visions of past glory feed the belief in absolute *virtus*, until Byron finally wraps himself in a blind and defiant self-confidence. Lost in rapture, defying the counsel of those who suspect La Fin's perfidy, Byron decides to return to court and so to judgment and eventual death. But if his trust in La Fin suggests an un- witting self-betrayal, his belief that the king will not dare confront him with a charge of treason suggests the irrational self-confidence of one who has lost touch with reality.

At court, Byron's protestations of innocence reemphasize his extraor- dinary self-delusion. Edward Grimeston states that he would not admit his guilt because "his courage was too great to stoope,"[22] but one recog- nizes that courage to be the blind self-confidence which a captain will soon describe with accuracy and point:

> C A P . : Yet doth that senseless apoplexy dull you?
>   The devil or your wicked angel blinds you,
>   Bereaving all your reason of a man,
>   And leaves you but the spirit of a horse
>   In your brute nostrils, only power to dare.
>
> [*T*. 4. 1. 106–10]

Byron's "possession" by visions of grandeur has loosed an unbridled spirit that has thrown reason, its master. We had heard the bestial passion moments before when Byron was told that the king had discovered the conspiracy:

> B Y R . : Blows, batteries, breaches, showers of steel and blood,
> Must be his downright messengers for me,
> And not the mizzling breath of policy;
> He, he himself, made passage to his crown
> Through no more armies, battles, massacres
> Than I will ask him to arrive at me.
>
> [*T*. 3. 1. 130–35]

The irrational epic thunder leaves no doubt that the beast the captain describes is the warrior's heroic spirit. Byron's "senseless apoplexy" has made him an Achilles *furens*.

The glorious vision of an aspiring death (C. 1. 2. 30–38)—that fatalistic vision in accord with the Achilles' paradigm of a brief, luminous heroic life—has suffered a degrading transformation. From the neo-Platonic ideals of transcendent spirit—of the *magus*, artist, self-creator, tamer of destiny—Byron's aspiration has plummeted to the sink of bestiality; by all appearances his heroic passion has been transformed into "the spirit of a horse," into a blind, instinctual compulsion to dare. But Chapman's purpose, I would again argue, is not simply to hold up Byron's descent for the moral ridicule of the audience. An examination of the three "bestial" analogies that stand out from the dramatic text as gems unset— that of the lion, the bird, and the boar—will indicate the dramatist's more even-handed appraisal of his hero.

The first occurs in the same context as the captain's description of "senseless apoplexy," at the moment when Byron has decided that he will not confess his guilt or flee into hiding to avoid the king's wrath.

> B Y R . :   Noble, happy beasts,
> That die, not having to their wills to live;
> They use no deprecations nor complaints,
> Nor suit for mercy; amongst them, the lion
> Serves not the lion, nor the horse the horse,
> As man serves man: when men show most their spirits
> In valour, and their utmost dares to do
> They are compar'd to lions, wolves, and boars;

> But, by conversion, none will say a lion
> Fights as he had the spirit of a man.
> Let me then in my danger now give cause
> For all men to begin that simile.
> For all my huge engagement I provide me
> This short sword only, which, if I have time
> To show my apprehender, he shall use
> Power of ten lions if I get not loose.
>
> [*T.* 4. 1. 138–53]

The self-irony implicit in the analogy is unavoidable, but one should also recognize the distinctions between Byron and the beast. Byron's defiant course of action may be irrational and deluded, but it is not blind instinct, not the bestial ignorance of men who drown their "eternal parts in sense / And sensual affectations" (*C.* 3. 3. 13–18). Rather, the delusion is precisely "senseless," the pledge of a man who would not be a beast but a titan. Byron would put aside his weak humanity—the will to live, to complain in the face of danger, to flee for survival—so that he might become pure spirit, pure hero, might become "in making all [his] ends eternity," like the legendary heroes of the past, a star (see *C.* 3. 3. 3–12).

Although it seems improbable that the man who is a beast according to our best moral judgment might somehow be perceived as a splendid titan in his defiance of the king and his opposition to imprisonment and death, Chapman nurtures this double response through a series of subtle shifts in dramatic emphasis. In the first place, morality has long before been put to rest as a dynamic issue; we have known from the early scenes of *The Tragedy* that Byron is wrong. With his arrest, moreover, we are no longer concerned with the safety of the king or the preservation of the ideals he embodies. And when Byron's opposition shifts from the king to death itself, our sympathies tend to embrace the hero who now must face our common enemy. There is, finally, the unsettling recognition of the superior man's absurd predicament, which La Bosse had remarked (*C.* 3. 3. 10–13) and Jean Jacquot finds emphasized in the final scenes of *The Tragedy*: "Mais après avoir justifié le triomphe de l'ordre, Chapman ne peut s'empêcher d'exprimer avec véhémence, dans les dernières scènes, sa révolte contre l'absurdité du monde et de la vie, où sont unis une chair corruptible et une âme éprise d'éternité."[23] To the extent that these shifts in dramatic emphasis mitigate one's moral censure of the "beast," the denouement of the action is viewed with a peculiar moral detachment, as if one were watching a spectacle. The audience is concerned with the tragic titan, interested to find out whether he will be true to his delusive vision of grandeur, whether his heroic spirit can indeed conquer his humanity and transcend death as a star. And, most likely, the audience is astonished that he succeeds so well for so long.

Byron plays out his arrest and the resignation of his sword with a dramatic flair reminiscent of Richard II. He is pathetic, but noble, retaining an inner integrity no matter the delusion on which it rests. Once in prison, however, Byron will not eat, sleep, or in any way accept confinement patiently; for imprisonment demeans his nature, and submission prostitutes his heroic spirit. Though his rage appears dumb and animalistic, and though his sights remain earthbound, equating freedom with physical liberty, still there is sympathy in the second of Chapman's splendid analogies:

> VID.: ... or rather as a bird,
> Enter'd a closet, which unwares is made
> His desperate prison, being pursu'd, amaz'd
> And wrathful beats his breast from wall to wall,
> Assaults the light, strikes down himself, not out,
> And being taken, struggles, gasps, and bites,
> Takes all his taker's strokings to be strokes,
> Abhorreth food, and with a savage will
> Frets, pines, and dies for former liberty:
> So fares the wrathful Duke. . . .
>
> [T. 5. 1. 118–27]

The identification of Byron with the frightened, trapped creature and with its spirited defiance elicits one's sympathy as well as astonishment. Owing to Chapman's clever use of personification, one's perception of the bird is transformed during the course of the passage from that of a pitiable little creature whose explosion of natural instinct is extraordinary to that of a voluntary agent whose savage resolution to be free is astonishing. Epic similes comparing a heroic warrior in a perilous strait to a wounded lion, stag, or boar were used to emphasize not what was base, but what was superhuman in his courageous resolve to fight and, if need be, to die valorously. The comparison to bestial instinct was thus a complimentary tribute to a heroic passion that would not submit to crafty wariness or craven scruple. In much the same way, the bird's savage instinct suggests Byron's superhuman spirit; or, to turn the simile as Byron would, the bird, like the lion, has been taught by Byron how to rage against captivity.

The third analogy, that of the wounded boar, is a more conventional epic comparison:

> D'ES.: And as a savage boar that (hunted long,
> Assail'd and set up) with his only eyes
> Swimming in fire, keeps off the baying hounds,
> Though sunk himself, yet holds his anger up,
> And snows it forth in foam; holds firm his stand,
> Of battailous bristles; feeds his hate to die,
> And whets his tusks with wrathful majesty:
> So fares the furious Duke, and with his looks
> Doth teach Death horrors. . . .

[*T*. 5. 3. 229–37]

Byron's heroic spirit is even more patently savage and irrational when confronting death as a cornered boar than it was when facing imprisonment as a trapped bird. But, again, warring against one's intellectual recognition of irony is a stronger emotional response to the pathetic, wrathful majesty of the beleagured beast. Once again personification forges an improbable link in the audience's response between the pathos one feels for the overmatched creature and the astonishment elicited by its titanic resolve to outface death. Byron continues to transcend human frailty by buckling himself to his heroic spirit, by losing himself in a vision of grandeur that "Doth teach Death horrors."

By pointing out Chapman's shifts in dramatic emphasis and then attempting to show how the dramatist evokes feelings of pathos and admiration for his "bestial" hero, I mean only to suggest that strict moral censure of Byron is a partial response to him. But by no means is the moral sensibility of the audience swept away on tides of sympathy or anaesthetized by the astonishing display of heroic spirit. The moral dimensions of *The Tragedy* are present to the end. Byron has cast off the Ulyssean ideal he had embraced in the final moments of *The Conspiracy*; in its stead, his heroic passion and diseased imagination, patching together visionary delusions of grandeur, have fashioned a portrait of defiance, of a heroic idealism tragically debased. At the same time that the moral debasement counteracts the audience's feelings of sympathy, moreover, a revelation of simple human frailty threatens Byron's heroic image. The pleas for mercy, the paroxysms of self-pity, the "deprecations and complaints" that he had disdained soon surface and, as Byron is enraged by his shameful weakness, create a psychological tempest of extraordinary ferocity (5. 3. 185–89). While the human being and his heroic conception of self wage this war of passions, the audience is led to believe that perhaps the psychological fury may act as a purgatorial fire:[24]

> VID.: O real Goodness, if thou be a power,
>   And not a word alone, in human uses,
>   Appear out of this angry conflagration,
>   Where this great captain, thy late temple, burns,
>   And turn his vicious fury to thy flame. . . .
>
>   [T. 5. 3. 205–9]

A universal reform of the microcosm must precede the return to a calm, rational state of mind; the passions must be purged in the surface conflagration so that the inner flame of goodness may reclaim its precinct in Byron's "temple." But the transformation from passionate defiance to rational resignation is never completed. The resources of the mind's empire do take the field, but Byron's heroic passion fights them to a standstill in the psychomachia of the final scene.

Byron approaches the scaffold relatively cool and pacified, but the officials know that new fuel, such as the binding of his wrists, could spark another explosion (T. 5. 4. 10–14). The sight of the bishop, a harbinger of death, triggers such an outburst: "Horror of death! Let me alone in peace. . . . " (T. 5. 4. 26–28), but the fury soon subsides into a quiet musing about the freedom of the soul and how it shall conquer death. Byron will "joyfully meet Death," speaking of himself, his body, and his earthly aspirations from a rational distance (T. 5. 4. 32–48). Nevertheless, the rational resolve of the mind's empire—the *contemptus mundi*, the "talk of knowledge," the momentary resignation—soon gives way to a spirited defiance and the heroic image of the warrior threatening the sun (T. 5. 4. 50–54). And so the pattern of vacillation continues with neither Ulysses nor Achilles gaining the advantage for long. On the one hand, Byron exhibits a calm of mind, a perspective on himself, a partial recognition of guilt, resignation to death, conventional wisdom; but on the other hand, the ceremonial trappings of death, the sensible fuel that forces Byron to look at death in the flesh (the bishop, the reading of charges, the stereotyped consolation, the appearance of the hangman), ignite a frantic reaction to claim innocence, to rage like the bird in confinement, like the boar facing death.

Byron's final speech reveals that to some extent goodness has rekindled its flame in the "temple," but the words and tone of resignation are animated by a lingering yearning for life and heroic integrity. If Byron has emerged from the purgatorial flames to embrace orthodox values, he retains at the same time the glow of a martyr; he does admit guilt, but the admission wields a sharp edge of complaint against the arbitrary powers of kings (*T.* 5. 4. 224–30). Conversely, even as he still clings to the discredited heroic image, he breaks through the self-encasing ego with thoughts of his brothers and friend. He resigns himself, finally, to eternal exile in a magnificent tonal passage:

> B Y R . : And so farewell for ever! Never more
> Shall any hope of my revival see me;
> Such is the endless exile of dead men.
> Summer succeeds the Spring; Autumn the Summer;
> The frosts of Winter the fall'n leaves of Autumn:
> All these and all fruits in them yearly fade,
> And every year return: but cursed man
> Shall never more renew his vanish'd face.
> Fall on your knees then, statists, ere ye fall,
> That you may rise again: knees bent too late,
> Stick you in earth like statues: see in me
> How you are pour'd down from your clearest heavens;
> Fall lower yet, mix'd with th'unmoved centre,
> That your own shadows may no longer mock ye.
> Strike, strike, O strike; fly, fly, commanding soul,
> And on thy wings for this thy body's breath,
> Bear the eternal victory of Death!
>
> [*T.* 5. 4. 245–61]

A deep but unmistakable desire for life threatens the calm resignation of the surface structure, but regal understanding does not lose command. He absorbs the yearning for life into a fuller recognition of what death means, and the result is a moving elegiac calm. Distanced from himself, he voices a *de casibus* epitaph on his career, which recalls the climax of *The Conspiracy*, the gigantomachy motif, the mocking delusions of the heroic spirit. But there remain hints of martyrdom in the phrase "pour'd down" from "clearest" heaven and hints of complaint in the extreme humiliation he recommends to all statists. The conventional wisdom still rankles his heroic spirit even as he knows it is right. If Byron's self-condemnation reinforces one's sense of a culpable hero partially re-deemed at the end of a *de casibus* tragedy, the quiet recollection of his heroic spirit, of his "wings" of valor and "breath" of aspiration, and the superb ambiguity of "the eternal victory of Death" elicit a response of admiration and pathos. That is, Chapman has not written a simple *de casibus* tragedy, but a heroic tragedy, and even to the end the antithetical values of the countergenres are reflected in the audience's mixed response of censure and awe and, perhaps, finally, that of pathetic waste.

Of the several choric pronouncements in the final scenes of *The Tragedy* the audience identifies most fully with Epernon's:

> E P . : Oh of what contraries consists a man!
> Of what impossible mixtures! Vice and virtue,
> Corruption, and eternnesse, at one time,
> And in one subject, let together loose!
> We have not any strength but weakens us,
> No greatness but doth crush us into air.
>
> [*T.* 5. 3. 189–94]

The broad philosophical framework encompasses one's feelings of moral censure and then extends beyond them as if to apologize for Byron's tragic heroism. The noble ideals of Byron's aspiration for eternity have all been corrupted: the neo-Platonic spark of deity, into satanic ambition; the spiritual ascent of the *magus*, into self-fascination; the creation of one's world, into Machiavellian temporizing; the creation of self, into self-delusion. The debasement of these noble ideals merits the moral condemnation that the dramatist provides from Prologue to conclusion. But Byron is no soulless, sensual beast, and one's condemnation of him is mitigated by the recognition of the superior man's absurd predicament. Vice and virtue are common to all of us, but when the virtue of a truly "rare spirit" aspires to eternity, his "faults" make him not just a man like the rest of us, but a tragic figure or, worse, a condemnable villain es-teemed no better than a moral beast. In Byron the "impossible mixture" of "Corruption, and eternnesse" set loose a unique bestial titanism.

Byron is the most Shakespearean of Chapman's tragic soldiers. As a deluded heroic myth-maker who attempts to unmetaphor an epic con-ception of self into actual chosen behavior, Byron is remarkably similar to Shakespeare's heroes at Troy. One might suggest, moreover, that when Chapman returns Byron to the community of men by having him reveal human fear and human sorrow in the face of death and admit to human frailty and failure, the dramatist approaches the Shakespearean point of view: that the hero's ability to recognize his own frailty and the folly of his pretensions to heroic grandeur is the condition of true human heroism. But such a suggestion would be mistaken. Byron's aspiration for eternity, even as it is debased by an unworthy enactment, remains an ennobling quality; and though the hero is burdened by a massive sense of failure, the audience is not encouraged to view his aspiration as colossal foolishness, as it is the heroic delusions of Othello, for example, either by Byron's own appraisal of his demise or by that of the other choric spokesmen. More important, perhaps, if the transcendent grandeur of Antony and Cleopatra's "rare spirits" proceeds from, and is finally indistinguishable from, the "taints" and "follies" of human nature, Byron's humanity at the end of *The Tragedy* is for Chapman only a normative conception. When Byron becomes a recognizable human being in his final moments, one is provided with an identifiable touchstone by which to measure retrospectively what has been contemptibly base and what has been astonishingly heroic in the career of a "rare spirit." Byron is, after all, one of us, and this recognition makes the overreacher's actions that much more condemnable deviations from the moral and social ideals governing our lives, and at the same time makes his extraordinary aspiration that much more awe-inspiring. If the beast warrants one's moral outrage, the aspirer gains one's acknowledgment of heroic grandeur.

THE ACHILLEAN HEROISM
OF CLERMONT AND ULYSSES

It is commonly thought that the years 1598 to 1604 mark the "heroic period" of Chapman's career, the period being set off by the celebration of Achilles and the laudatory epistle to Essex in 1598 and by Bussy's display of Achillean prowess in 1604. Thereafter Chapman disavowed this muscular brand of heroism, going so far—the argument continues—to condemn the Achillean heroism of Byron in 1608, to recant Bussy's titanic grandeur by offering Clermont D'Ambois as a Stoic corrective to Bussy in 1610–11, to withdraw sympathy from Achilles in the full translation of the *Iliads* in 1611, and to criticize Achilles indirectly by contrasting him to the pacifist, Stoic hero of the *Odysses* (ca. 1614). If our evaluation of the *Byron* plays as heroic tragedy shows this critical generalization to be simplistic, Chapman's systematic elevation of the

Achillean heroic spirit in the 1611 *Iliads*—as discussed at the beginning of Chapter 4—gives it the lie. Indeed, the Achillean element in Clermont's and Ulysses' heroism—to which we now turn—will underscore the continuing, fundamental importance of the heroic spirit and of "Predominant Perturbation" to Chapman's exemplary ideal of the "complete man."

Chapman did not retreat from the immoral and anarchic implications of "Predominant Perturbation" or from the distasteful physicality of "outward Fortitude," neither after *Bussy D'Ambois* nor, more pertinently, in the aftermath of Essex's tragedy on which *Bussy D'Ambois* reflects. Rather, the first decade of the seventeenth century found Chapman striving to understand and apologize for the tragic failure to which a "contemporary Achilles" like Essex, Bussy, and Byron was prone, while at the same time striving to find an ethical framework that would make the Achillean ideal palatable to his Christian society by reconciling it with "over-ruling Wisedome." It would appear that Chapman found such a framework in Tasso's *Gerusalemme Liberata* and in the "Allegory" Fairfax appended to the translation.

According to Tasso's tripartite psychology, we recall, the understanding and the ireful virtue are distinguishable yet fully complementary qualities. Just as Godfrey is superior to Rinaldo, the regal quality of the mind is superior to the heroic spirit, "her companion and handmaid"; but neither quality is self-sufficient: heroic wrath needs reason to guide it toward purposeful, moral action, and reason needs the heroic spirit to effect its commands. In much the same way, Chapman would claim, the Achillean ideal of "Predominant Perturbation" and the Ulyssean ideal of "over-ruling Wisedome" are distinguishable, complementary ideals. Neither mode of heroism excludes the other. "Outward Fortitude" is not irrational, for reason passes a favorable judgment on it; it is just wrath. "Over-ruling Wisedome" is not a dispassionate, apathetic ideal, for though Seneca and other Stoics have no use for the ireful passion, according to Tasso's "Allegory" and Chapman's idiosyncratic Stoicism, "Wisedome" is vain and ineffectual without the heroic spirit to carry out its instructions.

The confusing attempt at reconciling Achillean *virtus* and Ulyssean virtue in the climactic scene of *Bussy D'Ambois* and the moral ambiguity throughout the play suggest that Chapman saw the ideal of the "complete man" as if through a pessimistic glass darkly in 1604. In *The Conspiracy and Tragedy of Byron*, on the other hand, the precise replication of Tasso's tripartite psychology and the clear moral vision throughout the play intimate that Chapman's conception of the exemplary heroic ideal was now secure. Chapman might well have ventured in 1608 to portray a better version of the "complete man" than Bussy had been; but, instead, he chose to recast his conception of Essex in the tragic figure of Byron, a contemporary, recognizably similar, French soldier-hero. Nevertheless, the fully exemplary ideal was embodied soon thereafter (if rather clumsily) by Clermont and then—still later but more successfully—by Ulysses. These two heroes disclose the continuing centrality of the heroic spirit and of "Predominant Perturbation" in Chapman's thought, even as he has entered the so-called "Stoic period" of his career.

Clermont has often been sharply contrasted with Bussy, Ulysses with Achilles, but Chapman's conception of the heroic spirit, though somewhat refined, has undergone no essential change since either *Bussy D'Ambois* or the complete *Iliads* (1611). Although Clermont's disciplined virtue should be distinguished from Bussy's undisciplined *virtus*,[25] Clermont is still as close in conception to Bussy as he is to the imperturbable Cato of Chapman's *Caesar and Pompey*. Ulysses has also brought heroic passion under reason's governance, but even though the Achillean "Perturbation" is subservient to reason rather than "Predominant," Ulysses' heroic passion and "outward Fortitude" are nevertheless essential to his epic triumph. Soldiers as well as sages, Clermont and Ulysses are equipped to act well and to suffer well. They become exemplary heroes not by resigning Bussy's or Achilles' *virtus* in favor of Cato's Stoic virtue, but by achieving a delicate balance between heroic and Stoic dictates. "Learning" fosters in the heroes a perfect mental poise, a resolute serenity, enabling them to act or react equally well with fortitude and virtue, *no matter the situation*. Masters of the mind's empire, they are spiritually immune to social and political dislocation; context is nothing, mental poise is all.

Clermont is prepared for any situation, his learning enabling him "to do as well as say / Whatever fits a most accomplish'd man." When the trap is sprung on Clermont at Cambrai, both active and passive, heroic and Stoic, modes of behavior are celebrated. First, Clermont displays an astonishing zealous ire in resisting the capture:

> A U M . : What spirit breathes thus in this more than man,
> Turns flesh to air possess'd, and in a storm
> Tears men about the field like autumn leaves?

He turn'd wild lightning in the lackeys' hands,
Who, though their sudden violent twitch unhors'd him,
Yet when he bore himself, their saucy fingers
Flew as too hot off, as he had been fire.
The ambush then made in, through all whose force,
He drave as if a fierce and fire-given cannon
Had spit his iron vomit out amongst them.
    . . . till, all motion spent,
His fix'd eyes cast a blaze of such disdain,
All stood and star'd, and untouch'd let him lie,
As something sacred fallen out of the sky.

[4. 1. 11–39]

Clermont is all fire and air; his heroic spirit, reminiscent of Bussy's and Byron's, is equally as astonishing as theirs had been. Clermont is "possess'd" with heroic furor, with a divine spirit of greatness, with a wholly exemplary Achillean "Perturbation." This martial action wins him honor according to the code of heroic virtue. But after the capture the spirited tempest subsides into the cerebral calm of the Stoic sage lecturing his captors in philosophy. The different modes of heroic reaction are coupled as if they were chain shot. Each is exemplary, each sanctioned by reason, each fostered by "learning"; together, rational *virtus* and Stoic virtue define Clermont as a "complete man." The hero of Chapman's *Odysses*, the exemplar of *prudentia et pietas*,[26] shares the heroic ideal exhibited at Cambrai. If *pietas* enables Ulysses to suffer heroically, *prudentia* enables him to act heroically.

In the active life the Ulyssean ideal of "over-ruling Wisedome" is impotent without the aid of spirit. Right judgment means nothing, as Telemachus well knows, without the *"skill . . . To give . . . things fit their fact"* (*CH* 2. 18. 331–32)—the Chapman locution translates de Sponde's single word, *"prudentia"* (p. 264). To put knowledge into right action, however, requires an assertion of spirit which neither Telemachus nor Ulysses is capable of at the beginning of the epic. The first portrait of Ulysses is, in fact, a precise recollection of the rational but dispirited Bussy in his opening soliloquy. Minerva describes the hero in Calypso's thrall:

Eius filia infortunatum lugentem detinet.
Semper enim mollibus & dulcibus sermonibus
Demulcet, vt Ithaces obliuiscatur: caeterum Vlysses

163

Cupiens vel fumum exilientem videre
Suae terrae, mori desiderat.

[Loeb 1:55–59; de Sponde, p. 3]

His daughter tis who holds this homelesse-driven
Still mourning with her—evermore profuse
Of soft and winning speeches *that abuse*
And make so languishingly and possest
With so remisse a mind, her loved guest
Manage the action of his way for home.
Where he (*though in affection overcome*)
In judgement yet more longs to *shew his hopes,*
His countrie's smoke leape from her chimney tops,
And death askes *in her armes.*

[*CH* 2. 1. 94–103)

Calypso's charms have abused her guest, making him manage his home-coming languishingly and with negligence. Happily, Chapman has provided a gloss for this extraordinary circumlocution:

> This is thus translated the rather to expresse and approve the Allegorie driven through the whole *Odysses*—deciphering the intangling of the wisest in his affections and the torments that breede in every pious minde, to be thereby hindred to arrive so directly as he desires at the proper and onely true naturall countrie of every worthy man, whose haven is heaven and the next life, to which this life is but a sea in continuall aesture and vexation.
>
> [*CH* 2. 1. 97n.]

None of the other five references to Ulysses' enthrallment on Calypso's island suggests that Ulysses has been conquered by his sexual appetite, and one oversimplifies if he interprets the hero's problem as a typical struggle between rational judgment and base passions.[27] Throughout Chapman's translation, when "affection" as a base desire is at issue, the translator employs appetitive colorings—blood, passion, lust—to emphasize it.[28] This is not the case in the above passage. The "affection" Chapman refers to in the translated passage is an impulse of spirit—Charron's "subtle faculty for doing."[29] Though sound in judgment, Ulysses languishes dispiritedly, "in affection overcome." Quite simply, Ulysses has been unmanned. He knows his goal and hopes to reach it, but his rational desires are mocked by a massive failure of will. The particular torment breeding in Ulysses' pious mind is despair; like the men whom he will later inveigh against, those who *"fled their Faith so as they had no hart"* (CH 2. 18. 193), despair has sapped his spirit. The hero is *"ship-wrackt in his teares"* and *"drownd in discontent"* (CH 2. 5. 23, 201)—later Chapman interpolations of the same moment on Calypso's island. Ulysses cannot sail because of his tears, cannot swim because of his discontent; he has no *spirit*, no "faculty for doing," no vehicle, to put the commands of "the wisest in his affections" into motion. As at a dark moment before the safe arrival on the island of the Phaeacians, when a sudden storm springs up and "then bent / Ulysses' knees; *then all his spirit was spent. / In which despaire*, he thus spake ... " (CH 2. 5. 378–80)—so, too, an enervating despair has now sapped Ulysses' spirit, leaving him psychologically disabled with the mind's empire powerless to effect its wishes.

Ulysses' initial "retirement" is thus a dispirited collapse like Bussy's at the beginning of his tragedy. Minerva must rekindle his rational purpose, firing a new faith, new hope, and new spirit, so that the hero may again become "prudent." Significantly, in Chapman's translation *prudentia* and "spirit" are virtually synonymous. After Minerva has awakened Telemachus's spirit in Book 1, for example, it is not *"prudens Telemachus"* who announces to his mother that he is now in control of the household, and not *"prudens Telemachus"* who then turns to rebuke the suitors (as it is in de Sponde); rather, "to the Queene, replide / Inspir'd Telemachus" (CH 2. 1. 526–27) and "Telemachus *this new-given spirit* did passe / On their old insolence" (CH 2. 1. 562–63). Similarly, Telemachus's voyage becomes a heroic enterprise. It is a *"brave act"* (CH 2. 2. 433); Minerva does not *"vi concitabat"* each man (p. 24), but "she did with *spirit enflame*" (CH 2. 2. 575). Companions become *"souldiers"* (CH 2. 2. 605); the journey (*"iter"*—p. 24) becomes an *"honor'd action"* (CH 2. 2. 590). The men are not merely anticipating Telemachus's eagerness to depart ("tuam exspectantes alacritatem"—p. 24), but "all expected now / *He should the spirit of a souldier show*" (CH 2. 2. 587–88). Chapman means to suggest that Minerva has inspired Telemachus with heroic *virtus*.

As patroness of *prudentia* in the *Odysses*, Minerva is a goddess of many symbolic faces. At moments she seems to represent transcendent "wisedome"; to love her is to be not only a philosopher but a kind of Platonic mystagogue inspired by god-given grace.[30] More often, she is a symbol of worldly wisdom, sound judgment, and rational control over passion.[31] But what cannot be overstressed is that Chapman's Minerva is also Homer's Athena, patroness of wily Odysseus, man of wit, policy, craftiness, and white lies. Wariness, mistrust, and shrewd calculation are salient virtues in Chapman's *Odysses*.[32] Just as clearly and more to the immediate point, Minerva also symbolizes *prudentia* militant. She inspires Ulysses to deeds of "outward Fortitude," just as the deities in the *Iliads* inspired the warriors with godlike spirit. The best example occurs before the fight with the suitors, when Minerva, in the guise of Mentor, chides the hero for delaying the bloodletting:

> Non amplius tibi Vlysses robor firmum, neque aliqua fortitudo,
> Qualis quando pro Helen albis vlnis bono patre nata
> Nouem annis Troianis pugnasti assidue semper.
> Multos autem viros interfecisti in graui pugna,
> Tuo autem capta est consilio Priami ciuitas lata viis.
> Quomodo iam nunc quando tuum populum & possessiones
>   peruenisti
> Contra procos indignaris fortis esse.
>   [Loeb, 22:224–32; de Sponde, p. 313]

>   No more
> Thy force nor fortitude, as heretofore,
> *Will gaine thee glory.* When nine yeares at Troy
> White-wristed Helen's *rescue* did imploy
> *Thy armes and wisedome* still, and ever usde
> The bloods of thousands through the field diffusde
> *By thy vaste valor,* Priam's broad-waide Towne
> *By thy grave parts* was sackt and overthrowne—
> And now, amongst thy people and thy goods,
> Against the wooers' *base and petulant bloods*
> Stint'st thou thy valour? Rather mourning here
> *Than manly fighting?*
>   [CH 2. 22. 273–84]

The present need is for active fortitude, the kind of "vaste valor" and "manly fighting" that will win glory. Minerva is not inspiring an indiscriminate burst of passion, of course, but rational fervor of the kind displayed by Clermont at Cambrai. Just as Chapman's "wisedome" implies far more than de Sponde's "*consilio*," Helen's "*rescue*" and the wooers' "*base and petulant bloods*" provide a rational justification for the slaughters that the truly wise man of arms *ought to* recognize and *must* act upon. After the slaughter this same emphasis on "just wreake" transforms Homer's magnanimous warrior ("Non pietas interfectos ob viros superbire"—Loeb, 22:412; de Sponde, p. 317) into a cold, zealous exponent of righteousness (" It is no piety to bemone the proud"—*CH* 2. 22. 529). In these and other passages like them, Homer's courageous soldier becomes Chapman's proponent of *ira per zelum*.

"*Armes and wisedome*," "*vaste valor*" and "*grave parts*," *virtus* and virtue, heroic spirit and sound rational judgment—in the active life the "complete man" must be prepared for the "high exploite" of *ira per zelum* and the "high exploite" of rational restraint. Fully equipped, he can act heroically no matter the situation, giving "things fit their fact," realizing the ideal of *prudentia*. Of course, Ulysses is a passive saint as well as an active hero, but I have stressed his *prudentia* rather than his *pietas* in order to demonstrate that in spite of the emphasis given Stoic virtue in Chapman's late tragedies and his *Odysses*, heroic spirit is still essential to Chapman's conception of martial heroism, and outward fortitude and epic prowess still essential to his celebratory conception of the heroic genre.

7

SHAKESPEARE'S *CORIOLANUS*:

A TITAN POSSESSED WITH FRAILTY

Coriolanus has been a particularly puzzling play for modern critics. The difficulty extends beyond the play's interpretive problems (which are considerable, if the sheer number of diverse, irreconcilable responses is any measure) to a fundamental distaste for the tragic hero. After *Hamlet*, *King Lear*, *Macbeth*, and *Antony and Cleopatra*, one might expect to encounter in Shakespeare's final tragedy a central character of depth and perception; but one finds instead a titanic hero described in bloody, beastly, and mechanistic terms. Coriolanus is a creature of a different mold and different world, alien both to modern sensibilities and to Shakespeare's tragic characterization. Equally unsettling is the play's dramaturgy. There are few soliloquies, no real soul-searching, and no sense of the hero progressing through psychological stances while advancing to a new realization of self; rather, except for two important moments of fluctuation in character, plot functions to display a hero who is psychologically monolithic. Coriolanus undergoes no essential change when moving from the battlefield to the forum and from the forum to Antium. He moves through the plot rather than develops with it; his attitudes in both war and peace are predictable, indeed fiercely consistent, and his sense of self is fully developed. When considered together, the atypical characterization and dramaturgy foster the impression of a play more closely akin to Chapman's titanic tragedy than to Shakespeare's tragic art.

One might say, in fact, that Shakespeare's final tragedy is more truly titanic than either *Bussy D'Ambois* or the *Byron* plays, for in addition to alienating us from the tragic hero Shakespeare has also placed us at a critical remove from the values of the hero's society. No ideal vision of the Elizabethan court, no explicit norms of Christian humanism, no exemplary embodiment of the Christian monarch break in upon the pagan, politically primitive setting. The ethical conflict central to Chapman's titanic tragedies, that between the pagan ideals of epic heroism and the Elizabethan ideals of Christian humanism, never materializes in *Coriolanus*; for the ideals of epic heroism are fostered by the ethos of ancient Rome. That societal ethos, we know, was present in Shakespeare's source, Sir Thomas North's translation of Plutarch's "Life of Caius Marcius Coriolanus":

> Now in those dayes, valliantnes was honoured in Rome above all other vertues; which they called *Virtus*, by the name of vertue selfe, as including in that generall name, all other speciall vertues besides.[1]

This primitive, uncivilized *virtus* is the offspring of Homer's epic ideal, the *areté* of *The Iliad*, and it is reflected not only in Coriolanus's martial superiority but in the patrician political philosophy of a natural "aristocracy" (a word derived etymologically and conceptually from *areté*).[2] Shakespeare deliberately recreates the martial ethos of a pre-Christian Roman society, the very political structure of which is scaled to reflect individual worth; and though Coriolanus is repugnant, to be sure, Shakespeare's effort of the historical imagination[3] makes it difficult to criticize the titan according to normative moral and political standards such as one might invoke to censure Byron's immoral and anarchic ambition. Indeed, with more justification one might rather inveigh against Coriolanus because he is too idealistic, too noble, too honest, too superior, and hence, too inhuman; and yet, to do so would imply a more sweeping condemnation of the patrician ethos that nurtured him and an association with the spokesmen and exemplars of republicanism, the self-serving tribunes and the worthless rabble of plebeians.

In the face of a tragedy militating against sympathy for the tragic hero, in fact discouraging identification with him even to the extent of making it difficult to condemn him according to moral and political norms of behavior—that is, in the face of an alien hero in an alien world, with no sympathetic character to embrace and no normative values to espouse, the critic must inevitably raise questions about Shakespeare's dramatic *idea*. Why an awesome prodigy at the center of Shakespeare's final tragedy? Why the scrupulous adherence to his historical consciousness?

Why *Coriolanus* at this stage of Shakespeare's career? Several answers to these questions have been advanced, ranging from the dramatist's desire to write a political allegory to his disaffection with *Timon of Athens*.[4] My contention is that the atypical hero and the atypical dramaturgy of Shakespeare's final heroic tragedy might best be understood in light of Chapman's direct negative influence. *Coriolanus*, I shall argue, is an explicit response to the implications of titanic tragedy in general and to *The Conspiracy and Tragedy of Byron* in particular.

The most noteworthy theatrical event of 1608 was the scandal at the Blackfriars Playhouse. George Chapman's *Conspiracy and Tragedy of Byron* was at the center of the controversy, as the letter of the French ambassador relates: "Environ la micaresme ces certains comédiens à qui j'avois fait deffendre de jouer l'histoire du feu mareschal de Biron, voyant toutte la cour dehors, ne laissèrent de la faire, et non seulement cela, mais y introduisirent la Royne et Madame de Verneuil, la première traitait celle-cy fort mal de paroles, et luy donnant un soufflet. . . ."[5] This incident occasioned the ban on further productions by the Children of Blackfriars which, in turn, allowed the King's Men to move to the Blackfriars Theatre later that summer.[6] Beyond question, Shakespeare was aware of the *Byron* plays; the Children of Blackfriars was the strongest rival company to the King's Men, Chapman was the strongest rival tragedian to Shakespeare, and *The Tragedy of Byron* had become notorious. The *Byron* plays were composed and acted late in 1607 or early in 1608 (obviously no later than 8 April) and subsequently published in 1608,[7] and it may be that Shakespeare wrote his play for a Blackfriars performance in the autumn of 1608.[8] His intention may have been to "out-Chapman" Chapman in order to win a new audience, but there is reason to believe that his motivation was more than mercenary. With *Bussy D'Ambois* having been published in 1607 and a revival planned for 1609, with the performance of the *Byron* plays and the scandal at the Blackfriars in 1608, perhaps with word that Chapman was back at work on his *Iliads* (five new books were added to the original seven and printed the following year) and planning a sequel to *Bussy D'Ambois*, Shakespeare, I suspect, designed *Coriolanus* to respond not only to the *Byron* plays but to Chapman's theory of titanic heroism as well. This conjecture is supported by the generally accepted dating of *Coriolanus* as 1608–9.[9]

Less speculative support for the theory of direct influence arises from the substantial similarities and pointed distinctions between the two protagonists. First, both Byron and Coriolanus are exceptional soldiers and extraordinary social misfits; but whereas Byron's vaulting aspiration would subvert the social order, Coriolanus's heroic conception of self, as it is too exact an embodiment of the assumptions on which Roman society is based, would perfect the social order, stripping it of political lies, empty customs, and quaint myths and revealing it for what it really is, a necessarily rigid system of hierarchical strata defined by inherent superiority. Second, both soldiers berate the indolence and dissolution that spring up in peacetime, weakening the fiber of society, enfeebling traditional values; they imply that war is the proper environment for "virtue," a term that both heroes define as *virtus*.[10] Byron considers himself a man of Roman spirit and would advance on a *cursus honorum* to a social station reflecting his martial eminence; in a Christian monarchy, however, such an ambition is satanic or, to employ the Roman analogy, Catilinian. Coriolanus is a precise embodiment of epic *virtus*, a progeny of Hector when fighting for Rome, an Achilles or a Turnus when fighting against Rome; moreover, for the preeminent man of *virtus* to advance to the consulship is not only accommodated by, but encouraged by, the Roman political structure. Third, both soldiers assume that social status is defined by individual merit; although Byron's assumption is false and Coriolanus's is valid, they are both absolute (and tiresome) in their equation of social rewards and individual deserts. One way Byron justifies his desert is by appealing often to the many wounds he received while in the service of country. Shakespeare notices this, and his hero "outwounds" Chapman's Byron. Although Coriolanus is too modest to boast about his wounds, his supporters trumpet his signs of heroism, and, as the wounds are so numerous, their reckoning at one point leads to grotesquerie (2. 1. 137–72).

More telling is the characterization of Byron and Coriolanus in titanic dimensions and the insistence that their incendiary fury is a heroic property. The two protagonists equate ambition with self-fulfillment and defy all but personal edicts. They exhibit this titanic individualism in extreme form when they become Aristotle's "god-beasts," antisocial monsters,[11] seeking to create personal identities from the chaos of society and country. Byron in his godlike arrogance proclaims that "We must reform and have a new creation; / Of state and government, and on our Chaos / Will I sit brooding up another world" (*T.* 2. 1. 29–32); and Coriolanus will forge a new identity in Rome's flames: "He was a kind of nothing, titleless, / Till he had forg'd himself a name a' th' fire / Of burning Rome" (5. 1. 13–15). In both cases this anarchic individualism is fired by the heroic spirit. The fire imagery Chapman associated with heroic passion in *Bussy D'Ambois* and the *Byron* plays is present in *Coriolanus* as well. The tribunes plot their strategy around Coriolanus's wrath, much as lesser villains dupe Byron by igniting his choleric spirit. A. C. Bradley first noticed the stress on fire imagery in acts 4 and 5 of *Coriolanus* and linked it with the hero's fire-eyed vengeance.[12] But Shakespeare joins this implication with several significances of fire stressed in Chapman's heroic tragedies—the association of heroic spirit with divine furor, the physiological analogy of fire with choler, and the mythological allusion to Mars, the red planet and patron of warriors. Coriolanus is a "lonely dragon," a furious, beastly, winged warrior breathing the fire of his own indomitable spirit.

Still another similarity and distinction between Chapman's Byron and Shakespeare's Coriolanus resides in the nature of their aspiration for excellence. Chapman distinguished Byron's "breath," "exhalation," or "spirit" of aspiration from base appetite. Shakespeare also associates Coriolanus's breath with heroic spirit and with the trumpet and thunder of heroic exploit,[13] but his imagistic stress falls on the feeble "breath" of the plebeians. Their mouths are instruments of the belly; their foul breath is symbolic of base, dispirited, appetitive desire. This sharp contrast between Coriolanus and the rabble suggests to Paul A. Cantor that the Platonic distinction between appetitive passion and heroic spirit (*eros* and *thumos*) is operative in *Coriolanus*.[14] I would agree with Cantor and suggest in addition that Shakespeare incorporates the social and psychological hierarchies into his tragedy because they are pivotal to the *Byron* plays and essential to Chapman's sympathetic conception of the soldier-hero and of the heroic genre. As with Chapman's other emphases, Shakespeare adopts the distinction between base appetite and heroic passion in order to scrutinize it.

Coriolanus is deliberately shaped in the mold of Byron and then distinguished from him; he is every inch Chapman's hero, and then more. Not only has Shakespeare removed the titan from the moral and political contexts that warred against Byron's heroic grandeur, but he has also buttressed Coriolanus's heroic idealism with honorable, exemplary achievement rather than displaced it into unworthy modes of action. Equally important, the hero's epic deeds are presented on stage, not simply reported. Nowhere in Chapman's canon, much less in the *Byron* plays, will one find a heroic evocation so extensive and so impressive as Coriolanus's demonstration of epic prowess at Corioli (1. 4–10). It is as if Shakespeare set out to create a superior version of Chapman's hero so that he might criticize not only Bussy and Byron, but the defective epic ideals on which Chapman's conception of heroism is based.

Throughout most of Shakespeare's play, Coriolanus is perceived by the audience not as a man "possess'd . . . with greatness," as Byron was, but rather as a titan "possess'd" from time to time with human frailty. His weakness is that he can be swayed by his mother and friends, who would tie him ignobly to the community of men. Roman society finally repudiates him because he is too idealistic, too proud, and, as his pride is fully justified, too great; but the audience repudiates him because he is an alien, too godlike in his immunity against human weakness, too bestial in his insensitivity to the frailty of other men. At the climax of the tragedy, when the hero acknowledges that his true identity is that of a human being, suggesting that he had been "possess'd . . . with greatness" all along, and when he decides to spare Rome, submitting to the urge of natural affection—ironically, only then does he exhibit an identifiably human heroism. Shakespeare and the audience would account Coriolanus's display of human weakness his most heroic moment; conversely, what Chapman might account his greatest strength becomes his tragic weakness. For what is finally "most mortal" to the hero is his unwillingness to repudiate his heroic conception of self. He returns to the Volsces and to his death at the hands of Aufidius because his pride cannot brook the conception of living in a society that will celebrate him as a kind, affectionate, humane "hero." In act 5 of Shakespeare's final heroic tragedy, a human being and his heroic image are again placed in pointed and, in terms of Shakespeare's dramatic career, summary opposition. If by responding to the edicts of the heart the human being's merciful decision is heroic, the compulsive aspiration to fulfill an epic conception of self is tragic.

My proposal, then, is that Shakespeare's *Coriolanus* bears a closer resemblance to a Chapman tragedy than to plays typical of Shakespeare's tragic canon because it was conceived as a direct response to Chapman's epic biography of Byron and to the broader implications of titanic tragedy. The play suggests that no society, Roman or Renaissance, can tolerate the frightening ideal of heroic *virtus* once clothed in flesh; and, like *Antony and Cleopatra*, where the focus was on heroic love, this play of martial excellence demonstrates that true heroism does not reside in titanic excellence but in the willingness to accept human limitation and human frailty in oneself and others.

THE TITAN

In the opening scene of *Coriolanus* two spokesmen for the rebellious plebeians exchange views about Caius Martius's services to Rome:

1 . CIT . :   Though soft-conscienc'd men can be content to say it was for his country, he did it to please his mother, and to be partly proud, which he is, even to the altitude of his virtue.
2 . CIT . : What he cannot help in his nature, you account a vice in him.

[1. 1. 37–42]

The audience cannot determine causation as precisely as the first citizen might wish and is forced to puzzle over two incongruous motivations: (1) Martius's love for his mother, and (2) his pride in his natural prowess. Similarly, when the second citizen implies that Martius acts according to natural instinct, the term "nature" becomes ambiguous, referring both to the blood bond of affection and to the justifiable pride in his inherent *virtus*. This is not a syntactical oversight, but a typical Shakespearean strategy. The audience is kept in doubt about the protagonist (and thereby asked to question his motivation) at the same time that the thematic crux of Martius's two natural drives is introduced.

The implications of the citizens' brief exchange are more fully developed in the magnificent third scene of the play. Here Volumnia reveals the uncompromising drive for honor, fame, and individual excellence that typifies the aristocratic ethos in which Martius was nurtured. The ethos is cold, abstract, and strikingly grotesque as Volumnia voices it, for the Roman matron speaks in a quintessential domestic setting (see 1. 3. S.D.), and her martial ideal is superimposed on maternal images:

VOL.: If my son were my husband, I should freelier rejoice in that absence wherein he won honor than in the embracements of his bed where he would show most love.
   . . . I tell thee, daughter, I sprang not more in joy at first hearing he was a man-child than now in first seeing he had prov'd himself a man.
   . . . The breasts of Hecuba,
When she did suckle Hector, look'd not lovelier
Than Hector's forehead when it spit forth blood
At Grecian sword, [contemning].

[1. 3. 2–5, 15–17, 40–43]

Natural, human, life-giving acts and destructive, bloody, heroic deeds are yoked by violence together. Like Lady Macbeth, who would pluck her nipple from the child's gums and dash out its brains to fulfill her ambition, Volumnia reveals an extraordinary dedication to the Roman heroic ethos, a dedication that exceeds even the strongest of her natural, maternal instincts.

Volumnia's language reminds the audience that she was once a mother and that the awesome giant of act 1, scene 1, reflected in this scene by his son and namesake, little Martius, was once a boy himself, no doubt one who would rather "see the swords and hear a drum than look upon his schoolmaster" (1. 3. 55–56).[15] But though the subtle development of the maternal remembrances—from the marriage bed, to the moment of birth, to the period of suckling, to the Roman nursery—firmly establish the blood bond between mother and son, Shakespeare's stress clearly falls on the unnaturalness of the Roman heroic ideal. The audience is led to infer that there has been a second creation, the birth of another son, this one conceived in the love of war, born into manhood, suckled in blood, and educated for battle (2–5, 15–17, 40–43, 55–56). Volumnia subordinates the natural son and her maternal affection to this other Martius, a frightful abstraction composed of "honor," "renown," "fame," "good report." He is a creature "conceived" of heroic idealism; he is visionary and immortal (1. 3. 20–21), grotesque and inhuman:

> VOL.:   His bloody brow
> With his mail'd hand then wiping, forth he goes,
> Like to a harvest-man [that's] task'd to mow
> Or all or lose his hire.
>
> [1. 3. 34–37]

This is Volumnia's second "creation"; it is Martius's second nature. He is not only a child of flesh and blood but the product of a frightful ideal. Both natures confront the audience at the climax of the scene:

> VAL.: A' my word, the father's son. I'll swear 'tis a very pretty boy.
> A' my troth, I look'd upon him a' We'n'sday half an hour together; h'as such a confirm'd countenance. I saw him run after a gilded butterfly, and when he caught it, he let it go again, and after it again, and over and over he comes, and up again; catch'd it again: or whether his fall enrag'd him, or how 'twas, he did so set his teeth and tear it. O, I warrant, how he mammock'd it!
>
> [1. 3. 57–65]

The transformation of the pretty boy at play into the irrational monster, of the determined stare into the violent rage of a self-enclosed vision, underscores the grotesqueness of Martius's double nature as human being and inhuman hero. The second citizen claims that both the natural son, who would please his mother, and the awesome embodiment of *virtus*, who would please himself, are inextricably involved in his service to Rome.

The second Martius, the man of heroic *virtus* named Coriolanus, receives the dramatic stress in the first three acts of the tragedy. The human in him is overwhelmed by the bloody hero who cuts through battles like an automaton. He is a monstrous "thing of death," as impersonal as the symbols used to describe him: "sword," "whip," "steed." And yet, though alien to our sensibilities, Coriolanus is a consummate hero according to the ideals of his own society. The "shame culture" of Shakespeare's ancient Rome encourages the hero's aspiration for individual excellence, as Volumnia's language testifies and Cominius's public encomium verifies:

> COM.: . . . the deeds of Coriolanus
> Should not be utter'd feebly. It is held
> That valor is the chiefest virtue, and
> Most dignifies the haver; if it be,
> The man I speak of cannot in the world
> Be singly counterpois'd. At sixteen years,
> When Tarquin made a head for Rome, he fought
> Beyond the mark of others. . . .
>   His pupil age
> Man-ent'red thus, he waxed like a sea,
> And in the brunt of seventeen battles since
> He lurch'd all swords of the garland. For this last,
> Before and in Corioles, let me say,
> I cannot speak him home. . . .
>   His sword, death's stamp,
> Where it did mark, it took; from face to foot
> He was a thing of blood, whose every motion
> Was tim'd with dying cries. Alone he ent'red
> The mortal gate of th' city, which he painted
> With shunless destiny; aidless came off,

And with a sudden reinforcement struck
Corioles like a planet.

[2. 2. 82–89, 98–103, 107–14]

Deeds and feats, valor, the measurement of individual ability ("singly counterpois'd," "Beyond the mark of others," "Alone," "aidless"), impersonality ("like a sea," "death's stamp," "planet"), public display ("saw him," "in the consul's view"), public reward, and public encomium—all indicate that individual prowess operates in a congenial cultural domain, that individual aspiration may be fulfilled through public service, that is, through cruel and bloody, but self-confident and valiant deeds on behalf of society. Coriolanus's appeal to his soldiers similarly articulates a heroic ideal joining an individual taste for blood and relish for heroism with the concern for reputation and the patriotic desire to fight for one's country (1. 6. 66–75).

At the heart of the Roman cultural ideal is a traditional nexus between individual aspiration and public service. Deeds on behalf of society extend from an individual quest for honor. As long as the hero maintains a public consciousness, seeking and accepting honor as the public measurement of *virtus*, then public service makes ambition virtue. Volumnia suggests that unless one's honor is animated by the desire to win renown, fame, and good report, it is "no better than picture-like to hang by th' wall" (1. 3. 11); she would agree with Shakespeare's Ulysses that "to have done" or (from her point of view) to have not begun "is to hang / Quite out of fashion, like a rusty mail/ In monumental mock'ry" (*Tro.* 3. 3. 151–53). What distinguishes Coriolanus from his mother, his friends, and Roman society is that he rejects the conception of honor as a public reward, insisting that his deeds are answerable to his own evaluative standards.[16] By conceiving of honor as a personal dictate responsive to his own bosom integrity and by performing deeds in order to realize his own heroic conception of self, Coriolanus effectively severs his allegiance to self from his allegiance to country. This was the crux of Achilles' disastrous isolation in *The Iliad*, and it appears that Shakespeare pivots the first part of his tragedy on the contradiction inherent in the hero's double allegiance. The heroic ego that fires an individual aspiration for excellence cannot serve a second master.

The primacy of Coriolanus's allegiance to self is manifested in an extreme individualism that, though grounded in aristocratic premises,

177

soon comes to isolate him from all society. At the core of this individualism is the doctrine of judgment by merit. Coriolanus despises the plebeians because he judges them for what they are: "I love them as they
weigh" (2. 2. 74). He is reluctant to accept the people's "voices" for
a similar reason; his own desert, his deeds of heroic *virtus*, speak for
his candidacy. To receive the approbation of the plebeians' worthless,
dispirited "voices" is a noxious, antiquated social custom that is repugnant to his bosom integrity and antithetical to the principles of society's
aristocratic ethos.[17] The particular danger the tribunes notice resides in
this ominous link between the hero's individual idealism and his politics.
It is not surprising that the most superior titan among Shakespeare's
heroes is also the purest political theoretician in the canon:

> COR.:   This kind of service
> Did not deserve corn gratis. Being i' th' war,
> Their mutinies and revolts, wherein they show'd
> Most valor, spoke not for them.
>
>   [3. 1. 124–27]

The ascendancy of natural superiority was a familiar doctrine of the
ancient aristocracy and inseparable from the heroic code of *areté*; for
Coriolanus to become consul would be a fulfillment of the aristocratic
ethos, a public tribute to his singular *virtus*. Nevertheless, the tribunes'
point is well taken: a superior man acting in service of his country may be
a hero, but a hero who judges society according to his own conception of
self is likely to be an inhuman tyrant:

> BRU.:   You speak a' th' people
> As if you were a god, to punish; not
> A man of their infirmity.
>
>   [3. 1. 80–82]

The tribunes fear a tyranny of natural superiority, and their fears are
justified.

Given the aristocratic premise that one's status in society defines his
inner worth, Coriolanus's ascension to the consulship, a solitary eminence far above the masses (Shakespeare deliberately avoids mention of
any other candidate for the office), would formalize his absolute opposition to the people.

> MAR.:   Your virtue is
> To make him worthy whose offense subdues him,

And curse that justice did it. Who deserves greatness
Deserves your hate.

[1. 1. 174–77]

Martius suggests that by their demonstrative discontent, by their cursing of the nobility, the plebeians embody their own kind of anti-*virtus*, a code of inherent weakness and unworthiness that is precisely antiheroic. They do as they are; they are self-defined. According to his circular logic, moreover, their hatred of him above all others confirms his singular greatness. For Coriolanus, in other words, the consulship is defined by its "antipodal relationship" to the plebeians.[18] No doubt the tyranny would be absolute:

SIC.:   Where is this viper
That would depopulate the city and
Be every man himself?

[3. 1. 262–64]

If Coriolanus's display of *virtus* on the battlefield and his politics of *virtus* in the forum set him poles apart from the interests and values of the plebeians, they also distance him from the rest of the patricians. Menenius's analogy of the patricians to the belly of the body politic (1. 1. 96–163) suggests an organic interrelationship with the people as well as an ironical association with their appetitive interests.[19] The patricians are willing to grant the plebeians political representation in the body politic, acknowledging their needs and their right to make those needs known. The patricians may despise the plebeians as much as Coriolanus does, but they at least are willing to engage in a politics of accommodation. In Coriolanus's political vocabulary, however, "need" and "accommodation" have no place. The notion of "corn gratis" is abhorrent to his principles of inherent worth and just deserts because it is a synecdoche for the patricians' appallingly craven decision to feed the plebeians' indolence and inertia by giving them political representation gratis. And, unlike the patricians, Coriolanus is sickened by the very thought of complying (if only for "show") with social traditions, ceremonies, customs, forms (2. 2. 134–46) that would suggest his association with, not to mention dependence upon, the worthless rabble.

But perhaps the hero's attitude toward public adulation distinguishes him most from the rest of the patricians. Coriolanus is genuinely uneasy about receiving plaudits from others, and at the heart of this extraordinary modesty is a perverse pride that rankles at the notion that social consensus might define his worth. He fears that the dependence upon even the best of men for his public identity would compromise his heroic integrity. Though he will accept rewards from his peers, the name "Coriolanus" is the only gift equal to him, for it alone symbolizes his heroic identity. True reward, however, is found only in the fulfillment of personal standards of excellence:

> COM.:   Our spoils he kick'd at,
> And look'd upon things precious as they were
> The common muck of the world. He covets less
> Than misery itself would give, rewards
> His deeds with doing them, and is content
> To spend the time to end it.
> MEN.:   He's right noble.
>
> [2. 2. 124–29]

But Menenius will later say that "His nature is *too noble* for the world" (3. 1. 254; my emphasis), for Coriolanus's titanic individualism is tantamount to a self-imposed banishment from Roman society, plebeians and patricians alike. He is correct when he proclaims "I banish you," for his attempt to define himself is inescapably an attempt to isolate himself from society and its normative standards of behavior and standards of judgment. In striving to realize his own heroic conception of self, Coriolanus is following a course that leads inevitably to his social dislocation. The hero's progress is at once a noble ascent and a dehumanizing retreat into a self-enclosed world.

More so than in *Troilus and Cressida*, in *Coriolanus* Shakespeare elaborates on the soldier's "self-possession," suggesting in precise ways how the retreat from reality into a visionary world of epic myth has caused both a social dislocation and a psychic displacement. Volumnia's grotesque imagery introduces the artistic design according to which the real self is displaced by a heroic conception of self; that is, natural human needs and sources of gratification—sex, sustenance, love, community— are displaced by an unnatural, dehumanizing, individualistic appetite for honor, fame, renown, and heroic excellence. Volumnia's substitution of valor's rewards for the pleasures of the marriage bed, for example, anticipates the moments when Coriolanus and Aufidius testify that they are Bellona's bridegrooms:

MAR.:   O! let me clip ye ·
In arms as sound as when I woo'd, in heart
As merry as when our nuptial day was done
And tapers burnt to bedward!

[1. 6. 29–32]

AUF.:   Know thou first,
I lov'd the maid I married; never man
Sigh'd truer breath; but that I see thee here,
Thou noble thing, more dances my rapt heart
Than when I first my wedded mistress saw
Bestride my threshold.

[4. 5. 113–18]

Both greetings anticipate a forthcoming battle, a "consummation" in military action.[20] Shakespeare exaggerates the conventional language of warriors, as he had the dedication of the Roman matron, to alert the audience to the unnatural code they exemplify.

Volumnia also describes Coriolanus's initiation into manhood as a second birth (1. 3. 15–18), and war indeed becomes his surrogate mother. We watch Coriolanus take on a heroic identity through the extended *aristeia* of act 1; he is born, suckled, and baptized in the bloody ceremony of war and afterward named "Coriolanus" to symbolize his new identity.[21] The mother's language had anticipated Martius's second creation; now she vaguely discerns that her natural son has become somehow alien to her:

VOL.: My gentle Martius, worthy Caius, and
By deed-achieving honor newly nam'd—
What is it?—Coriolanus must I call thee?

[2. 1. 172–74]

Finally, war itself is likened to a kind of grotesque nourishment for the heroes. Like Hector, the exemplars of the heroic code leave and take from the grim feast of war, feeding a compulsive appetite for glory, honor, renown, heroic image. The heroic quest is bloody, destructive, and—as it is juxtaposed grotesquely with "eating," an image normally associated with a social ceremony of human sustenance and community —unnatural, inhuman, ravenous, bestial. Only a blind partisan of tradition could fail to see the reality of brute passion beneath the so-called heroic aspiration for excellence. For Coriolanus the aristocratic ethos has grown into war's huge belly, the womb of heroes and storehouse of heroic sustenance.[22]

Martius's search for identity in this alien heroic world parallels his insistence on individualism and independence from society. Shakespeare seems to have taken the hint for such self-absorption from Aristotle's heroic ideal of "ennobled self-love,"[23] and then portrayed its excess. Perhaps the clearest depiction of its excess is found in the Coriolanus-Aufidius relationship, for each represents to the other a standard of comparison threatening his own preeminence. From the beginning, the warriors' love-hate affair isolates them from society. Roman and Volscian mean little to them; theirs is a private feast.[24] As long as Aufidius lives, Coriolanus must share his heroic stature with him, and vice versa; for this reason the heroes' rivalry is a fierce hatred. But the hatred also suggests a perverse form of self-love, not simply because they respect a common nobility ("I would wish me only he"), but because they are forced to share their admiration of self with a second identity.[25] What each loves most in himself he sees in the other, and just as in the face-to-face encounters of Hector and Achilles in *Troilus and Cressida*, when that self-love is extended outward to a second identity, as if to a mirror image, the psychological impulse is radically narcissistic. When the heroes meet in Actium, Shakespeare chooses to depict the narcissism as a friendship, clearly twisting the notion that friendship presupposes a recognition of oneself in another.[26] But it is a grotesque friendship; the "one soul in bodies twain" ideal is described literally (4. 6. 194–200) and in terms of public stature, for this momentary relationship cannot survive the acquisitive pull for honor that the gigantic egos will exert. Love and hate, then, are the twin offspring of an essential self-love, hardly a "doit" between them, and the uneasy sharing of identity cannot long survive the force of heroic ego asserting its absolute individuality.

One recognizes, therefore, that Aufidius, the individual whom Coriolanus admires and seeks to emulate most, is really a creature reflecting Coriolanus's own heroic image. The external world has no meaning to Coriolanus except as it defines his heroic identity. He stands completely alone, totally absorbed in a visionary world of heroism. The impact of his terrifying isolation, of his titanic independence from human society and bloody "self-creation" in war, does not strike home fully until after his banishment, when he renounces the last tie with Rome—the name "Coriolanus"—withdraws completely from the Roman ethos, and closes himself off in the world of ego:

COM.:   Coriolanus
He would not answer to; forbade all names;
He was a kind of nothing, titleless,
Till he had forg'd himself a name a' th' fire
Of burning Rome.

[5. 1. 11–15]

"A kind of nothing" is total self-absorption. He will not permit a public identity because no name will now fit him. This is why he expects his mere presence to identify him to Aufidius (4. 5. 57–60). No longer a man of human infirmity nor a member of the human community, a "kind of nothing" is at the same time a kind of everything, godlike in his self-sufficiency, but impersonal, inhuman, unnatural:

COM.: He is their god; he leads them like a thing
Made by some other deity than Nature,
That shapes man better.

[4. 6. 90–92]

Having listened to Volumnia in act 1, scene 3, one might associate the "other deity" with Rome's unnatural heroic ethos. More accurately, perhaps, the aristocratic heroic ideal has rough-hewn Martius, but by moving beyond that ideal Coriolanus has shaped his own end. He is a heroic man grown into a dragon in the isolation of his own sick ego. The titan would be self-created and renounce all ties with nature, family, humanity:

COR.:   . . . I'll never
Be such a gosling to obey instinct, but stand
As if a man were author of himself,
And knew no other kin.

[5. 3. 34–37]

Shakespeare has carried to its logical conclusion this second Martius, the unnatural creation of pride and *virtus*. Together, the heroic ethos and a heroic conception of self have shaped him better than Nature had intended and *therefore* worse. Coriolanus is the beast-man apotheosized, both titanic and inhuman, at the same time Chapman's hero and Shakespeare's criticism of him.

Byron's favorite hero was Alexander. This was in keeping with the heroic legacy: Hercules was the intermediary between the divine deeds of his father Zeus and the warrior princes of Greece and Rome; his heroical perfection was embodied most fully in literature by Achilles, in history by Alexander.[27] Shakespeare's response is pointed:

> MEN.: When he walks, he moves like an engine, and the ground shrinks before his treading. He is able to pierce a corslet with his eye, talks like a knell, and his hum is a battery. He sits in his state, as a thing made for Alexander. What he bids be done is finish'd with his bidding. He wants nothing of a god but eternity and a heaven to throne in.
>
> SIC.: Yes, mercy, if you report him truly.
>
> [5. 4. 18–25]

This is the final, terrifying vision of Chapman's superman, but one from which Martius had momentarily retreated in the previous scene and one which Shakespeare had renounced long before.

THE BOY

Shakespeare's response to Chapman's awesome titan centers on the other Martius, the natural son of a natural mother, the vulnerable human being whose instinct and affection belie the heroic ideal he would impersonate. As we have seen in act 1, scene 3, Coriolanus's human nature is brought forward in a series of domestic images—the marriage bed, the mother's joy at birth, the suckling of the child—and in the vignette of the innocent boy chasing the butterfly. Although these images are used to enhance the strength of the Roman ethos and although Martius's humanity receives little notice in the first acts of the tragedy, Shakespeare establishes the hero's ties with the community of men early in the play as preparation for Coriolanus's psychological conflict at the climax in act 5.

In an important way, Martius's double nature as titanic hero and vulnerable human being is reflected by his paradoxical relationship with society. Although he can isolate himself from the human community, he can never be fully independent of the people he abhors. He needs and actively seeks their hatred in order to define himself according to the political philosophy of *virtus*: ". . . but he seeks their hate with greater devotion than they can render it him, and leaves nothing undone that may fully discover him their opposite" (2. 2. 18–21). And he also needs their praise so that he might reject it, distancing himself from the unworthy bestowers of praise according to the doctrine of inherent merit.

But no matter the distance he puts between himself and society by his peculiar kind of negative definition, he still remains dependent on it for his heroic identity. Shakespeare is at pains to make this clear. Listen to the tribune Brutus describe Martius's triumph:

> B R U . : All tongues speak of him, and the bleared sights
>   Are spectacled to see him. Your prattling nurse
>   Into a rapture lets her baby cry
>   While she chats him; the kitchen malkin pins
>   Her richest lockram 'bout her reechy neck,
>   Clamb'ring the walls to eye him; stalls, bulks, windows
>   Are smother'd up, leads fill'd, and ridges hors'd
>   With variable complexions, all agreeing
>   In earnestness to see him. Seld-shown flamens
>   Do press among the popular throngs, and puff
>   To win a vulgar station; our veil'd dames
>   Commit the war of white and damask in
>   Their nicely gawded cheeks to th' wanton spoil
>   Of Phoebus' burning kisses—such a poother
>   As if that whatsoever god who leads him
>   Were slily crept into his human powers,
>   And gave him graceful posture.
>
> [2. 1. 205–21]

This stunning description, which pictures feminine, common, domestic, urban plebeians acclaiming the conqueror-god, is a deliberate evocation of the antiheroic. One cannot imagine a reception more repugnant to Coriolanus: from "tongues" to "popular throngs" to "veil'd dames" to "nicely gawded cheeks" to "Phoebus' burning kisses." The extraordinary series of urban domestic photographs, which soon grows into a democratic portrait, drives home the fact that Coriolanus's heroic identity, public renown, and the consulship itself—which Volumnia has just introduced—are dependent on these the least of his brethren.

To reemphasize his dependence on society, a messenger then issues a further report on the triumph:

> M E S S . : I have seen the dumb men throng to see him, and
>   The blind to hear him speak. Matrons flung gloves,
>   Ladies and maids their scarfs and handkerchers,
>   Upon him as he pass'd; the nobles bended,

> As to Jove's statue, and the commons made
> A shower and thunder with their caps and shouts.
> I never saw the like.
>
> [2. 1. 262–68]

The hero is likened to Jove himself, or rather to a "statue" of Jove. For this god has been created, not born; he is defined by the veneration of the nobility, not self-defined; and worse, this god of weather, the Jove who reigns over the mutable heavens, relies for his power on the "shower and thunder" which the plebeians create for him.

The darker side of Coriolanus's dependent relationship with society emerges through a complex metaphor:

> SIC.:   This, as you say, suggested
> At some time when his soaring insolence
> Shall teach the people—which time shall not want,
> If he be put upon't, and that's as easy
> As to set dogs on sheep—will be his fire
> To kindle their dry stubble; and their blaze
> Shall darken him for ever.
>
> [2. 1. 253–59]

Coriolanus's furious opposition to the people will spark a self-immolation, for his individuality is so intimately bound up with its public context that the destruction of the context would be a kind of self-destruction. Volumnia says much the same thing at the climax in act 5. She had earlier spoken of a son who existed in others' "good report" (1. 3. 20–21), and later asserts that the immolation of Rome will be suicidal for the hero, a blaze that will darken his reputation forever:

> VOL.: ... If thou conquer Rome, the benefit
> Which thou shalt thereby reap is such a name
> Whose repetition will be dogg'd with curses;
> Whose chronicle thus writ: "The man was noble,
> But with his last attempt he wip'd it out,
> Destroy'd his country, and his name remains
> To th' ensuing age abhorr'd."
>
> [5. 3. 142–48]

Coriolanus's titanic independence from the people and heroic conception of self are, then, but one side of the coin; the hero depends on the

186

"voices" of the people he hates for his heroic identity and is bound to the community of men he would transcend.[28]

This same dependence and same bond are revealed in the relationship of mother and son. Despite Volumnia's extraordinary dedication to the heroic code, she bears a closer resemblance to the rest of the patricians than to her son. One thinks, for example, of her willingness to compromise, her political duplicity, her use of language and eloquence. But as a threat to Coriolanus's heroic identity Volumnia is most like the plebeians. She brings out the "boy" in him, the ignoble, weak dependence on humanity that his pride cannot brook. This is evident in the first confrontation of mother and son in act 3, when Volumnia asks him to apologize to the people. For Coriolanus to obey his mother would be to betray himself: "Would you have me / False to my nature? Rather say, I play / The man I am" (3. 2. 14–16). When he donned the gown of humility earlier, in his own mind he had compromised his integrity and played false to his heroic nature (2. 2. 144–46, 148–49; 2. 3. 112–24). Nevertheless, he had salvaged some self-respect and preserved his heroic integrity to some extent by employing a kind of double-talk, by not showing his wounds, and by never actually "begging" for the people's voices. But the compromise to his integrity that Volumnia recommends is complete; he must become a pure actor both in speech and gesture:

> V O L . : Because that now it lies you on to speak
> To th' people; not by your own instruction,
> Nor by th' matter which your heart prompts you,
> But with such words that are but roted in
> Your tongue, though but bastards, and syllables
> Of no allowance, to your bosom's truth. . . .
> 　　I prithee now, my son,
> Go to them, with this bonnet in thy hand,
> And thus far having stretch'd it (here be with them),
> Thy knee bussing the stones (for in such business
> Action is eloquence, and the eyes of th' ignorant
> More learned than the ears), waving thy head,
> Which often thus correcting thy stout heart,
> Now humble as the ripest mulberry. . . .
> 　　　　　　　　　　　　　　　　　[3. 2. 52–57, 72–79]

But Coriolanus's language, we know, is forged in the same furnace as his martial valor; his words and actions in the forum, like his valorous deeds on the battlefield, as they are expressions of essence and affirmations of a heroic identity, are inseparable from his bosom integrity.

The enormity of the self-betrayal is apparent to Coriolanus. He knows it is a "lie" and a "part" absolutely untrue to himself:

> COR.: I will not do't,
> Lest I surcease to honor mine own truth,
> And by my body's action teach my mind
> A most inherent baseness.
>
> [3. 2. 120–23]

Coriolanus fears that this betrayal of heroic integrity might lead to a fatal betrayal of heroic identity. It would be as if some ignoble, alien power were to "possess" him with baseness instead of greatness:

> COR.: Well, I must do 't.
> Away, my disposition, and possess me
> Some harlot's spirit! My throat of war be turn'd,
> Which quier'd with my drum, into a pipe
> Small as an eunuch, or the virgin voice
> That babies lull asleep! The smiles of knaves
> Tent in my cheeks, and schoolboys' tears take up
> The glasses of my sight! A beggar's tongue
> Make motion through my lips, and my arm'd knees,
> Who bow'd but in my stirrup, bend like his
> That hath receiv'd an alms!
>
> [3. 2. 110–20]

The fragmented glimpses of the warrior's heroic image ("throat of war," "drum," "arm'd knees," "tent," "stirrup") are swallowed up in the scathing, abusive vision of self. Volumnia has asked him to become weak, mean, effeminate, and boyish—variants of the domestic, democratic, antiheroic imagery that was remarked earlier, the sum total of which may be characterized by the word "plebeian." This is the nature of the alien force that his mother wants to "possess" him, and this is why he does not want to play such a part. And yet, paradoxically, even as he goes on to reject his mother's request in the lines following this passage, he reveals precisely the aspect of his nature that finally does capitulate. The "boy" in Coriolanus will agree to do as he is asked, confirming his association, however repugnant, with the multitude of sheep.

Perhaps the most interesting aspect of the confrontation resides in Volumnia's misunderstanding of the nature of the power she exerts over her son. She pictures Coriolanus as playing a role according to her own script; the script is new in this case, but the essential relationship between actor and playwright has not changed. To her mind he is still her heroic offspring fulfilling her dreams of grandeur for him:

> V O L .: I prithee now, sweet son, as thou hast said
> My praises made thee first a soldier, so,
> To have my praise for this, perform a part
> Thou hast not done before.
>
> [3. 2. 107–10]

Coriolanus grew up with no father, and Volumnia nurtured him in the heroic ethos. She helped frame his heroic identity by asking him to live up to her conception of excellence, and there is a peculiar sense in which she shares that identity with him. He has become so much a part of her conception that she seems to participate in his battles; her pride in his wounds suggests that she has suffered ("labored" might be the better verb) through every one of them. Moreover, hardly had he gained his victory and returned home in triumph than she envisions for him and reveals to him, as a playwright to an actor, what the next stage of his heroic career ought to be (2. 1. 147–49, 198–202). The mother has given birth to the boy, but she has also "conceived" the son's career, as if plotting a heroic biography.

For this reason Volumnia is both hurt and perplexed at Coriolanus's hesitancy to play out her device, distinguishing the heroic *virtus* she nurtured from the alien ego with its own absolute standards: "Do as thou list; / Thy valiantness was mine, thou suck'st it from me; / But owe thy pride thyself" (3. 2. 128–30). Volumnia attacks his ingratitude, using the metaphor of maternal nurture to serve her main point, that she was the source of his heroic identity. Although her attack leads to a change of heart in Coriolanus, Volumnia, more concerned with her hero's renown than with her natural son's desires, never understands why her rebuke succeeds. Coriolanus severs the martial valor from the maternal image in the metaphor; his decision to apologize to the people is based on love and affection for the offended mother who once nursed him. One knows this because quite unconsciously he had revealed moments before that a compromise would be tantamount to that repulsive string of democratic images of weakness and dependence. This is exactly the case: the "boy" backs off from the titanic role and compromises the "hero" to please his mother.

The forces at conflict in the second and final confrontation between mother and son are carefully laid out. Throughout acts 4 and 5, Coriolanus has been described as a demideity. Aufidius and the Volscians emphasize his sovereignty of nature, his titanic power, his heroic constancy, his burning vengeance. This winged dragon is set against the other Martius, Nature's creation, an antiheroic human being capable of mercy, forgiveness, kindness, pity, and familial love. When the confrontation is concluded, Aufidius reiterates in an aside, and Menenius after him (5. 4. 26–29), the crux of the conflict within Coriolanus: "I am glad thou hast set thy mercy and thy honor / At difference in thee. Out of that I'll work / Myself a former fortune" (5. 3. 200–202). Shakespeare seems to have been struck by North's emphasis on "nature" and "natural affection" in the translation of Plutarch,[29] and then to have designed his entire tragedy so that the natural man and his heroic image would collide at this climactic moment when mother again confronts son. Coriolanus's double nature is both the source and the central issue of the tragic conflict.

The playwright transports the women and the boy from the domestic setting of act 1, scene 3, to confront the hero on his throne of state. Volumnia's martial and maternal images, once yoked by violence together, are now unloosed, unmetaphored as dramatic conflict. The physical placement of the boy and women standing apart from and in opposition to the hero on stage is a dramatic emblem of Coriolanus's own psychomachia at this moment. As much as he would remain a solitary titan, human affections well up in him, urging the hero to capitulate:

COR.:   But out, affection,
All bond and privilege of nature, break!
Let it be virtuous to be obstinate.
What is that curtsy worth? or those doves' eyes,
Which can make gods forsworn? I melt, and am not
Of stronger earth than others. My mother bows,
As if Olympus to a molehill should
In supplication nod; and my young boy
Hath an aspect of intercession, which
Great Nature cries, "Deny not."

[5. 3. 24–33]

Coriolanus survives this moment, girding himself against nature and human weakness; but the theatrical metaphor of act 3, scene 2, is soon reversed, signaling a crucial change in his perception of self: "Like a dull actor now / I have forgot my part, and I am out, / Even to a full disgrace" (5. 3. 40–42). The other Martius, the man of nature and natural affection, breaks through the heroic role he had played so long and so completely that he had thought it to be his essential self. But one sees him now, as he seems to discover himself, as a man who had been "possess'd . . . with greatness" all along. Nevertheless, despite the affectionate greeting given his family and Valeria, he steels himself again, and the internal struggle continues.

For the most part, Volumnia's long, rhetorical plea serves as background accompaniment for the real conflict carried on in silence (5. 3. 148, 153, 164, 168, 182 S.D.). The appeal to Coriolanus is advanced merely by the presence of the family, and the fact that his mother makes the request of him and rebukes him means more than the logic of the discourse.[30] The words meet his ears, but the mother hits his heart, and his silent decision will speak from the heart. Still, the most effective thrust of her plea, beginning with her final rebuke (5. 3. 169–82), criticizes his pride, isolating the surname "Coriolanus," symbol of his "self-creation," from familial and natural bonds of affection. She isolates him from family and Rome, her rebuke at the same time an appeal to his deepest natural instincts. Coriolanus's long, silent decision to spare Rome must be approached indirectly. Earlier in the scene Coriolanus had articulated "Great Nature's" appeal, but now the forces of natural affection at work in him are hidden from the audience. What one finally hears is a second thought, a distanced interpretation of the decision both after the fact and from an opposing point of view:

COR.:   O mother, mother!
What have you done? Behold, the heavens do ope,
The gods look down, and this unnatural scene
They laugh at. O my mother, mother! O!
You have won a happy victory to Rome;
But, for your son, believe it—O, believe it—
Most dangerously you have with him prevail'd,
If not most mortal to him. But let it come.

[5. 3. 182–89]

This is the "hero" sitting in judgment on the "boy's" decision. The immediate misgivings and regrets indicate that he is unwilling to repudiate his heroic identity even as it has been overwhelmed at this crucial moment by the natural instincts of love and affection.

The mother he addresses in accusatory tones—"What have you done?" —has once again asked him to compromise his integrity. The deities are not simply celestial spectators of the world stage; they are the Homeric gods who "sit in hourly synod about [Coriolanus's] particular prosperity" (5. 2. 68–69), the gods who watch over and have a stake in the epic hero's destiny. They perhaps thought that they were watching a titanic drama, but the retreat from the titanism and the newly asserted allegiance to human values turn the drama into an "unnatural scene," a farce, and the gods who are watching laugh to see the imposter to starry immortality melt with affection. Coriolanus's vision of their derisive laughter expresses the enormous shame he feels (as he earlier had felt "disgraced" by his show of emotion) for having submitted to Nature's command. Shakespeare's audience, however, recognizes that the painful decision to retreat from an epic conception of self is in its own way a heroic action.

The new kind of heroism Coriolanus exhibits at the climax of the drama is won at the expense of—is indeed defined by its rejection of —martial prowess, self-assertion, epic individualism, titanic independence. In opting for peace, in acting on behalf of Nature, Coriolanus has stripped himself of the very qualities that had set him apart from and above mortal men; he has broken through the self-encasing ego and has rejoined the human community. Such a transformation is repugnant to the hero. He senses that this compromise of his heroic image has somehow meant a final submission, and he is reviled by the abhorrent feelings of dependence, vulnerability, and baseness with which he is now possessed. The many variants of the natural, domestic, plebeian imagery examined earlier are brought to a focus in the word "mortal"; to be human is to be weak, dependent, vulnerable, and, from the "hero's" point of view, unnatural and antiheroic. "But let it come"—the grandeur of Coriolanus's submission can be fully understood only when one recognizes all that is denied by that simple adversative "But." Menenius, who has yet to learn of Coriolanus's capitulation, gets it backward:

MEN.: There is difference between a grub and a butterfly, yet your butterfly was a grub. This Martius is grown from man to dragon: he has wings, he's more than a creeping thing.

[5. 4. 11–14]

The grub has become a butterfly—winged, beautiful, fragile, sympathetic —and the dragon has become a man, a weak, vulnerable, creeping thing, yet heroic in his own way. At the climax of *Coriolanus*, Shakespeare has transformed Chapman's conception of a bestial titan, elevating what is bestial and at the same time reducing what is titanic to a human stature with which a sympathetic audience might identify. Unlike that of Byron, Coriolanus's final display of humanity does not function as a touchstone by which one might distinguish the hero's aspirations for excellence from those of mere mortal men; rather, antiheroic humanity is the ineluctable source of what Shakespeare would define as true heroism, true grandeur.

Coriolanus also foresaw that the compromise to his heroic image would be fatal, "most mortal," to him, but in this respect he was dead wrong. By setting his mercy and his honor at difference, he may have allowed Aufidius to work himself a former fortune among the Volscians; but Aufidius's victory in no way necessitates Coriolanus's death. What is "mortal" to Coriolanus is the fact that, even though he has submitted to Nature's command at this moment, he still hopes to preserve his heroic conception of self. He has not been transformed by his decision, nor has the climax of the tragedy been a moment of pure reconciliation with mother, family, and Rome.[31] He will die at the hands of Aufidius and the Volsces because he cannot stomach the vision of living in Rome as an unnatural hero; the approving "voices" of the Romans, celebrating his mercy and compassion, will seem to him a chorus of ridicule. And so, Coriolanus returns to the Volsces and to his eventual death; unlike Antony, he is unable to reconstruct a new heroic image and new system of values on the ruins of his former conception of self. The butterfly expects to remain a dragon, and *that* is "most mortal" to him.

So much of what we hear in the final scene of the tragedy is Aufidius's "construction" that our evaluations of Martius tend to be muddled. Shakespeare portrays both sides of the protagonist, refusing to the end to accept the sentimental solution of the hero's absolute reconciliation with his humanity. On the one hand, Martius's new relationship with the commoners and new interest in the language of discourse are reassuring:

AUF.:   Him I accuse
The city ports by this hath enter'd, and
Intends t' appear before the people, hoping
To purge himself with words.

[5. 6. 5–8]

Enter CORIOLANUS *marching with Drum and Colors,*
the COMMONERS *being with him.*
[5. 6. 69 S.D.]

Coriolanus feels the need to clear himself before the people, and he is now comfortable with their allegiance. But the seeming transformation of the impersonal titan into a democratic human being, the seeming redemption offered the tragic figure in this scene, is but a partial and relative assessment. For Coriolanus still clings to his heroic identity; after all, he intends to argue with his "words" that he in no way betrayed the Volscians nor his own heroic integrity.

Aufidius thinks otherwise. He lashes out at Coriolanus's self-betrayal by calling him Martius, the "son" who submitted to the mother at the expense of the "hero," and then increases the intensity of his attack against the Volscian "traitor":

> A U F . : You lords and heads a' th' state, perfidiously
> He has betray'd your business, and given up,
> For certain drops of salt, your city Rome,
> I say "your city," to his wife and mother,
> Breaking his oath and resolution like
> A twist of rotten silk, never admitting
> Counsel a' th' war; but at his nurse's tears
> He whin'd and roar'd away your victory,
> That pages blush'd at him, and men of heart
> Look'd wond'ring each at others.
>
> [5. 6. 90–99]

Aufidius's exaggerated imagery and his judgment by absolute standards of heroism recall Coriolanus's earlier self-accusations of frailty and meanness. He denies Martius any semblance of heroic honor and integrity by divesting him of "Coriolanus," stolen from Corioli and not won through heroic deeds, and by distinguishing the "boy" from true "men of heart."

The spark is struck. Coriolanus had never repudiated his heroic identity; his decision had been an uneasy reconciliation of his two natures, compromising his heroic identity, to be sure, but not denying it. In the closing moments, what had been the thematic crux of his characterization is recognized as the heart of his tragedy: Coriolanus's two natures are irreconcilable. The hero's choler bursts forth at Aufidius's lies:

COR.:   Hear'st thou, Mars?
AUF.: Name not the god, thou boy of tears!

[5. 6. 99–100]

The final, sharp juxtaposition of titanic and infantile identities, recollecting the military and domestic imagery throughout the drama, announces the demise of the hero. Coriolanus's great spirit takes wing, and even as he recalls the martial grandeur of the past, the butterfly is "mammock'd," and the dragon shown to be a creeping thing most mortal.

THE COMMAND OF GREAT NATURE

Dramatic provenance and the numerous similarities and distinctions remarked at the beginning of this chapter have convinced me that Chapman had a demonstrable negative influence on Shakespeare's final heroic tragedy. But whether or not the reader shares my conviction about Chapman's explicit negative influence, it seems especially fruitful to read *Coriolanus* in the context of Chapman's conception of titanic heroism in general and his *Byron* plays in particular. Like Bussy and Byron, Coriolanus is granted the single-minded aspiration for excellence and the special gifts that distinguish a superior hero from the rest of mortal men. The unflinching commitment to heroic image transforms society into a battlefield where the hero might assert his heroic excellence; as the soldier would project his personal epic myth into a world where reality is defined by social consensus, his eccentric behavior inevitably leads to social dislocation and situational conflict reminiscent of Chapman's heroic tragedies. Yet Coriolanus is not only similar to Bussy and Byron, but in some respects he is perceived by the audience as being even more titanic than Chapman's heroes. His martial excellence, for example, is witnessed on stage rather than reported by *nuntius*. The actions proceeding from his heroic spirit are never unworthy of it and never ironically base; if anything, they are too good, too excellent, too exact an enactment of heroic *areté*. Furthermore, given the "shame culture" of ancient Rome, the audience is discouraged from a moral perspective of the kind that would censure Bussy's amoral *virtus* and condemn Byron's vaulting ambition.

The truth is, nonetheless, that Shakespeare deliberately conceives Coriolanus in the mold of Chapman's heroes not to praise but to bury that conception of heroism. Shakespeare's paragon of epic *virtus* is an inhuman, unfeeling war machine whose heroic conception of self fosters attitudes and actions that not only jar against social consensus but, more important, countermand the laws of nature. Like Chapman's heroes, Shakespeare's titan is most godlike when he is most unnatural, when he is a bloody automaton in war and an egocentric anarchist in peace. To grant the terrifying creature the stature of epic hero, Shakespeare would say, is to grant him very little; for, as *Troilus and Cressida* had demonstrated and *Coriolanus* now reaffirms, a social ethos that prizes such a heroism is itself unnatural.

Given Shakespeare's emphasis on the unnaturalness of the hero and of the Roman heroic ethos, it is not surprising that the human values warring against Coriolanus's titanic conception of self speak for nature and natural affection. At the climax of the play, the dramatist's shift from a presentational characterization typical of Chapman's tragedies to a psychological characterization typical of his own tragedies announces what is, in the terms of this study, Shakespeare's summary portrayal of a human being confronting his heroic conception of self. The "boy," who capitulates to the "command of Great Nature" and mercifully spares Rome, displays true grandeur; the "hero," who judges the decision sparing Rome to be weak, shameful, even ridiculous, and so would continue living a personal epic myth, displays a delusion of grandeur. If the momentary commitment to human values defines Coriolanus's true heroism, the continuing allegiance to an unnatural heroic image fates him to tragedy.

At the climax of *Coriolanus*, the hero must make a choice between "honor" and "mercy"—the two terms being generic signatures for entirely different visions of the world. He may continue to live a personal epic myth in a heroic drama something like Marlowe's *Tamburlaine* or he may, by relenting, play the despicable role of "boy" in an "unnatural scene." For the "hero" to back down at this moment would be to act improbably, incongruously. It would be as if a different hero with antipodal values had been borrowed from a countergenre and indecorously inset at the climax of the titanic drama in order to mock the "hero" and the heroic genre. The genre in Shakespeare's canon that speaks most forcefully for nature, natural affection, humanity, familial blood bonds, mercy, and the other symbolic associations with "boy" is tragicomic romance or comedy of forgiveness, by either name the genre to which Shakespeare had already turned his attention in 1609. At their deaths,

Antony and Cleopatra, facing the world of empire with a comedic and romance vision of reality and confronting Caesar's version of heroical history with the values of those countergenres, had transformed a *de casibus* tragedy into a romantic tragedy. But Coriolanus, even as he momentarily capitulates to "Great Nature's command," is unable to renounce his heroic conception of self in favor of romance values and a human identity. He would rather return to the Volsces as a "hero" than remain in Rome as a "boy." Turning his back on the source of his true heroism and true grandeur, he soon dies a deluded heroic fool.

8

CONCLUSION: CHAPMAN AND SHAKESPEARE

AT JOURNEY'S END

The different conceptions of heroism and evaluations of epic embodied by
Byron and Coriolanus, by Chapman's aspiring overreacher and Shakespeare's fire-breathing dragon, perhaps indicate that the disagreement
focused on the Achilles of Chapman's *Iliads* and the Achilles of Shakespeare's *Troilus and Cressida* remained strong after a decade of rethink-
ing. One can never know for certain, but the "contemporary Achilles,"
the Earl of Essex, may well have been at the root of the dramatists'
disagreement. Byron is twice linked specifically to Essex (*T.* 4. 1. 33–38;
T. 5. 3. 139–47), and T. M. Parrott has remarked the obvious, that
"nothing is more striking in the tragedy of Byron (as in the story of
Essex of which Chapman must have been reminded at every turn) than
the overweening self-confidence, drunken and blinded with conceit of
his own importance."[1] Chapman was sincere in describing Essex as the
"now living Instance of the Achilleian vertues"; Essex's "divine temper . . . in godlike pursute of Eternitie" was no different in kind from
Achilles'. Chapman chose Byron, the French warrior-hero so much like
Essex, to be the torchbearer of that same heroic legacy, and if this time
moral and political contexts placed the hero's "eternnesse" in relation to
his "Corruption" (*T.* 5. 3. 191), the dramatist's sympathetic apology for
Byron's heroic spirit is nonetheless extensive and compelling. The bestial
titan is as much noble and pathetic as morally reprehensible, and the
audience is made to ponder the pathetic waste at his demise. Above all,
his titanic grandeur is indisputable—or so, at least, Chapman might have
thought.

What seems to have attracted Shakespeare's attention especially was
the portrayal of Byron as a "beast-man apotheosized."[2] Byron's grandeur

reflects his titanic excess, and both grandeur and excess might be measured best not by the astounding moments of self-assertion, but by the elements of his characterization that link him to the audience of mortal men. Byron's pleas for mercy, his fear of death, and his admission of failure in the final moments of *The Tragedy* were a manifestation of human weakness, which, perhaps like Essex's final recantation, tended to encourage one's moral censure of him. He was, after all, a human being, and he ought to be held accountable to the standards of morality he deliberately transgressed. At the same time, however, by returning Byron to the community of men at the end of his tragedy, Chapman allows the audience to reflect on the astonishing spirit it has witnessed. Byron's aspiration for excellence, the attempt to overreach human limitations, sets him apart from and above ordinary men. This distance between what is human and what is heroic measures Byron's grandeur just as it had Bussy's. Shakespeare, as if granting Chapman's conceptions of tragic grandeur and extending from them, creates a tragedy of social dislocation issuing from the actual achievements of a true titan rather than from the failure of a deluded aspirer. But the very qualities that define Coriolanus as an astonishing Achillean hero are redefined by Shakespeare as unnatural, bestial, and destructive, both of self and of society.[3]

Shakespeare's last word in the dialogue with Chapman could not be more pointed. At the climax of Shakespeare's final heroic tragedy, an inhuman, unnatural, Chapmanesque titan, wrapped in a heroic conception of self and armed with the values of the epic genre, confronts his real self, the "boy," symbolizing the limitations, frailty, and vulnerable beauty of human nature. The decision to spare Rome followed by the decision to continue living a personal epic myth suggests that Chapman has got it all backward: the human being possessed with frailty is heroic, and Chapman's titanic hero is unnatural, inhuman, and—like the warriors at Troy who were also "possess'd . . . with greatness"—as tragically deluded about the nature of heroic grandeur as is Chapman the translator and tragedian about heroic passion and the value of Achillean individualism.

Shakespeare was mistaken if he had written *Coriolanus* assuming that the sequel to *Bussy D'Ambois* would promote another Achillean hero like Bussy and Byron. Clermont D'Ambois may be a spirited soldier of exceptional prowess, but his self-governance and steadfast devotion to moral virtue are equally awe-inspiring and, owing to the grimly Senecan world of the play, more insistent. A fully equipped exemplary hero, Clermont possesses the martial *virtus* necessary for honorable action and the Stoic fortitude necessary for patient endurance in adversity. The hero of Chapman's *Odysses* is a kindred conception; the man of *prudentia et pietas* has also brought heroic *virtus* and moral virtue into exemplary accommodation.

If Chapman's heroic tragedies document a search for a new heroic ideal after the Essex tragedy of 1601, then in Clermont and Ulysses he has found his "complete man." Equally important for us, though, *The Revenge of Bussy D'Ambois* and the translation of *The Odyssey* constitute Chapman's last word in the dialogue with Shakespeare, projecting an implicit response to the persistent antiheroic bias of Shakespeare's heroic tragedies. Clermont and Ulysses are not passionate beasts, but men of godlike spirit governed by godlike reason. They are not unnatural; that term more properly describes the depraved world the heroes strive to enlighten or, failing that, in which they struggle to survive with honor and virtue intact. Nor are they inhuman; they aspire to perfect their humanity without overreaching human capacity and without defying the commandments of heaven. In short, Clermont and Ulysses are men of heroic spirit and of refined moral sensibility; they not only respond implicitly to Shakespeare's critique of heroism, but also serve as exemplary models for contemporary society, confirming epic as the high genre of approbation.

Just as Shakespeare's *Coriolanus* writes large the pejorative conceptions of heroic passion and social deviancy first advanced in *Troilus and Cressida* and in the character of Hotspur, in the portrayals of Clermont and Ulysses Chapman reverts to his stance in the *Iliads* (1598). In *The Revenge* and the *Odysses*, Chapman readdresses the Essex paradigm of ancient virtue displaced in a degenerate milieu; but unlike Bussy and Byron, pathetic misfits for whom only an apology is warranted, Chapman's final soldier-heroes are fully exemplary heroes. Both Clermont, an exemplary heroic martyr, and Ulysses, an exemplary epic hero, wear on their sleeves Chapman's newly restored, unqualified esteem for ancient virtue and his full commitment to the exemplary heroic genre, in this respect broadening rather than narrowing the disagreement with Shakespeare over the value of epic and of the epic tradition.

Of course, for Chapman to speak in defense of epic is to speak in defense of himself, of his literary idealism, of his exalted mission as heroic poet and tragedian. The celebratory conception of self in the poetic epilogue to the *Odysses* is perhaps predictable:

So wrought divine Ulysses through his woes,
So crown'd the Light with him his Mother's Throes,
As through his great Renowner I have wrought,
And my safe sail to sacred Anchor brought.

[CH 2:421]

Chapman's analogy between the long and difficult journeys of hero and poet suggests that the translation has been a heroic Ulyssean enterprise. Additionally, drawing on a conventional *topos*, Chapman self-consciously calls to mind the "voyages" of Spenser, Tasso, Ariosto, and Dante so that he might take his place of honor among them. This epic evocation, doubly heroic, celebrates Chapman's own "godlike pursute of Eternitie," begun in earnest in 1598 and, with the completion of the *Odysses*, "to sacred Anchor brought." One might be tempted to intimate the "self-idolatry" in Chapman's conception of self, but looking back across the works discussed in this volume and recognizing that scarcely a word has been written about *The Widow's Tears* and *The Gentleman Usher*, two unqualified successes, nor about the pioneer of the comedy of humours nor about the narrative poet, one might rather be inclined to grant Chapman his heroic image.

That image, we know, is one that Shakespeare did not covet. Shakespeare's conception of self and the literary "quest" in the latter half of his career seem precisely opposite to those of Chapman. The remarkably self-effacing personality that one associates with an authorial presence so quietly unassertive as to seem an absence suggests that Shakespeare might well have thought that Chapman's celebratory conception of self and sense of literary mission were heroic pretensions to greatness. Similarly, although Shakespeare's seventeenth-century plays in general document no single, discernible quest, *Troilus and Cressida* and the heroic tragedies followed by the tragicomic romances do seem to point at an aversion to heroic individualism, a growing awe for the resilient qualities of human nature, and a demonstrable commitment to social values.

One might suggest, in fact, that Shakespeare in his later years inverts the hierarchy of values implicit in the classical-Renaissance paradigm defining pastoral and comedy as low genres and epic and tragedy as high genres. Increasingly, the sound and fury of tragic men attempting to carve out their own destiny is rejected in favor of a forgiving, repentant, humble stance in the presence of a mysterious but beneficent Providence. Ambition is made virtue and military ventures are justified only when the fight is to preserve society and is either sanctioned by Providence or blessed by Nature or both, as are Malcolm's fight in *Macbeth* and that of Guiderius, Arviragus, and Posthumus in *Cymbeline*. Increasingly, the dramatist exalts the Providence associated with comedy and "mouldy tales" and the Nature associated with the low genre of pastoral. For us, then, it seems only fitting that Shakespeare would have abjured his rough magic, drowned his book, and rejoined the community of men in Stratford-upon-Avon just at the time when the heroic Chapman was completing his "godlike pursute of Eternitie."

CITATIONS

Citations for Shakespeare's works are to *The Riverside Shakespeare*, ed. G. Blakemore Evans, Harry Levin, et al. (Boston: Houghton Mifflin Co., 1974). Shakespeare's sources are quoted from *Narrative and Dramatic Sources of Shakespeare*, ed. Geoffrey Bullough, 7 vols. (London: Routledge & Kegan Paul, 1957–73), hereafter cited as Bullough.

I quote Chapman's poetry from *The Poems of George Chapman*, ed. Phyllis Brooks Bartlett (New York: MLA, 1941); Chapman's translation of Homer from *Chapman's Homer*, ed. Allardyce Nicoll, 2 vols. (Princeton: Princeton University Press, 1956), hereafter cited as *CH*. Citations for Homer are to *The Iliad*, trans. A. T. Murray, Loeb Classical Library, 2 vols. (Cambridge, Mass.: Harvard University Press, 1924–25), and to *The Odyssey*, trans. A. T. Murray, Loeb Classical Library, 2 vols. (Cambridge, Mass.: Harvard University Press, 1919), hereafter cited as Loeb. The Latin translation of Homer's epics is taken from Jean de Sponde, *Homeri quae extant omnia* . . . (Basel, 1583), hereafter cited as de Sponde.

Citations for *Bussy D'Ambois* are to The Revels Plays, ed. Nicolas Brooke (Cambridge, Mass.: Harvard University Press, 1964). All other citations for Chapman's dramas are to *The Plays of George Chapman: The Tragedies*, ed. Thomas Marc Parrott, 2 vols. (1910; New York: Russell & Russell, 1961) and to *The Plays of George Chapman: The Comedies*, ed. Thomas Marc Parrott, 2 vols. (1913; New York: Russell & Russell, 1961).

NOTES

INTRODUCTION

1. Sir Philip Sidney, "An Apologie for Poetrie," pp. 159–60.

2. George Puttenham, "The Arte of English Poesie," pp. 42–43.

3. The quotations are from Puttenham, "The Arte of English Poesie," pp. 36–37; see also Thomas Heywood, "An Apologie for Actors," sig. B3; and Andrew R. Anderson, "Hercules and His Successors," pp. 7–58.

4. Rosalie Colie, *The Resources of Kind*, p. 114.

5. Ibid., p. 115.

6. Ibid., p. 118. In this paragraph I have adapted Colie's provocative comments on *Don Quixote* (pp. 118–19).

7. Sir Ernst H. S. Gombrich, *Symbolic Images*, p. 5.

8. Aristotle's brief comparison of tragedy and epic in his *Poetics* conformed to the Horatian-rhetorical tradition's placement of the genres in the "high" category of literature, a category characterized by an elevated style appropriate to the matters of gods, heroes, and kings. The sixteenth-century critical controversy concerning the superiority of epic or tragedy assumed their generic kinship. For a review of this critical material, see Bernard Weinberg, *A History of Literary Criticism in the Renaissance*.

9. Pertinent comments on the coalescence of tragedy and epic may be found in H. T. Swedenberg, *The Theory of the Epic in England, 1650–1800*, pp. 8–9; Graham Hough, *A Preface to the Faerie Queene*, pp. 48–49; Richard C. Crowley, "*Coriolanus* and the Epic Genre," pp. 114–30; John M. Steadman, *Epic and Tragic Structure in Paradise Lost*, pp. 29 ff. The likely influence of "arms and the man" on Elizabethan tragedy has been suggested by Paul A. Jorgensen, *Shakespeare's Military World*, p. 206.

10. Eugene Waith, *Ideas of Greatness*, chapter 2, is a recent treatment of *Tamburlaine* and the heroic romance. Among discussions of the history plays, the most pertinent to this study is David Riggs, *Shakespeare's Heroical Histories*.

11. Although there were some critics who insisted that war was the only suitable subject matter for epic (see Swedenberg, *Theory of the Epic*, p. 9), the admission of the Italian romance into the epic genre (an entrance more forced by literary practice than begged by critical theory) inevitably defined love as an equally appropriate subject matter. Even Minturno, who thought that the romance was an ignoble barbarism (in the strict Latinate sense), acknowledges that the actions and loves of the knights were of themselves "worthy of epic poetry"; see Allen H. Gilbert, *Literary Criticism*, p. 277. Tasso argued that of the

two heroic feelings, wrath and love, the latter was the better subject matter for a heroic poem; see either Gilbert, ibid., pp. 484–87, or, preferably, Tasso, *Discourses on the Heroic Poem*, pp. 44–49. In "An Apologie for Poetrie," Sidney seemed to mix romance and epic indiscriminately, exhibiting the "comprehensive unity of the heroic tradition" (Waith, *Ideas of Greatness*, p. 29). As Spenser's epic confirms, love and war were both matters for heroic poetry.

12. The output of military manuals during the latter years of Elizabeth's reign is startling; see Maurice J. D. Cockle, *A Bibliography of English Military Books up to 1642*. The most comprehensive review of the handbooks as they relate to the portrayal of the soldier on stage is Jorgensen's *Shakespeare's Military World* (chapter 6 is especially instructive on the soldier's dislocation). See also Lily B. Campbell, *Shakespeare's "Histories,"* pp. 255–305.

13. See Barton's review of Howard Felperin, *Shakespearean Representation*, pp. 135–37.

CHAPTER 1

1. Bacon repeatedly characterized Essex as an Elizabethan Icarus. See the letter from Bacon to Essex (20 July 1600) in G. B. Harrison, *The Life and Death of Robert Devereux, Earl of Essex*, p. 268; "Sir Francis Bacon His Apologie . . ." (1604) in Edwin A. Abbott, *Bacon and Essex*, App. 1, p. 5; Bacon's official state declaration on the Essex affair, "A Declaration Touching the Treasons of the Late Earl of Essex and His Accomplices" (1601), in ibid., App. 2, p. 2; and his metaphor of the tragic stage in ibid., pp. 18–19.

2. For descriptions of Essex's character see Abbot, *Bacon and Essex*, pp. 23–36; Ray Heffner, "Essex, the Ideal Courtier," pp. 7–36; and Harrison, *Life and Death of Essex*, pp. 130–34, 179–81, 274–75.

3. Quoted from *The Civil Wars*, p. 312.

4. *CH* 1:504.

5. See Madeleine Doran, *Endeavors of Art*, pp. 112–13. The patriotic exuberance following the defeat of the Armada had an undeniable effect on the English history play, but it probably should not be considered a formative cause of the genre. See E. M. W. Tillyard, *Shakespeare's History Plays*, pp. 98–101; see also Irving Ribner, *The English History Play in the Age of Shakespeare*, pp. 6–7. Lindsay Boynton, *The Elizabethan Militia*, chapters 5–6, discusses the financial burdens and practical difficulties of preparing for the on-again, off-again Spanish threat during the 1590s.

6. The interest in the science of warfare and some practical applications of new military theory are outlined in F. L. Taylor, *The Art of War in Italy, 1494–1529*, and in Sir Charles Oman, *A History of the Art of War in the Sixteenth Century*. The use of mercenaries and the introduction of artillery, firearms, Swiss pikes, and scientific fortifications made the chivalric warrior and chivalric warfare obsolete. For a more general discussion of the decline of the chivalric warrior see Sidney Painter, *French Chivalry*, chapter 1.

On the humanistic influence in the transformation of the warrior noble into the English gentleman, see esp. Robert P. Adams, *The Better Part of Valor*, and Fritz Caspari, *Humanism and the Social Order in England*. For my purposes the most useful study on the decline of the English warrior, discussing the military, political, and educational influences, is Arthur B. Ferguson, *The Indian Summer of English Chivalry*. Also pertinent is Laurence Stone, *The Crisis of the Aristocracy, 1558–1641*, pp. 71–82, 264–66.

The clearest dramatic embodiment of the old-style soldier is Talbot in Shakespeare's *1 Henry VI*; see David Riggs, *Shakespeare's Heroical Histories*, esp. pp. 22–23.

7. There is little question that *Philotas* reflected on Essex's tragic downfall; see Laurence Michel's introduction to Samuel Daniel, *The Tragedy of Philotas*, pp. 45–62. As I read the tragedy, moreover, there is little wonder that Daniel had to apologize for it. Aside from the chronology established for the composition of *Philotas*, Daniel's formal "Apology," a predictable performance, should not be taken seriously.

8. Matthew Proser's discussion of *Othello* anticipates in many respects these observations on the soldier's dislocation; see *The Heroic Image in Five Shakespearean Tragedies*, esp. pp. 92–95.

9. The topic of honor is familiar to students of Renaissance drama. Among the more pertinent works are Ruth Kelso, *The Doctrine of the English Gentleman in the Sixteenth Century*, esp. pp. 96–110; Hiram Haydn, *The Counter-Renaissance*, pp. 555–612; Curtis Brown Watson, *Shakespeare and the Renaissance Concept of Honor*; Paul N. Siegel, *Shakespeare in His Time and Ours*, chapter 5; and Norman Council, *When Honour's at the Stake*, esp. pp. 11–35. To my mind the most comprehensive treatment of the topic, with a bibliography of the primary sources and some perceptive comments on Chapman, is Alice Shalvi, *The Relationship of Renaissance Concepts of Honour to Shakespeare's Problem Plays*.

The point to be stressed is that the dramatists were not concerned with defining commonplace ideas about honor but with using the various conceptions of honor for dramatic point: to convey heroic idealism, to signal crucial changes in character, and, especially, to emphasize the individual's conflict with society. Conceptions of honor issuing from the inner dictates of reason, conscience, or instinct might be used to buttress an individual code of behavior; on the other hand, when honor was conceived of as a reward bestowed by society on the individual who exemplifies its standards of behavior, then it might symbolize the highest values of an ethical system. Honor might stand as a principle of an individualistic code of conduct or as the symbol of social consensus; it might be invoked to support epic ideals of individual heroism or society's ethical and political ideals. For Chapman and Shakespeare, in other words, the ambiguous nature of honor made it a supple and useful expressive system for articulating the kinds of conflict that were essential to the mixed genre of heroic tragedy.

10. Proser, *Heroic Image*, pp. 3–9.

11. On countergenre see Claudio Guillén, *Literature as System*, esp. pp.

146–58; also Rosalie Colie, *The Resources of Kind*, pp. 93–94, and for genre as a "set" on the world, pp. 114–15.

12. George Puttenham, "The Arte of English Poesie," Bk. 1, chapter 15, pp. 34–35.

13. John Steadman, *Milton and the Renaissance Hero*, esp. pp. 23–41.

14. I am indebted to Werner W. Jaeger, *Paideia*, 1:1–8.

15. *The Tragedies of George Chapman.*

16. See Plato's *Republic*, 435–41; Tasso's *Discourses on the Heroic Poem*, pp. 46–47, and his "Allegory" (1581) appended to the Fairfax translation of *Gerusalemme Liberata*; and Hiram Haydn's discussion of Tasso in *The Counter-Renaissance*, pp. 578–85.

17. Of special interest on this broad topic of Renaissance love are Steadman, *Milton and the Renaissance Hero*, pp. 108–36; and Mark Rose, *Heroic Love*.

18. Since the aesthetics and not the ideology is of concern here, I want to put aside for a moment the notion that Chapman's dramatic *idea* reflects a Platonic mystagogue's insight into a transcendent truth. For background on *idea*, see esp. Erwin Panofsky, *Idea*, and Annabel M. Patterson, "Tasso and Neoplatonism," pp. 105–33. On Chapman's neo-Platonic aesthetics, see Raymond B. Waddington, *The Mind's Empire*, esp. chapter 1.

19. The narrative structure of Marlowe's *Tamburlaine* serves to exhibit the astonishing hero. As if they are so many rhetorical *exempla*, the episodes articulate heroic aspiration and prowess, cumulatively enlarging the hero to titanic proportions; but at the end of each episode, the hero remains essentially unchanged. A natural death ends hero and plot alike, and given the nature of *Tamburlaine*'s excellence and the nature of the episodic structure, there could be no other coherent closure. The influence of rhetoric on Marlowe's presentational dramaturgy has been argued persuasively by Riggs, *Shakespeare's Heroical Histories*, pp. 55–59. The use of plot to exhibit character also anticipates that of the Restoration heroic play; see Eric Rothstein, *Restoration Tragedy*, pp. 55–59.

20. Robert B. Heilman, *Tragedy and Melodrama*, esp. pp. 79–86, would use the terms "melodrama" and "tragedy" in drawing a similar distinction. No matter the terminology, however, the distinction is relative, not absolute. On the complication of melodramatic patterns in *Bussy D'Ambois* and the inclusion of melodramatic elements in *Othello*, *Antony and Cleopatra*, and *Coriolanus*, see Heilman, pp. 33, 151, 164–65, 195–96. Recognizing that Chapman was an originator of humour comedy, one might suggest that the entanglement of a static character in situational conflict is a comedic device. From the first blast of bravado the audience knows that a comic discrepancy exists between the claims of the *miles gloriosus*—the pertinent example—and his real abilities. He is dehumoured when comic wits or circumstances push him into a situation where mere words will not cut the mustard. The risible soldier may be said to have talked himself into trouble, but basically a shift in situation springs the ironic trap on him.

21. For a synchronic overview of the psychological organizations that make a character (say, Othello) possible, see J. Leeds Barroll, *Artificial Persons*. In the

following paragraphs my diachronic description of a character (Othello) within a play (*Othello*) is diametrically opposed to Barroll's approach but in no way incompatible to it.

22. See Michael Goldman's remarks on character "selving" in *Shakespeare and the Energies of Drama*, chapter 2, and his interesting discussion of Cleopatra and Othello in *The Actor's Freedom*, pp. 141–47.

CHAPTER 2

1. See Philip Henslowe, *Henslowe's Diary*, pp. 47, 121. For the Troy-related plays, see Alfred Harbage, *Annals of English Drama, 975–1700*, pp. 68–69; and J. S. P. Tatlock, "The Siege of Troy in Elizabethan Literature, Especially in Shakespeare and Heywood," pp. 676–78. The Troy vogue is reviewed by Robert K. Presson, *Shakespeare's Troilus and Cressida & The Legends of Troy*, pp. 3–5; Robert Kimbrough, *Shakespeare's Troilus and Cressida and Its Setting*, pp. 26–27; and Bullough, 6:84.

2. The fragment of the Admiral plot is reprinted in Philip Henslowe, *Henslowe Papers*, p. 142; W. W. Greg, *Dramatic Documents from Elizabethan Playhouses*, plot 5; Bullough, 6:220–21. On Heywood's *I Iron Age* as a revision of the "troye" drama of 1596, see especially Allan Holaday, "Heywood's *Troia Britanica* and *The Ages*," pp. 430–39, which reviews previous opinion and concludes that the revision remains a distinct possibility.

3. Chaucer's and Henryson's poems were published together in 1532 and later reprinted by Thomas Speght in 1598 and 1602. Caxton's translation of Raoul LeFevre (ca. 1474) was published in a new edition by Thomas Creede in 1596.

4. Bullough, as well as Kenneth Muir, *Shakespeare's Sources*, 1:78–96, accept Presson's general thesis, but are careful to balance the debt to Chapman against the clear debts to Chaucer and Caxton especially.

5. Among important works dealing with Chapman's translation of *The Iliad* are H. M. Regel, "Über George Chapmans Homerübersetzung"; Franck L. Schoell, *Etudes sur l'humanisme continental en Angleterre à la fin de la Renaissance*, chapter 6; Donald Smalley, "The Ethical Bias of Chapman's Homer"; Phyllis B. Bartlett, "Chapman's Revisions in His *Iliads*," "The Heroes of Chapman's Homer," and "Stylistic Devices in Chapman's *Iliads*"; H. C. Fay, "Chapman's Materials for His Translations of Homer," and "Poetry, Pedantry and Life in Chapman's *Iliads*"; Edward Phinney, Jr., "Continental Humanists and Chapman's *Iliads*"; Millar MacLure, *George Chapman*, pp. 158–91; Reuben Brower, *Hero and Saint*, pp. 63–81.

6. See Raymond B. Waddington, *The Mind's Empire*, esp. chapter 1.

7. "Achilles natura fuit superbus & animo elatiore, vnde toties a Poetis atrox, animosus, saeuus, peruicax, immitis, indomitus, indocilis, inexorabilis, appellatur" (Io. Spandanus, *Homeri quae extant omnia . . .* , p. 173, note d). Here as elsewhere the translation of de Sponde's commentary is mine. Although the Latin translation of Homer was actually that of Andreas Divus, Chapman

thought it was Jean de Sponde's, and I refer to it as such. In transcribing the translation and commentary I will fill in de Sponde's elisions.

When comparing Chapman's translation with the original, I quote the literal Latin translation rather than the Greek in de Sponde's parallel text edition. Chapman likely relied on the Latin as much, or more, than the Greek. For the convenience of those readers who wish to compare Chapman with the Greek text and a literal translation of Homer, I have included citations to the Loeb edition. I will also have occasion to use Johann Scapula's *Lexicon Graeco-Latinum novum* (1580). I have consulted the Basel edition of 1615.

8. MacLure, *George Chapman*, pp. 163, 164.

9. See ibid., p. 169; Waddington, *The Mind's Empire*, p. 40.

10. Chapman's attitude toward Achilles' outward heroism in the second half of *The Iliad* will be discussed at the beginning of Chapter 4.

11. "Passion of the mind" is a phrase suggested to me by "The Teares of Peace" (lines 184–90). I use it to describe a rational and wholly justifiable zeal. Its Christian analogue is "zealous ire"; see, for example, Eugene Waith, *The Herculean Hero*, pp. 44–45, and M. Thomas Hester's illuminating essay, " 'Zeal' as Satire."

12. MacLure, *George Chapman*, p. 174. De Sponde had written: "Certamen istud in Achille fuit Rationis & partis irascibilis. Illa irae moderationem suadebat: haec ad vindictam stimulabat. Exitus quoque certaminis duplex fuit. Nam ab Ira primum Ratio superata est: deinde a Ratione Ira. Rationem enim per Mineruam liceat allegorice interpretari. Hoc postremum nobis imitandum est, alterum vero fugiendum. Etenim diis proximus ille est, quem ratio, non ira mouet, inquit ille" (p. 11, note b). (The rational and irascible parts of Achilles were at odds, reason urging a moderation of wrath, passion stirring him toward revenge. And the inward strife had a double issue: first, reason was overwhelmed by wrath, then wrath bridled by reason. For it is permissible to take Minerva as an allegorical figure of Reason. The second result we should imitate, the first avoid. For it is said that that man is close to the gods whom reason, not passion, motivates.)

13. As noted by all careful examiners of Chapman's translation, he uses periphrasis extensively to give Homer's characters an unmistakable ethical dimension. For Chapman's defense of the device, see "To the Reader" (*CH* 1:507) and especially "The Preface to the Reader" (*CH* 1:16–17).

14. "In hac autem Achillis oratione iracundi hominis status satis exprimitur, docemurque, eum qui se impetui & furori irae concesserit effraenem ore fieri, sine superiorum reuerentia, quam id circo Regi Achilles non praestat, iniuriosas in eum contumelias effutiens . . . cum eum verbis alioqui non lacessisset contumeliosis Agamemnon solo vocabulo "ἐκπαγλότατε" vsus, pro quo longe acerbiora Achilles rependit. Agamemnon itaque ea in re modestior fuit" (p. 9, note a). (In this speech Achilles clearly portrays for us the tendencies of a passionate man, who looses his unbridled tongue without deference to superiors once he has yielded to the furious compulsion of anger; and we may learn here how Achilles does not conduct himself with the eminence of the king, when he

spews out unjust invective against him. . . . Besides, Agamemnon does not provoke Achilles with abusive language, using only the single phrase "terriblest of men" [1. 150], but for this Achilles pays him back with far harsher words. And so, Agamemnon in this situation proved himself the more temperate man.)

15. *CH* 2:4.

16. De Sponde had translated the passage (Loeb 1:408–12) this way:

Si aliquo modo velit Troianis auxiliari:
Ad puppes vero vsque & ad mare expellere Achiuos
Caesos, vt omnes fruantur rege,
Noscat autem & Atrides late dominans Agamemnon
Suum detrimentum, quod fortissimum Achiuorum nihili fecit.

[p. 19]

17. "Nihil aliud quaerit Achilles quam vt Graecorum dispendio gloriae suae faciat compendium, quod quidem minime laudandum, minusque probo viro imitandum est" (p. 19, note h).

18. De Sponde translated: ". . . donec Achiui / Filium meum honorent augeantque eum honore" (p. 22).

19. "Hanc vocem non esse sapientis docebunt Ethici doctores. . . ." De Sponde then goes on to advocate the Stoic ideal of constancy, tranquillity, and freedom from the perturbations and cares of mind (see p. 172, note g). "Seen" from Chapman's perspective, of course, these are precisely the qualities Achilles does exhibit at this moment.

20. Donald Smalley has commented extensively on Achilles' "just wrath" in "The Ethical Bias of Chapman's Homer," esp. pp. 174–82. On this particular passage, see also Elias Schwartz, "Seneca, Homer, and Chapman's *Bussy D'Ambois*," p. 173.

21. "Preface" to the 1598 edition (*CH* 1:504).

22. J. A. K. Thomson, *Shakespeare and the Classics*, pp. 211, 214, phrases this point more strongly. See also T. J. B. Spencer, " 'Greeks and Merrygreeks,' " p. 232.

23. *CH* 1:504.

24. *The Mind's Empire*, pp. 108–12.

25. G. B. Harrison, *The Life and Death of Robert Devereux, Earl of Essex*, chapters 10–12.

26. Robert K. Presson, "Wrestling with This World," stresses Chapman's identification with his tragic heroes.

27. Una Ellis-Fermor, *The Frontiers of Drama*, pp. 56–76.

28. R. J. Kaufmann, "Ceremonies for Chaos," pp. 139–40. Kaufmann agrees with Ellis-Fermor that the painful reconstruction of Shakespeare's imaginative world occurs during the period of his tragedies. The final paragraphs of this chapter, describing in generic terms the progression from *Troilus and Cressida* to the heroic tragedies, support their contention.

29. E. R. Dodds, *The Greeks and the Irrational*, pp. 17–18, 28–50.

30. On this point see esp. Alvin Kernan, *The Cankered Muse*, p. 197.

31. Many critics have noted the peculiar intellectual detachment with which Shakespeare views the world of *Troilus and Cressida*. See *The New Variorum Troilus and Cressida*, pp. 519–48; and esp. Brian Morris, "The Tragic Structure of *Troilus and Cressida*," pp. 482–83.

32. I share Geoffrey Bullough's conviction that Shakespeare's parody of heroic bombast and his distortion of heroic characterization had Chapman's *Iliads* as its target. See Bullough, 6:87, 100, 111; also Brower, *Hero and Saint*, p. 275n.

33. Many critics have written on the ironic structure, the incongruous styles, and the thematic emphasis on the inadequacy of language in *Troilus and Cressida*. Among the more cogent essays are Derick R. C. Marsh, "Interpretation and Misinterpretation"; T. McAlindon, "Language, Style, and Meaning in *Troilus and Cressida*"; Elias Schwartz, "Tonal Equivocation and the Meaning of *Troilus and Cressida*"; Lawrence Danson, *Tragic Alphabet*, chapter 4. Richard D. Fly, "Cassandra and the Language of Prophecy in *Troilus and Cressida*," stresses the prophecy of inescapable ruin in an interpretation much in accord with Ellis-Fermor's, Kaufmann's, and my own. See also M. T. Jones-Davies's discussion of Shakespeare's use of myth for ironic counterpoint in "Discord in Shakespeare's *Troilus and Cressida*."

34. Richard D. Fly, *Shakespeare's Mediated World*, chapter 2, pivots a challenging essay on the metaphors of poetics in the play. His metadramatic thesis does not convince me, however, for these particular metaphors say more about the heroes who voice them than about the dramatist. An earlier essay associating Shakespeare with Troilus's poetic imagination is Winifred M. T. Nowottny's "'Opinion' and 'Value' in *Troilus and Cressida*."

35. On the issue of self-idolatry, see esp. J. Leeds Barroll, *Artificial Persons*, pp. 169–71. Though his comments on Tasso seem to me to be misleading, Norman Council's remarks on the heroes' self-created behavioral code are precisely to the point; see his *When Honour's at the Stake*, esp. pp. 75–81. If David Kaula is correct, Shakespeare appears to strengthen and amplify the central theme of self-idolatry with a symbolic overlay drawn from the Bible; see Kaula's "'Mad Idolatry' in Shakespeare's *Troilus and Cressida*."

36. Guillaume DuVair, *The Moral Philosophy of the Stoicks*, p. 79. My guess is that Ulysses is not reading Plato, but this 1598 pocket edition of DuVair.

37. Ibid., pp. 79–82.

38. Ibid., p. 79.

39. According to theorists on honor, the bestower of honor must be equally as judicious and virtuous as the recipient. See esp. Robert Ashley, *Of Honour*, pp. 66–71.

40. The reasons for Shakespeare's conscious romanticism of "the matter of Troy" are many, the most obvious being that chivalry and romance were present in the sources, in Chaucer, Caxton, and John Lydgate. More important, chivalry is the Elizabethan mode of heroic idealism, and Shakespeare was not inclined to distinguish between classical and medieval ideals when dramatizing an ideological world reflecting the dictates of heroic passion. Though the incorporation of medieval romance into the epic setting appears to move Shake-

peare's Troy saga beyond Homeric heroism and Chapman's *Iliads*, the truth is that the playwright has simply added a complementary medium to express the heroes' appetitive passion. Chivalry provided a common metaphorical vocabulary and atmospheric milieu that would accommodate both love plot and war plot and the heroic passion they reflect.

41. Kaufmann, "Ceremonies for Chaos" (pp. 148–52), has some shrewd observations on chivalry in this regard.

42. S. L. Bethell's symbolic interpretation of this incident is precisely to the point; see his *Shakespeare and the Popular Dramatic Tradition*, pp. 103–4. Adrien Bonjour, "Hector and the 'One in Sumptuous Armour,' " pp. 104–8, argues for a naturalistic interpretation in which the incident heightens Hector's chivalry, making his death the more pathetic; but a romantic redemption of Hector (or of Troilus, for that matter) will not hold up to a careful examination of the character throughout the play.

43. On the subject of Troilus's self-infatuation and its aftermath, see especially David Kaula, "Will and Reason in *Troilus and Cressida*," pp. 271–83; Robert Ornstein, *The Moral Vision of Jacobean Tragedy*, pp. 242–45; and Emil Roy's psychoanalytic reading of Troilus in "War and Manliness in Shakespeare's *Troilus and Cressida*," pp. 110–12.

44. Rolf Soellner, *Shakespeare's Patterns of Self-Knowledge*, pp. 211–13, provides a lucid discussion of Troilus's psychic cleavage. In general, my discussion of Troilus extends from Barroll's observations (*Artificial Persons*, pp. 183–87).

45. I see nothing of value in Troilus's final moments, but for an opposing view see Nowottny, " 'Opinion' and 'Value' in *Troilus and Cressida*," pp. 293–94, and Morris, "The Tragic Structure of *Troilus and Cressida*," pp. 489–91.

46. See Harry Levin, *The Overreacher*, p. 161; also Barroll's discussion of "affections" in *Artificial Persons*, pp. 36–39.

47. See Rosalie Colie, *The Resources of Kind*, pp. 115–16.

48. See Rosalie Colie's excellent discussion of *Troilus and Cressida* in *Shakespeare's Living Art*, chapter 8.

CHAPTER 3

1. Othello's social consciousness has been stressed recently by E. A. J. Honigmann, *Shakespeare*, pp. 94–96, and by Michael Long, *The Unnatural Scene*, esp. pp. 52–53.

2. Like Cassio's "reputation" and Iago's "good name," Othello's honor is an attribute of a public persona. Whether associated with deserts ("demerits") in the service of state (1. 2. 18–24) or with the signiory's estimation of him as a dutiful soldier (1. 3. 267–75), honor for Othello is a societal tribute, a symbolic recognition of his stature in Venetian society. On "good name" and honor in *Othello*, see esp. Brents Stirling, *Unity in Shakespearean Tragedy*, pp. 111–21; Madeleine Doran, "Good Name in *Othello*," esp. pp. 198–203; David L. Jeffrey

and Patrick Grant, "Reputation in *Othello*," pp. 197–208. I find myself in substantial agreement with Norman Council, who suggests that at Othello's pivotal turn in character he abandons a rational pursuit of virtue for an "honorable" pursuit of vengeance; but I would note that Othello's rational virtue had been allied with social ideals and public values from the start. See Council's *When Honour's at the Stake*, pp. 124–32.

3. Wolfgang Clemen points out the tendency toward self-reference in Othello's language in *The Development of Shakespeare's Imagery*, pp. 120–21, 124, 128–29. Although the accusation of a self-dramatizing pride in Othello's character has become a critical commonplace, Matthew Proser's discussion, though typical, seems especially well argued; see *The Heroic Image in Five Shakespearean Tragedies*, esp. pp. 104–5. The cool confidence that I associate with Othello the soldier has also been interpreted in light of Othello's Stoic self-sufficiency; see Ruth Levitsky, "All-in-All Sufficiency in *Othello*," and Katherine S. Stockholder, "Egregiously an Ass."

4. Robert Ornstein, *The Moral Vision of Jacobean Tragedy*, p. 223.

5. Long, *The Unnatural Scene*, esp. pp. 41–44.

6. Although I am indebted to Arthur M. Eastman's illuminating essay on Othello's martial mentality, I think that he overstates the Moor's conscious duplicity early in the play. Othello will come to embrace the cynical vision of Iago, the play's master ironist, after the temptation scene, but at this stage in the play one should distinguish the soldier's wary mentality from deceitful opportunism by its fundamentally defensive posture. See Eastman's "Othello as Ironist."

7. Leonora Brodwin in *Elizabethan Love Tragedy*, pp. 201–5, believes that Desdemona's willfulness is the cause of the discord in Othello at this moment and that the consummation disruptions are symbolic of this and other hidden discords in the love relationship. Although Brodwin's larger point about the differences between the loves, and especially the estimation of Desdemona's ideal love, is to the point, her severe condemnation of Othello's egotistical self-regard led her to these challenging but overly subtle attempts to uncover the "defect" of love. In this respect, she follows, among others, G. R. Elliott, *Flaming Minister*, pp. 29–30, 63–65; Leo Kirschbaum, "The Modern Othello," pp. 290–93; F. R. Leavis, *The Common Pursuit*, pp. 147–48; and Albert Gerard, "'Egregiously an Ass,'" pp. 103–5. Norman Rabkin's view of Othello's love as something like an act of faith is more to the point; see his *Shakespeare and the Common Understanding*, p. 63.

8. The love-war nexus in *Othello* is discussed at some length by Elliott, *Flaming Minister*, pp. 33–35; Robert B. Heilman, *Magic in the Web*, pp. 182–93; G. R. Hibbard, "'Othello' and the Pattern of Shakespearian Tragedy," p. 41; and Reuben Brower, *Hero and Saint*, pp. 7–9.

9. R. A. Yoder, "The Two Worlds of Othello," pp. 218–19, discusses the transition to the comic stage and notes recent criticism on the comic elements in *Othello*.

10. Rosalie Colie and Robert G. Hunter call attention to the Venus-Mars myth

in relation to the arrival on Cyprus; see Colie's *Shakespeare's Living Art*, pp. 150–53, and Hunter's *Shakespeare and the Mystery of God's Judgment*, pp. 136–39.

11. See Colie's discussion of Shakespeare's use of sonnet language and ideals at this moment in *Shakespeare's Living Art*, pp. 154–58. Ultimately the love ideals for which the sonnet genre speaks are allied with the values for which tragedy must speak; Othello will kill the heroic fool in testimony to them.

12. Paul A. Jorgensen, " 'Perplex'd in the Extreme,' " is particularly helpful on this point.

13. Frank Kermode calls attention to J. C. Maxwell's perceptive commentary on this point; see his introduction to *Othello* in *The Riverside Shakespeare*, p. 1201.

14. Brodwin, *Elizabethan Love Tragedy*, pp. 211–12, stresses Othello's betrayal of Desdemona and its subsequent reflection in the handkerchief symbolism.

15. Brower (*Hero and Saint*, pp. 12–13) makes the general point about the profanation of the heroic and sacred at this moment.

16. Proser (*The Heroic Image*, pp. 131–32) and others have stressed the pretension of justice in the public persona Othello now assumes.

17. Stirling's analysis of Othello's self-deception at this moment is especially pointed; see *Unity in Shakespearean Tragedy*, pp. 129–33.

18. The charges of self-dramatization and self-cheering (that is, the Eliot-Leavis Othello) are appropriate here, but Othello eventually rejects the self-puffery, and it does not resurface in the calm of objectivity and understatement at the end. See T. S. Eliot, *Selected Essays*, pp. 110–11, and Leavis, *The Common Pursuit*, pp. 150–52.

19. Derick R. C. Marsh, *Passion Lends Them Power*, p. 119, correctly suggests that only a massive act of will can keep Othello on the unnatural course he has chosen. See also Hunter, *Shakespeare*, pp. 151–52.

20. See Colie, *Shakespeare's Living Art*, esp. pp. 159–60, 162–63.

CHAPTER 4

1. See *CH* 1:43.
2. *CH* 2:5.
3. Hector may emerge from the 1611 translation as the most likable character (as he is in Homer as well), but Achilles remains the hero of the *Iliads*. See Phyllis B. Bartlett, "Chapman's Revisions in His *Iliads*."
4. This point is crucial to an understanding of the *Iliads* and of the quality of "spirit" that animates Bussy, Byron, and, as we shall see, Clermont and Ulysses as well. The following examples are either interpretive colorings or outright expansions of Homer's text, each emphasizing divine inspiration of, or divine possession of, the mortal warriors: *CH* 1. 5. 1–4; 5. 128; 9. 657; 11. 11–12; 13. 54, 60, 78; 15. 53–54;15. 238–47; 15. 541–42; 15. 558–62; 16. 603–4; 17.

180–83; 17. 463–65; 17. 499–500; 19. 370–73. As an afterthought, I have checked about a dozen moments when mortals urge on other mortals; with an equally impressive (though not total) uniformity, Chapman does *not* use the related cluster of locutions ("inspire," "animate," "infuse spirit," and the like) in these instances, reserving that terminology only for special moments when he wishes to convey a sense of divine *inflatus*.

5. The time-honored critical theory of progressive influences, dividing Chapman's career into neo-Platonic, heroic, and—with the advent of Jacobean pessimism—Stoic parcels, has long outlived its usefulness. The second half of the *Iliads* (1611) celebrating Achilles' heroic wrath was translated after Chapman came under the "dominant" influence of Stoicism, and indeed a careful evaluation of Clermont suggests that he was conceived as a perfect Achillean hero as well as a Stoic sage. Furthermore, the *Iliads* of 1598 and the opening scene of *Bussy D'Ambois* (as I shall document at length in the following notes) demonstrate that in the so-called neo-Platonic and heroic periods of his career Chapman's knowledge of neo-Stoicism was extensive. By the time he wrote *Bussy D'Ambois*, his familiarity with Cicero and DuVair, Seneca and Lipsius—both active and passive strains of neo-Stoicism—seems assured, especially since Stoic conceptions frame the ideational structure of the tragedy. Bussy's Stoic discourse in the opening scene and the resonant echoes of *Hercules Oetaeus* at the conclusion enclose an unmistakable quest pattern, the Stoic pursuit of virtue across Fortune's stormy seas. On the active and passive strains of neo-Stoicism, see Peter Bement, "The Stoicism of Chapman's Clermont D'Ambois"; see also his *George Chapman*, pp. 183–90.

6. In the large context of the "state of things" and in view of the large dichotomy presented in the first three words, the Reason under challenge by Fortune (1. 1. 1) is the Stoic equivalent of Providence, the rational principle that inheres in the cosmos and gives purpose to all things as they unfold in time. Universal Reason is the foundation of Stoic philosophy. At the same time, however, the Stoics linked Reason with the generative rational principle in each of us, the divine "seed" (1. 1. 4), man's central force regulating all activity in accordance with the universal Reason. See, among others, Seneca, *Epistulae*, 41. 4, 73. 16, 10. 29; M. Aurelius, *Meditations*, 9. 1; E. Vernon Arnold, *Roman Stoicism*, p. 161.

With authoritative precedent Bussy contends that only "Need" (1. 1. 3) can truly nurture man's divine spark within. "Need" may refer here to cosmic necessity and to the Stoic submission to the inevitable (the course of virtue), but most likely the context of the soliloquy evokes the Cynic life of austerity and simplicity which the Stoics adopted. "Need," associated with the golden age existence (Seneca, *Epistulae*, 90. 14) and the term used to describe the ideal of conforming to the basic requirements of the body as nature dictates them, helps man to live a virtuous life. See Seneca, *Epistulae*, 8. 5, 87. 2–4, 9; Epictetus, *Discourses*, 3. 22; Laertius, *Lives*, 7. 130.

A life of "Virtue" (1. 1. 32) was lived in accordance with Reason and the law of nature. In that large sense, it was inseparable from them and encompassed all the moral virtues that display it. Cicero's *De Officiis* (esp. 1. 2–10, 5–31) provides the most thorough review of the primary and secondary virtues comprising Stoic "Virtue."

7. The Stoic life of retirement, for which Seneca was an especially forceful advocate (*Epistulae*, esp. 48, and *Moralia*, esp. "De Otio"), seems to have been conflated with the Horatian retirement. Seneca's country life of simplicity, solitude, and contemplative retreat paralleled the satirist's retreat to the life of frugality, piety, and moral virtue (see, for example, Horace's *Carmina* 3. 3. 1–4; *Epode* 11; and *Epistulae*, 1. 10, 1. 14, 2. 6). Persius also learned the value of the simple life from his Stoic mentor, Cornutus (*Satirae*, 5, 6). As Hallett Smith points out in *Elizabethan Poetry*, pp. 13–14, the Horatian retreat to simple virtue was known to the sixteenth-century English poets; however, Montaigne seems closer in spirit to the Stoic contemplative retreat (*Essayes*, "Of Solitariness"). A full description of the Stoic retirement is found in J. Lipsius's *De Constantia*, 2. 1–3, where he describes the pleasant surroundings of a garden by a river at the same time that he insists on the proper kind of contemplative "recreation." Bement provides an excellent description of Stoic retirement in *Chapman*, pp. 185–86, associating it with the Horatian *beatus vir*; but, though he outlines the conventions of the *beatus vir* and of the melancholy man informing Bussy's soliloquy, Bement chooses not to league the *beatus vir* with a Stoic retirement at the beginning of *Bussy*, despite the heavily contemplative and philosophical tone of the soliloquy. See his fine essay on *Bussy* in ibid., pp. 104–43.

8. Nicolas Brooke's introduction to the Revels Edition is especially helpful on this point; he uses the poetic ambiguity of the soliloquy to develop the larger conflict between *virtù* and virtue. I will use the terms *virtus* and virtue, but my point of departure is the same (see Brooke, pp. xxix–xxxiii).

9. See Seneca, *Epistulae*, 8. 2, 14. 14, 68. 2, 10, and *Moralia*, "De Otio," 1. 4–3. 5, 5. 1–18; Lipsius, *De Constantia*, 2. 3.

10. Despite the benefits of the contemplative retreat, the Stoic ideal was an active life of heroic struggle against vice. Cicero, Laertius, and Seneca make the point forcefully (*De Officiis*, 1. 21. 70–72; *Lives*, 8. 121; *Moralia*, "De Providentia," 4. 9–6. 5, and "De Vita Beata," 22. 1–5). The Stoics recognized Hercules as the reformer and savior of the world (see Cicero, *De Officiis*, 3. 5. 25), but they emphasized that his activity exhibited, above all else, self-control and wisdom. Seneca states, for example, that Cato, Ulysses, and Hercules were alike in that they were "wise men . . . unconquered by struggles, were despisers of pleasure, and victors over all terrors" (*Moralia*, "De Constantia," 2. 1, quoted from *Moral Essays*, 1:51. As Eugene Waith has documented, this is the Hercules that the Christian Renaissance adopted; see *The Herculean Hero*, pp. 30–38, 40–48, and the interpretive essay on *Bussy*, chapter 4; see also Raymond B. Waddington, "Prometheus and Hercules" (in *Journal of English Literary History*), pp. 21–48, somewhat condensed for *The Mind's Empire*, chapter 2. Later citations for Waddington are to the journal article.

11. "Ardour" appears to be the calor which man and the stars shared; see

Johnstone Parr, *Tamburlaine's Malady, and Other Essays on Astrology in Elizabethan Drama*, pp. 15–19. Janet Spens, "Chapman's Ethical Thought," pp. 142–48, and Eugene Waith, *Ideas of Greatness*, pp. 126–27, provide apt commentaries on this passage. Spens sanctions Bussy's natural compulsion by appealing to Cicero's theory that each individual has his own unique law of nature which he must fulfill (*De Officiis*, 1. 30. 107). Indeed, the concept was indicative of the Stoic concern for individualism; Chrysippus espoused it before Panaetius, whose work Cicero translated in *De Officiis*, and Seneca also adheres to it (see Laertius, *Lives*, 8. 89 and Seneca's *"naturam suam"* of *Epistulae*, 12. 7–9). According to the Stoics, however, the fulfillment of one's particular nature never became a blind, compulsive drive; it was always subsumed under the wider ideal of progress toward virtue. On this point, see Cicero, *De Officiis*, 1. 31. 110, and Geneviève Rodis-Lewis, *La Morale Stoicienne*, pp. 20–21, 82. The emphasis is not on the sanction of the strong individual, as Spens may lead one to believe, but on each man's having a uniquely appropriate course to virtue. Antipater's epitaph for Zeno is pertinent to this point: "Here lies great Zeno, dear to Citium, who scaled high Olympus, though he piled not Pelion on Ossa, nor toiled at the labours of Heracles, but this was the path he found out to the stars—the way of temperance alone" (Laertius, *Lives*, 7. 29, 2:141).

12. Bussy begins the play lamenting the perversion of an Aristotelian concept of honor similar to Othello's notion of social estimation ("Reward goes backwards, Honour on his head"), but thereafter he moves progressively to more personal and idiosyncratic codes of behavior. Monsieur tempts him by suggesting that exemplary, patriotic behavior will win him a "good name" among his peers (1. 1. 64–81), but when Bussy goes to court, intending to act honestly and virtuously, he invokes a generally Stoic conception of personal honor to which external rewards are irrelevant. After the duel, however, he defends his actions according to the code of the *duello*, that is, by appealing to a law of reputation based on a romantic conception that to defend one's honor is a noble instinct. This code of manly individualism sets Bussy apart from and in opposition to society's moral and legal standards of acceptable behavior. Later, when he chides Tamyra for allowing herself to knuckle under to a guilty conscience and sense of dishonor ("Sin is a coward, madam"), his attitude approximates the naturalistic notion that a mistaken conception of honor as a symbol of social consensus fosters an inhibiting social code, something like the Ten Commandments, which is imposed on man to blunt the confident assertion of natural desires.

13. See, for example, Erwin Panofsky, *The Life and Art of Albrecht Dürer*, pp. 157–59 and plate 214; Lawrence Babb, *The Elizabethan Malady*, pp. 11–13.

14. See Cedric H. Whitman, *Homer and the Heroic Tradition*, chapter 7.

15. C. L. Barber, "The Ambivalence of *Bussy D'Ambois*," sees the conflict between public and private conceptions of honor as central to the play's ambiguity. Insofar as we understand honor as an expressive vocabulary for social conflict in Chapman's play, and not a central concern per se, Barber's remarks are to the point.

16. *Epistulae*, 90. 44–46; quoted from *Seneca's Epistles*, 2:429–31. Emphasis added.

17. Those critics who accept Bussy as an ideal protagonist at the outset of the play inevitably turn their opprobrium against Nature or, more pertinently here, the corrupt society that destroys him. A recent example of the latter critical tendency is Roger Truscott Burbridge, "Speech and Action in Chapman's *Bussy D'Ambois*"; also, Lordi's introduction to the Regents Edition of *Bussy D'Ambois*, pp. xxvi–xxvii. Robert Ornstein, *The Moral Vision of Jacobean Tragedy*, sets up the apparent "moral design" of Chapman's tragedy in terms of an ideal protagonist in a degenerate society (p. 51); although I have suggested why Bussy and his ineffectual philosophy are not ideal, Ornstein's sense of the moral anarchy in a play without a definitive norm is to the point.

18. See J. Leeds Barroll's perceptive comments on such "service" in *Artificial Persons*, p. 169.

19. Allen Bergson provides an excellent analysis of Bussy's diminished self-awareness while role-playing at court; see his "The Ironic Tragedies of Marston and Chapman," pp. 616–17; Waddington, "Prometheus and Hercules," pp. 29–37, is especially illuminating on the question of Bussy's self-parody.

20. Chapman appears to have been influenced by the skeptical and libertine tradition of the late sixteenth century; see Louis I. Bredvold, "The Naturalism of Donne in Relation to Some Renaissance Traditions." Other critics have commented on Chapman's pessimistic vision of nature in *Bussy*: James Smith, "George Chapman (II)," pp. 49–53; R. H. Perkinson, "Nature and the Tragic Hero in Chapman's Bussy Plays," pp. 265–70; Elias Schwartz, "Seneca, Homer, and Chapman's *Bussy D'Ambois*," pp. 164, 168–71; Irving Ribner, *Jacobean Tragedy*, pp. 21–35.

21. Jean Jacquot discusses the moral reverberations of the conjuring scene in his introduction to *Bussy D'Amboise* (pp. lxxi–lxxiii) and in a restatement in "*Bussy D'Ambois* and Chapman's Conception of Tragedy," pp. 133–34. Angus Fletcher's remarks on the supernatural in *Allegory*, pp. 149–50, seem pertinent to this moment in *Bussy*.

22. See Brooke's discussion, pp. xlix–l.

23. I have quoted the Seneca passage above; see also *Republic*, 374 f.

24. See, for example, 2. 2. 184–85. "Opinion" is bodily knowledge, sense impressions that charade as real without the informing judgment of man's rational faculties. See Laertius, *Lives*, 7. 45–51; Lipsius, *De Constantia*, 1. 1; and Peter Ure, "A Note on 'Opinion' in Daniel, Greville, and Chapman."

25. See Jacquot's edition of the play, pp. lxxxi–lxxxiv, and his "*Bussy D'Ambois*," pp. 134–35.

26. The ethical conflict is not resolved in the *Iliads* either. In a fascinating passage in the second half of the translation, one catches Chapman struggling to reconcile the ideals, but with no more success than he has in the final scene of *Bussy D'Ambois*. Having traced his lineage, Aeneas says that blood lines are blood lines, "But as for valour, it is Zeus that increaseth it for men or minisheth it, even as himself wisheth, seeing he is mightiest of all" (quoted from Homer, *The Iliad*, 2:389). What Zeus bestows and takes away is ἀρετή, in the Homeric context the strength and valor of one endowed with naturally superior prowess;

de Sponde translates the word as *virtus*, and Chapman faces a knotty interpretive problem. To solve it, Chapman expands the passage:

> But Jove gives vertue; he augments and he empaires the worth
> Of all men, and his will, their Rule; he, strong'st, all strength affords.

> [CH 1. 20. 223–25]

The translation has the effect of glossing "vertue" twice, defining it first according to the broad subcategory of "worth" and obedience to God's command, and then the more specific subcategory of "strength." The translator retains the sense of martial *virtus*, yet, in subsuming it under "worth," he suggests that it might be construed as moral strength.

CHAPTER 5

1. Many critics have commented on this paradox, but see especially David Daiches, *More Literary Essays*, p. 95.

2. Among the many discussions of the mythic dimension of *Antony and Cleopatra* are Raymond B. Waddington, "*Antony and Cleopatra*"; Janet Adelman, *The Common Liar*, esp. pp. 68–101; Maynard Mack, "*Antony and Cleopatra*," pp. 96–99. Harold Fisch, "*Antony and Cleopatra*," would like us to understand the mythic pretensions of Antony and Cleopatra within a framework of irony.

3. See Edgar Wind, *Pagan Mysteries in the Renaissance*, pp. 73–80.

4. Ovid, *Metamorphoses*, 9. 773–84; Dio Cassius, *Roman History*, 50. 25; and Diodorus Siculus, 1. 11. 1–3, identify Isis as a moon goddess, but it is likely that Shakespeare's conception derived from a conflation of the lunar identification in Plutarch's "Isis and Osiris" (*Moralia*, 372) with the *myrionymos* Isis in Apuleius, *The Golden Ass*, 11. 5. Cartari's discussion of Diana in *Le Imagini de gli dei* . . . also associates the moon goddess with Isis, noting specifically that Isis's multicolored robe was a symbol of her various shapes and power of transformation. Michael Lloyd, "Cleopatra as Isis," examining the play in light of Apuleius's catalog of Isis's myriad associations with Roman deities, comments on many of Cleopatra's Isiac faces. For a full account of Isis's endless diversity and various powers, see R. E. Witt, *Isis in the Graeco-Roman World*.

5. I am generally indebted here to Arnold Stein, "The Image of Antony." Stein is careful to point out, however, that the lyric imagination is "not exempt from the force of fact, and must pay the price for the rightness of feeling" (p. 606).

6. Because Shakespeare has retained the outline of the *de casibus* history, many critics choose to view the play, as Caesar would, from the historical perspective. J. Leeds Barroll, "Shakespeare and Roman History," and James E. Phillips, *The State in Shakespeare's Greek and Roman Plays*, pp. 198–200, have pointed out that history celebrated Augustus Caesar as an ideal prince who brought order to chaos; those critics who share this historical perspective inevitably condemn Antony and Cleopatra as threats to political order and stability, a good example being David Stempel, "The Transmigration of the Crocodile." This perspective

also supports the moral condemnation of Antony and Cleopatra, the tacit assumption of which being that Antony has deviated from the normative values that would otherwise have assured his Roman honor and historical reputation. The most virulent condemnation from this perspective is Franklin M. Dickey, *Not Wisely But Too Well*, chapters 10–12. Both political and moral criticism are of Caesar's party, the latter sometimes without knowing it.

7. Essays of particular relevance to Fortune and the different time-senses in the play include Michael Lloyd, "Antony and the Game of Chance"; David Kaula, "The Time Sense of *Antony and Cleopatra*"; Marilyn L. Williamson, "Fortune in *Antony and Cleopatra*"; James E. Siemon, " 'The Strong Necessity of Time' "; also, Charles A. Hallett, "Change, Fortune, and Time."

8. See Kaula, "Time Sense," p. 222. Robert Ornstein, elaborating on Cleopatra's early "dying fits" while looking ahead to act 5, points out that separation from Antony is a "form of death" for Cleopatra, leading to sleep, reverie, and dreams of Antony; see his excellent essay, "The Ethic of the Imagination," p. 43. It should also be noted that Cleopatra's presence is similarly a form of death for the Roman Antony.

9. See Wind, *Pagan Mysteries*, pp. 91–93.

10. The *concordia discors* of Cleopatra's characterization prompted S. L. Bethell, *Shakespeare and the Popular Dramatic Tradition*, to describe her as a "metaphysical conceit" (p. 155); Maynard Mack, in his introduction to the Pelican Edition of *Antony and Cleopatra*, used the term "absolute oxymoron" (p. 19); in *Shakespeare and the Students*, p. 87, D. J. Enright notes that there are two realities in the Cydnus description, fancy and nature.

11. See the discussion of Cleopatra in Derick R. C. Marsh, *Passion Lends Them Power*, pp. 159–60, 169.

12. Paul Cantor makes some fine points about "The Liberation of Eros" in *Shakespeare's Rome*, esp. pp. 155–62.

13. Michael Lloyd, "The Roman Tongue," delineates the Roman and Egyptian styles and the values they project. Among the many other essays dealing with the question of style in *Antony and Cleopatra*, see esp. Madeleine Doran, "The Language of Hyperbole in *Antony and Cleopatra*," rpt. *Shakespeare's Dramatic Language*, pp. 154–81; Mack, "Antony and Cleopatra," pp. 90–92; Julian Markels, *The Pillar of the World*, chapter 6; and for a large view of the significance of Asiatic and Attic styles in the play, Rosalie Colie, *Shakespeare's Living Art*, pp. 168–207.

14. See Ray L. Heffner, Jr., "The Messengers in Shakespeare's *Antony and Cleopatra*," p. 158.

15. On martial heroism as an anachronistic ideal in Augustan Rome, see William Rosen, *Shakespeare and the Craft of Tragedy*, pp. 112, 144; Matthew Proser, *The Heroic Image in Five Shakespearean Tragedies*, pp. 182–83; Ornstein, "The Ethic of the Imagination," pp. 35–36; and esp. Adelman, *The Common Liar*, pp. 132–39, and Cantor, *Shakespeare's Rome*, pp. 127–36.

16. Mack makes the point in "Antony and Cleopatra," p. 107; see also J. Oates Smith's discussion of Antony's heart in "The Alchemy of *Antony and Cleopatra*," p. 39; and Marsh, *Passion Lends Them Power*, pp. 151–52.

17. Mack, *"Antony and Cleopatra,"* p. 109.

18. This is Enright's observation in *Shakespeare and the Students*, p. 95.

19. Lloyd, "Cleopatra as Isis," p. 92, and Robert G. Hunter, "Cleopatra and the 'Oestre Junonicque,' " comment on the derogatory simile of the cow, an animal sacred to Isis.

20. Rage is Antony's chief Herculean characteristic in the play; see Eugene Waith, *The Herculean Hero*, pp. 115–17. Antony characteristically invokes Hercules as a reflexive assertion of a heroic image that has been lost.

21. Bullough, 5:305.

22. Ibid., p. 308.

23. This is only one of several love paradoxes Shakespeare dramatizes in the play. The lovers' relationship has been discussed extensively in terms of celestial-demonic, creative-destructive, spiritual-bestial polarities; see Maurice Charney, *Shakespeare's Roman Plays*, pp. 96–101; Charles Lyons, *Shakespeare and the Ambiguity of Love's Triumph*, pp. 160–86; Michael Payne, "Erotic Irony and Polarity in *Antony and Cleopatra*"; J. L. Simmons, *Shakespeare's Pagan World*, pp. 111–24.

24. Bullough, 5:307.

25. Adelman notes the allusion to Spenser but does not pursue its appropriateness to the "fiction" Antony is living; see *The Common Liar*, pp. 65–66.

26. On the harmonious love relationship extending from the arming episode through the victory celebration, see esp. Lloyd, "Cleopatra as Isis," p. 89; Proser, *The Heroic Image*, p. 201; Thomas McFarland, *Tragic Meanings in Shakespeare*, pp. 118–19; Markels, *The Pillar of the World*, pp. 137–39; T. McAlindon, *Shakespeare and Decorum*, pp. 193–97.

27. M. W. MacCallum, *Shakespeare's Roman Plays*, p. 409.

28. On the general topic of apocalyptic allusions in the play, see Ethel Seaton, "*Antony and Cleopatra* and The Book of Revelation."

29. The grandeur of Antony's magnanimity is stressed by Stein, "The Image of Antony," p. 594; Markels, *The Pillar of the World*, pp. 135–36; Ornstein, "The Ethic of the Imagination," pp. 40–41; and Enright, *Shakespeare and the Students*, p. 106.

30. See John Livingston Lowes, "The Loveres Maladye of Hereos."

31. Proser points out Antony's playacting in these final moments and Cleopatra's role in upstaging him. Proser's sense of ironic burlesque in the monument scene is close to my own; see *The Heroic Image*, pp. 208–13.

32. Derek A. Traversi's judgment about Antony's romantic "evasion" of reality seems wholly justified (*Shakespeare*, p. 175); so, too, Rosen's assertion that Antony's claim to a former stature is no more than a reverie (*Shakespeare and the Craft of Tragedy*, pp. 144–46, 155–56). Notwithstanding Stein's generous suspension of rebuttal and debate at the moment of death ("The Image of Antony," p. 599), Simmons appears correct in saying that Antony must be judged a "fool" at this moment (*Shakespeare's Pagan World*, pp. 148–49). Paradoxically, however, Markels is also justified in asserting that Antony has reached a transcendent plane of existence (*The Pillar of the World*, pp. 139–41).

33. As he did with Enobarbus's divided response, fatal choice, final repentance, and tribute to love, Shakespeare employs what Adelman has called "the structure of assent" (*The Common Liar*, pp. 157–68), steering the audience response toward recognition and approval of love's value.

34. Proser (*The Heroic Image*, p. 183) and Simmons (*Shakespeare's Pagan World*, p. 159) also point out the fusion of soldier and lover in the dream.

35. Ornstein suggests that Cleopatra and Shakespeare share an artistic vision and mythic imagination at this moment; see "The Ethic of the Imagination," p. 45. However, later we must distinguish the drama Cleopatra would write from that which is in fact enacted in her final moments.

36. Bullough, 5:307.

37. For these Isiac identities, see n. 4.

38. See esp. Thomas Heywood, "An Apologie for Actors," sig. B3.

CHAPTER 6

1. See Peter Ure, *Elizabethan and Jacobean Drama*, p. 129.

2. Derek Crawley, *Character in Relation to Action in the Tragedies of George Chapman*, pp. 65–69, makes a similar point about the confrontation of styles in the *Byron* plays.

3. Typical of the critical theory that Chapman was recanting the Achillean ideal of active heroism are Ennis Rees, *The Tragedies of George Chapman*, pp. 51–54; Elias Schwartz, "Chapman's Renaissance Man," pp. 613–14; Peter Bement, *George Chapman*, pp. 144–48.

4. Torquato Tasso, *Jerusalem Delivered*, p. 498.

5. Ibid., p. 499. On Tasso's views of martial heroism, see C. P. Brand, *Torquato Tasso*, pp. 83–85.

6. I am obviously indebted to D. P. Walker's analysis of Ficino's spiritual magic in *Spiritual and Demonic Magic from Ficino to Campanella*, pp. 3–23.

7. Eugene Waith has pointed out the echo of *Hercules Furens*, lines 1038–39: "Quis hic locus, quae regio, quae mundi plaga / ubi sum?" See his discussion of *Byron* in *Ideas of Greatness*, pp. 133–38.

8. Millar MacLure employs the Hercules analogy in *George Chapman*, p. 138. His is the most suggestive reading of Byron as a Herculean hero (see pp. 135–43).

9. Crawley, *Character*, pp. 79–80, also stresses the opposition between the clime of truth and the hellish vapors of flattery.

10. The king's prognosis of "choler adust" (C. 2. 2. 43) provides a physiological account of Byron's diseased imagination. The melancholiac's strong but corrupted powers of the imagination were commonplace. See Robert Burton, *The Anatomy of Melancholy*, 1:253–58; also Lily B. Campbell, *Shakespeare's Tragic Heroes*, section II, and Lawrence Babb, *The Elizabethan Malady*, pp. 42–54. On the other hand, self-fascination suggests that Byron's distemper is psychological, not physiological, that melancholy is a result, not a cause, of the diseased imagination. As Chapman knew, the mind could also affect

the body (see *Sir Giles Goosecap, Knight*, 5. 2. 1–25 ff.). The passions make the imagination their instrument, the imagination then seeks to blind the eye of the rational judge, and reason, once deceived by the imagination, not only justifies the imaginative vision (as Byron does with complete sincerity), but also stirs up the passions in its defense. Burton, for example, provides a relevant account, under "causes of melancholy," of the effect that pride or vainglory (like Byron's) have on the imagination (1:292–300). Most likely, Chapman's source for this idea, which one also finds expressed in *Bussy D'Ambois*, 5. 1. 42–53, is Agrippa's *De Occulta Philosophia*, 1. 64–65; 2. 63. Indeed, Jean Jacquot claims that Chapman knew Agrippa's opinion on this very issue; see Jacquot's edition of *Bussy D'Amboise*, p. lxxi. Also relevant is Hardin Craig's comment on Agrippa's notion of "self-fascination" in *The Enchanted Glass*, p. 46.

11. See Giovanni Pico della Mirandola, *Oration On the Dignity of Man*, sects. 32–33.

12. Alexander was famous as one whose virtue conquered Fortune; the *locus classicus* was Plutarch, *Moralia*, "De Alexandri Magni Fortuna aut Virtute, I–II." Franck L. Schoell, *Etudes sur l'humanisme continental en Angleterre à la fin de la Renaissance*, appendix II, examines Chapman's extensive debt to Plutarch in the *Byron* plays; see also Schoell's comment on Byron's identification with Alexander earlier in the study (p. 85). The importance of the Fortune-virtue dialectic to the thematic structure of the *Byron* plays was first argued convincingly by Peter Ure, *Elizabethan and Jacobean Drama*, pp. 123–44.

13. *Moralia*, 335C–336B.

14. Nesca Robb, *Neoplatonism of the Italian Renaissance*, p. 27, finds the germ of this emphasis on the poet's supremacy in Petrarch, but in any event Tasso, Sidney, Puttenham, and a host of other Renaissance critics used the commonplace analogy of the poet as a second creator.

15. On Ficino's notion of the contemplative imagination and creative melancholy, see esp. Paul O. Kristeller, *The Philosophy of Marcilio Ficino*, pp. 224–25, or Kristeller, *Eight Philosophers of the Italian Renaissance*, pp. 43–45; and Babb, *The Elizabethan Malady*, pp. 58–67. MacLure, *George Chapman*, pp. 33–35, relates creative melancholy specifically to Chapman's poetics; see also the more general discussion of Chapman's neo-Platonic aesthetic in Raymond B. Waddington, *The Mind's Empire*, chapter 1.

16. On this point see especially Ernst Cassirer, *The Individual and the Cosmos in Renaissance Philosophy*, chapter 3.

17. *T.* 1. 1. 77–86. This passage is suggested by Chapman's source, Jean de Serres, *A Generall Historie of France*, p. 1100.

18. Francis Vian, *La guerre des géants*, p. 289. Bacon's understanding of the gigantomachy as the monarch's suppression of open rebellion is typical of the political emphasis given the myth (see *The Advancement of Learning*, Bk. 2. 4. 4). Among the play's critics, Bement, *George Chapman*, pp. 144–81, is especially cogent in stressing the importance of law, justice, and social institutions in the play's vision of civil ideals. Natale Conti's moral interpretation of the gigantomachy, emphasizing the giants' self-love and impiety, is also relevant to

the moral vision of the *Byron* plays; see *Mythologiae sive explicationis fabularum*, p. 652; see also Wayne A. Rebhorn, "Structure and Meaning in *The Praise of Folly*," p. 467. In "The Teares of Peace" Chapman associates the giants with those monsters of outward forms who scorn a life of goodness and true humanity:

> Where are our Scarre-crowes now, or men of ragges,
> Of Titles meerely, Places, Fortunes, Bragges,
> That want and scorne both? Those inuerted men?
> Those dungeons; whose soules no more containe
> The actuall light of Reason, then darke beasts?
> Those Cloudes, driuen still, twixt Gods beame and their brests?
> Those Giants, throwing goulden hils gainst heauen?
> To no one spice of true humanitie given?
>
> [401–8]

The blind, ambitious giants are most like the "active men" who aspire beyond nature, whose life is consumed in seeking "State-height," an ascent that leads inevitably to a tempestuous death (413–27). Heaven's lightning will disperse "Those Cloudes," her thunderbolt cast down "Those Giants" who aspire to a divine virtue and immortality they do not merit (1108–11).

19. See Hesiod, *Works and Days*, lines 156–201.

20. Those critics who respond to the *Byron* plays simply as moral drama inevitably accent the devastating irony attending Byron's heroic pretensions. As a result their descriptions of the tragic hero range from that of a simpleton with a total lack of spiritual resources (Rees, *Tragedies*, pp. 67, 72, 84) to a naive dreamer (Schwartz, "Chapman's Renaissance Man," pp. 617–23) to something akin to a comic buffoon (Robert Ornstein, *The Moral Vision of Jacobean Tragedy*, p. 62; Crawley, *Character*, pp. 108–9).

21. See especially Hardin Craig, "Ethics in the Jacobean Drama," pp. 24–46.

22. De Serres, *A Generall Historie of France*, p. 1108.

23. Jean Jacquot, *George Chapman*, p. 154.

24. See Janet Spens, "Chapman's Ethical Thought," pp. 157–58.

25. Although I agree with Albert H. Tricomi, "The Revised Version of Chapman's *Bussy D'Ambois*," that the revisions for the revival of *Bussy D'Ambois* in 1609 tend to denigrate Bussy's heroic behavior, the "shift in point of view" might rather be considered a slight adjustment reflecting the clearer moral perspective and the better understanding of the psychology of the heroic spirit that Chapman displayed in the *Byron* plays; to my mind, it has nothing at all to do with Chapman's supposed conversion to Stoicism after 1607–8, as Tricomi claims.

26. Jean de Sponde, *Homeri quae extant omnia*, p. 5.

27. See CH 2. 4. 751–54; 5. 23–26; 5. 201–9; 7. 344–66; and 9. 55–66 (where the "inflaming affections" belong to Calypso and Circe). I disagree with George de Forest Lord's suggestion that Ulysses has become entangled in the desires of the flesh on Calypso's island; see his *Homeric Renaissance*, pp. 41–44.

28. See Lord's discussion of appetitive imagery in *Homeric Renaissance*, pp. 62–69.

29. Pierre Charron, *Of Wisdom Three Books*, p. 56. Charron's entire discussion of "spirit" is germane (see chapter 14).

30. See Chapman's extended expansion, *CH* 2. 460–71. In the interpretive translation following the expansion, Ulysses appears to be one of the elect; see *CH* 2. 13. 481–87 and MacLure's remarks in *George Chapman*, p. 197.

31. According to the allegorical tradition, Ulysses' marvelous immunity to Circe illustrated rational control over appetitive passion; in this respect Chapman's emphasis in the Circe episode is traditional (see *CH* 2. 10. 439–45, 452–54). But there are several expansions at other points in the epic that reflect Chapman's untraditionally strong emphasis on rational control; see, for example, *CH* 2. 17. 313–14; 20. 19–35; et al. In the fascinating episode concerning the cattle of the sun god, when Ulysses is put to sleep, his companions were without governance: *"there wak't no meane to curb / Their headstrong wants,"* and Eurylochus *"that did disturb / My rule* in chiefe at all times" led them astray (*CH* 2. 12. 482–84). *"To themselves alone / My rude men left ungoverned"* (*CH* 2. 12. 534–35), the companions did an impious deed. Chapman's expansions turn the episode into an allegory in which Ulysses represents Reason.

32. See *CH* 2. 1. 320; 2. 180; 3. 165; 5. 239–41; 13. 371–72; 13. 420–23; and Chapman's apology for Penelope's wariness in 13. 173–76, 335–61.

CHAPTER 7

1. Quoted from Bullough, 5:506.

2. See Werner W. Jaeger, *Paideia*, 1:1–5. Jaeger links Aristotle's concept of the "magnanimous" man to heroic *areté*, and Roy W. Battenhouse, *Shakespearean Tragedy*, pp. 362–74, relates the pagan ideal of magnanimity to *Coriolanus* specifically. The heroic ideal is also at the heart of Reuben A. Brower's discussion of the play in *Hero and Saint* and of Eugene Waith's chapter in *The Herculean Hero*. See also William Rosen, *Shakespeare and the Craft of Tragedy*, pp. 163–66, and Richard C. Crowley, "*Coriolanus* and the Epic Genre." Crowley's conception of the tragedy is close to my own.

3. T. J. B. Spencer has called *Coriolanus* one of the "great feats of the historical imagination in Renaissance Europe," and his appraisal is seconded by Roy Battenhouse (see Spencer, "Shakespeare and the Elizabethan Romans," pp. 34–35, and Battenhouse, *Shakespearean Tragedy*, p. 309). On this point the reader might also consult Gilbert Highet, *The Classical Tradition*, p. 198; H. S. Wilson, *On the Design of Shakespearean Tragedy*, pp. 87–88; and Allan Bloom, *Shakespeare's Politics*, pp. 76–78.

4. For Bullough's theory that Shakespeare discarded *Timon* for *Coriolanus*, see Bullough, 5:455; see also Paul A. Jorgensen, *Shakespeare's Military World*, pp. 292–93. Several critics have suggested, of course, that the dramatic conception of *Coriolanus* should be related to Shakespeare's other Roman plays. Especially

important are its similarities and contrasts with *Antony and Cleopatra*. For observations generally stressing the contrasts between *Coriolanus* and *Antony and Cleopatra*, see Bullough 5:455; Derek A. Traversi, *Shakespeare*, p. 230; Waith, *The Herculean Hero*, p. 140; and especially Paul A. Cantor, *Shakespeare's Rome*. On the other hand, Norman Rabkin, "The Tragedy of Politics," pp. 195, 212, and G. Wilson Knight, *The Imperial Theme*, pp. 154–94, are among those who find *Coriolanus* similar in conception to *Antony and Cleopatra*. My own suggestion is that despite the fact that one play is concerned with heroic love and the other with martial heroism, Shakespeare's attitude toward heroism and his concept of tragic grandeur are essentially the same in both plays. On this general question about the inspiration for *Coriolanus*, see also J. Dover Wilson's introduction to the New Cambridge Edition of the play, pp. xvii–xix.

5. Quoted from John B. Gabel, "The Original Version of Chapman's *Tragedy of Byron*," p. 434. See also J. J. Jusserand, "Ambassador La Boderie and the 'Compositeur' of the Byron Plays," p. 204, or E. K. Chambers, *The Elizabethan Stage*, 3:257–58.

6. The series of events is outlined in Irwin Smith's *Shakespeare's Blackfriars Playhouse*, chapter 9. See also Chambers, *The Elizabethan Stage*, 2:53–54, 509–10.

7. The entry in the Stationers' Register is for 5 June 1608.

8. The King's Men's lease at Blackfriars began in August 1608, and although repairs and the plague delayed performance until 1609 (Smith, *Blackfriars*, chapter 12), it is possible that Shakespeare may have been writing *Coriolanus* for an autumn performance. The first King's Men tragedy would respond to the last tragedy of the Children, and Shakespeare would respond to Chapman.

9. On the date of *Coriolanus* I follow E. K. Chambers, *William Shakespeare*, 1:480; Bullough, 5:453–54; Wilson, p. x; and M. W. MacCallum, *Shakespeare's Roman Plays*, p. 462. Their dating ranges from early 1608 to early 1609.

10. Byron expounds his view on peace in *T.* 1. 2. 1–16, 4. 1. 1–28; Coriolanus in 1. 1. 229–30 and later, by proxy, in 4. 5. 233–50. Such ideas were commonplace in contemporary treatises; war as a purge of society's "musty superfluity" was characteristic of the soldier-hero's ideology, and clearly both Byron and Coriolanus share that ideology. See Jorgensen, *Shakespeare's Military World*, pp. 187–91.

11. Aristotle, *Politics*, Bk. 1. 1252a; see also Annibale Romei's *The Courtiers Academie*, p. 247. Among critics who have examined the concept's applicability to *Coriolanus* are F. N. Lees, "*Coriolanus*, Aristotle, and Bacon"; Bloom, *Shakespeare's Politics*, pp. 83–86; Cantor, *Shakespeare's Rome*, pp. 101–3; and Maurice Charney, *Shakespeare's Roman Plays*, p. 187.

12. A. C. Bradley, *Coriolanus* (1912), rpt. in *A Miscellany*, p. 104.

13. See 1. 4. 59; 1. 6. 25–27. Several descriptions of Coriolanus emphasize that both his words and his valor spring from the same fiery source: 3. 1. 76–80, 256–59; 3. 2. 54–57; 3. 3. 27–30. In act 1, scene 1, Coriolanus's tirade is an expedient substitute for the sword, which he would prefer to use against the plebeians (197–200). He is always ready to vent his wrath through activity, and language in the forum is as much a form of activity as swordplay on the

battlefield (see Waith, *The Herculean Hero*, pp. 126–27). Coriolanus's antieloquence goes hand in hand with his soldier's education and martial spirit: 1. 3. 55–56; 2. 2. 72; 2. 2. 82–83; 3. 1. 318–20; 4. 2. 17–19. The soldier's language of action is contrasted with the citizen's language of conventional discourse, as in act 1, scene 1, when they "sigh'd forth proverbs" (205) and with worthless, ineffectual breath "vented their complainings" (210).

14. See Cantor, *Shakespeare's Rome*, pp. 30–39, 63–77.

15. The facts that the schoolmaster is mentioned at all, that Volumnia feels compelled to lecture Virgilia, and that Virgilia's love and concern for her husband are human suggest to some critics that the wife is representative of the silent, hidden nature of Coriolanus; see Matthew Proser, *The Heroic Image in Five Shakespearean Tragedies*, p. 155, and Katherine Stockholder, "The Other Coriolanus," p. 230. I would point out in addition that Shakespeare, having given Coriolanus maternal, conjugal, and paternal relationships, provides the titan with a context that will allow him to become far more human than Chapman's Byron, who had no familial ties except for the relatively unimportant memory of his heroic sire.

16. Several critics have pointed out Coriolanus's personal standards of behavior and have then proceeded into an analysis of language or into a discussion of "self-creation." See Proser, *The Heroic Image*, pp. 147–61; Terence Eagleton, *Shakespeare and Society*, pp. 104–7; James L. Calderwood, "*Coriolanus*"; Carol M. Sicherman, "*Coriolanus.*"

17. The distinction between Coriolanus's deeds and the plebeians' voices, between an honor based on merit and an honor based on popular opinion, has been developed well in several essays. I will not belabor the point here. See Rosen, *Shakespeare and the Craft of Tragedy*, pp. 167–73; D. J. Gordon, "Name and Fame," pp. 45–49; Rabkin, "Tragedy of Politics," pp. 202–3.

18. See Waith, *The Herculean Hero*, pp. 123–25.

19. For a recent discussion of this ironical suggestion see esp. Cantor, *Shakespeare's Rome*, pp. 64–66.

20. Although I do not agree with some particular points of his analysis, the premise of Ralph Berry's essay, "Sexual Imagery in *Coriolanus*," is sound. Shakespeare did indeed perceive that sex and aggression were profoundly linked, though it seems to me that *Troilus and Cressida* (as remarked in chapter 2) exemplifies that perception even more fully than *Coriolanus*. Michael Long, *The Unnatural Scene*, pp. 63–68, 184–86, discusses this topic in relation to *Coriolanus* and to Shakespeare's unnatural villains.

21. The new identity as "Coriolanus" has been stressed by Gordon, "Name and Fame," p. 51; see also Manfred Weidhorn, "The Relation of Title and Name to Identity in Shakespearian Tragedy," p. 313.

22. For a general discussion of the food and eating imagery in the play, see Charney, *Shakespeare's Roman Plays*, pp. 143–57. My point complements rather than refutes Charles Mitchell, who links the swollen belly and the selfish feasting of war with Coriolanus's "great appetitive love of self"; see his excellent article, "*Coriolanus*," pp. 201, 213–14.

23. Jaeger calls the ideal that of an "ennobled self-love" in *Paideia*, 1:10.
24. Aufidius and Coriolanus have no social loyalties (1. 1. 232–35; 1. 10. 3–5). Eagleton reminds us that they have no need of social definition (*Shakespeare and Society*, pp. 111–13).
25. Waith refers to Aufidius as "almost an alter ego" of Coriolanus (*The Herculean Hero*, p. 131); Mitchell, "*Coriolanus*," p. 202, suggests that Coriolanus sees Aufidius as "an image of his own ideal self; so that his love for Aufidius mirrors his love of himself." See also Michael McCanles's interpretation of the love-hate relationship in "The Dialectic of Transcendence in *Coriolanus*," pp. 45–46.
26. For example, see Cicero, *De Amicitia*, 7.
27. See David Riggs's discussion in *Shakespeare's Heroical Histories*, pp. 7–10; also Andrew R. Anderson, "Hercules and His Successors."
28. Coriolanus's conception of "service" also suggests his dependence on society. He needs purpose and direction for his action. The need to serve is among the many reasons he went to Aufidius after his banishment; see 4. 4. 26; 4. 5. 104.
29. See Bullough, 5:538–40; and Hermann Heuer, "From Plutarch to Shakespeare," p. 55.
30. Among others, the point is made by H. C. Goddard, *The Meaning of Shakespeare*, pp. 605–10, and J. Dover Wilson in his introduction to the New Cambridge Edition, p. xxxiv. As suggested above, the women and boy stand as a dramatic emblem for the natural instincts that argue their point silently within Coriolanus.
31. Weighty spokesmen for reconciliation are Bradley, *A Miscellany*, p. 93, and Knight, *The Imperial Theme*, p. 196. Other critics, perhaps the majority, have read a far darker ending in which nothing of value is salvaged; see, for example, Waith, *The Herculean Hero*, pp. 138–42, and Mitchell, "*Coriolanus*," pp. 221–22. My interpretation is closest in agreement with E. A. M. Colman, "The End of *Coriolanus*," pp. 1–12, and Lawrence Danson, *Tragic Alphabet*, pp. 161–62.

CONCLUSION

1. Parrott, *The Tragedies*, 2:607. Among critics who have discussed the Byron-Essex analogy, see Jean Jacquot, *George Chapman*, pp. 31, 42, 149; Paul A. Jorgensen, *Shakespeare's Military World*, esp. p. 276; and Millar MacLure, *George Chapman*, pp. 133–34.
2. Roy Battenhouse's phrase in *Shakespearean Tragedy*, p. 320.
3. Plutarch had compared Coriolanus's rage to that of Achilles, and both Reuben Brower, *Hero and Saint*, esp. pp. 360, 372, 377, and Battenhouse, *Shakespearean Tragedy*, pp. 369–70, see Achilles as Coriolanus's archetype. A. P. Rossiter, *Angel with Horns*, p. 248, and Terence Eagleton, *Shakespeare and Society*, pp. 104–5, also notice Coriolanus's similarity to the Achilles of *Troilus and Cressida*.

BIBLIOGRAPHY

Abbott, Edwin A. *Bacon and Essex*. London: Seeley, Jackson & Halliday, 1877.
Adams, Robert P. *The Better Part of Valor*. Seattle: University of Washington Press, 1962.
Adelman, Janet. *The Common Liar: An Essay on Antony and Cleopatra*. New Haven: Yale University Press, 1973.
Agrippa, Cornelius. *De Occulta Philosophia*. Translated by J. Friske. London, 1651.
Anderson, Andrew R. "Hercules and His Successors." *Harvard Studies in Classical Philology* 39 (1928): 7–58.
Apuleius. *The Golden Ass*. Translated by W. Adlington, 1566; rev. S. Gaselee. Loeb Classical Library. Cambridge, Mass.: Harvard University Press, 1971.
Aristotle. *Nicomachean Ethics*. Translated by H. Rackham. Loeb Classical Library. London: William Heinemann Ltd., 1926.
————. *The Politics*. Translated by H. Rackham. Loeb Classical Library. London: William Heinemann Ltd., 1932.
Arnold, Edward Vernon. *Roman Stoicism*. Cambridge, England: Cambridge University Press, 1911.
Ashley, Robert. *Of Honour*. Edited with introduction by Virgil B. Heltzel. San Marino: Huntington Library, 1949.
Aurelius, Antoninus Marcus. *Meditations*. Translated by C. R. Haines. Loeb Classical Library. London: William Heinemann Ltd., 1916.
Babb, Lawrence. *The Elizabethan Malady*. East Lansing, Mich.: Michigan State University Press, 1951.
Bacon, Francis. *The Advancement of Learning and New Atlantis*. Edited by Arthur Johnston. Oxford: Clarendon Press, 1974.
Barber, Cesar Lombardi. "The Ambivalence of *Bussy D'Ambois*." *Review of English Literature* 2 (1961): 38–44.
Barroll, John Leeds. *Artificial Persons: The Formation of Character in the Tragedies of Shakespeare*. Columbia, S.C.: University of South Carolina Press, 1974.
————. "Shakespeare and Roman History." *Modern Language Review* 53 (1958): 327–43.
Bartlett, Phyllis B. "Chapman's Revisions in His *Iliads*." *Journal of English Literary History* 2 (1935): 92–119.
————. "The Heroes of Chapman's Homer." *Review of English Studies* 19 (1941): 257–80.
————. "Stylistic Devices in Chapman's *Iliads*." *Publications of the Modern*

Language Association of America 57 (1942): 661–75.

Barton, Anne. Review of Howard Felperin, *Shakespearean Representation: Mimesis and Modernity in Elizabethan Tragedy*. *Renaissance Quarterly* 32 (1979): 135–37.

Battenhouse, Roy W. *Shakespearean Tragedy*. Bloomington, Ind.: Indiana University Press, 1969.

Bement, Peter. *George Chapman: Action and Contemplation in His Tragedies*. Salzburg: University of Salzburg Press, 1974.

———. "The Stoicism of Chapman's Clermont D'Ambois." *Studies in English Literature* 12 (1972): 345–57.

Bergson, Allen. "The Ironic Tragedies of Marston and Chapman: Notes on Jacobean Tragic Form." *Journal of English and Germanic Philology* 69 (1970): 613–30.

Berry, Ralph. "Sexual Imagery in *Coriolanus*." *Studies in English Literature* 13 (1973): 301–16.

Bethell, Samuel Leslie. *Shakespeare and the Popular Dramatic Tradition*. Durham, N.C.: Duke University Press, 1944.

Bloom, Allan. *Shakespeare's Politics*. New York: Basic Books, 1964.

Bonjour, Adrien. "Hector and the 'One in Sumptuous Armour.' " *English Studies* 45 (1964): 104–8.

Boynton, Lindsay. *The Elizabethan Militia*. Toronto: University of Toronto Press, 1967.

Bradley, Andrew Cecil. *A Miscellany*. London: Macmillan, 1929.

Brand, Charles Peter. *Torquato Tasso: A Study of the Poet and of His Contribution to English Literature*. Cambridge, England: Cambridge University Press, 1965.

Bredvold, Louis I. "The Naturalism of Donne in Relation to Some Renaissance Traditions." *Journal of English and Germanic Philology* 22 (1923): 471–502.

Brodwin, Leonora. *Elizabethan Love Tragedy*. New York: New York University Press, 1971.

Brower, Reuben A. *Hero and Saint: Shakespeare and the Graeco-Roman Heroic Tradition*. New York: Oxford University Press, 1971.

Bullough, Geoffrey, ed. *Narrative and Dramatic Sources of Shakespeare*. 7 vols. London: Routledge & Kegan Paul, 1957–73.

Burbridge, Roger Truscott. "Speech and Action in Chapman's *Bussy D'Ambois*." *Tennessee Studies in Literature* 17 (1972): 59–65.

Burton, Robert. *The Anatomy of Melancholy*. Everyman's Library. 3 vols. New York: Dutton, 1932.

Calderwood, James L. "*Coriolanus*: Wordless Meanings and Meaningless Words." *Studies in English Literature* 6 (1966): 211–24.

Campbell, Lily B. *Shakespeare's "Histories": Mirrors of Elizabethan Policy*. San Marino: Huntington Library, 1947.

———. *Shakespeare's Tragic Heroes*. Cambridge, England: Cambridge University Press, 1930.

Cantor, Paul A. *Shakespeare's Rome: Republic and Empire*. Ithaca, N.Y.: Cornell University Press, 1976.

Cartari, Vincenzo. *Le Imagini de gli dei. Imagines deorum*. Lyons, 1581.

Caspari, Fritz. *Humanism and the Social Order in England*. Chicago: University of Chicago Press, 1954.

Cassirer, Ernst. *The Individual and the Cosmos in Renaissance Philosophy*. Translated by Mario Dimandi. 1927; rpt. Philadelphia: University of Pennsylvania Press, 1972.

Cassius, Dio Cocceianus. *Dio's Roman History*. Translated by Ernest Cary. Loeb Classical Library. 9 vols. London: William Heinemann Ltd., 1914–27.

Chambers, Sir Edmund Kerchever. *The Elizabethan Stage*. 4 vols. Oxford: Clarendon Press, 1923.

————. *William Shakespeare*. 2 vols. New York: Oxford University Press, 1930.

Chapman, George. *Bussy D'Amboise*. Edited by Jean Jacquot. Paris: Aubier, 1960.

————. *Bussy D'Ambois*. The Revels Plays. Edited by Nicolas Brooke. Cambridge, Mass.: Harvard University Press, 1964.

————. *Bussy D'Ambois*. The Regents Edition. Edited by Robert J. Lordi. Lincoln: University of Nebraska Press, 1964.

————. *Chapman's Homer*. Edited by Allardyce Nicoll. 2 vols. Princeton: Princeton University Press, 1966.

————. *The Plays of George Chapman: The Comedies*. Edited by Thomas Marc Parrott. 1913; rpt. in 2 vols. New York: Russell & Russell, 1961.

————. *The Plays of George Chapman: The Tragedies*. Edited by Thomas Marc Parrott. 1910; rpt. in 2 vols. New York: Russell & Russell, 1961.

————. *The Poems of George Chapman*. Edited by Phyllis Brooks Bartlett. New York: MLA, 1941.

Charlton, Henry Buckley. *Shakespearian Tragedy*. Cambridge, England: Cambridge University Press, 1948.

Charney, Maurice. *Shakespeare's Roman Plays*. Cambridge, Mass.: Harvard University Press, 1961.

Charron, Pierre. *De la sagesse*, 1601. *Of Wisdom Three Books*. Translated by Samson Lennard. London, ca. 1612.

Cicero, Marcus Tullius. "De Amicitia." *De Senectute, De Amicitia, De Divinatione*. Translated by William Armistead Falconer. Loeb Classical Library. Cambridge, Mass.: Harvard University Press, 1971. Pp. 108–211.

————. "De Officiis." Translated by Walter Miller. Loeb Classical Library. Cambridge, Mass.: Harvard University Press, 1968.

Clemen, Wolfgang. *The Development of Shakespeare's Imagery*. Cambridge, Mass.: Harvard University Press, 1951.

Cockle, Maurice J. D. *A Bibliography of English Military Books up to 1642*. 2d edition. London: Holland Press, 1957.

Colie, Rosalie. *The Resources of Kind: Genre-Theory in the Renaissance*. Berkeley: University of California Press, 1973.

————. *Shakespeare's Living Art*. Princeton: Princeton University Press, 1974.

Colman, E. A. M. "The End of *Coriolanus.*" *Journal of English Literary History* 34 (1967): 1–12.

Comes, Natalis (see Conti, Natale).

Conti, Natale. *Mythologiae sive Explicationis Fabularum.* Frankfort, 1596.

Council, Norman. *When Honour's at the Stake: Ideas of Honour in Shakespeare's Plays.* London: Allen & Unwin, 1973.

Craig, Hardin. *The Enchanted Glass.* New York: Oxford University Press, 1936.

——. "Ethics in the Jacobean Drama: The Case of Chapman." In *The Parrott Presentation Volume,* edited by Hardin Craig. Princeton: Princeton University Press, 1935. Pp. 24–46.

Crawley, Derek. *Character in Relation to Action in the Tragedies of George Chapman.* Salzburg: University of Salzburg Press, 1974.

Crowley, Richard C. "*Coriolanus* and the Epic Genre." In *Shakespeare's Late Plays,* edited by Richard C. Tobias and Paul G. Zolbrod. Athens, Ohio: Ohio University Press, 1974. Pp. 114–30.

Daiches, David. *More Literary Essays.* Chicago: University of Chicago Press, 1968.

Daniel, Samuel. *The Civil Wars.* Edited by Laurence Michel. New Haven: Yale University Press, 1958.

——. *The Tragedy of Philotas.* Edited with introduction by Laurence Michel. New Haven: Yale University Press, 1949.

Danson, Lawrence. *Tragic Alphabet: Shakespeare's Drama of Language.* New Haven: Yale University Press, 1974.

Dickey, Franklin M. *Not Wisely But Too Well: Shakespeare's Love Tragedies.* San Marino: Huntington Library, 1957.

Dio (see Cassius Dio Cocceianus).

Diodorus Siculus. *Geography.* Translated by C. H. Oldfather. Loeb Classical Library. 2 vols. Cambridge, Mass.: Harvard University Press, 1933–67.

Dodds, Eric Robertson. *The Greeks and the Irrational.* Sather Classical Lectures, No. 25. Berkeley: University of California Press, 1951.

Doran, Madeleine. *Endeavors of Art.* Madison: University of Wisconsin Press, 1954.

——. "Good Name In *Othello.*" *Studies in English Literature* 7 (1967): 195–217.

——. "The Language of Hyperbole in *Antony and Cleopatra.*" *Queen's Quarterly* 22 (1965): 26–51.

——. *Shakespeare's Dramatic Language.* Madison: University of Wisconsin Press, 1976.

DuVair, Guillaume. *The Moral Philosophy of the Stoicks.* Translated by T[homas] I[ames]. London, 1598.

Eagleton, Terence. *Shakespeare and Society.* New York: Schocken Books, 1967.

Eastman, Arthur M. "Othello as Ironist." In *In Honor of Austin Wright.* Carnegie Series in English, No. 12. Pittsburgh: Carnegie-Mellon University Press, 1972. Pp. 18–29.

Eliot, Thomas Stearns. *Selected Essays.* New York: Harcourt, Brace & Co., 1932.

Elliott, George Roy. *Flaming Minister: A Study of Othello as Tragedy of Love and Hate*. Durham, N.C.: Duke University Press, 1953.

Ellis-Fermor, Una. *The Frontiers of Drama*. London: Methuen, 1945.

Enright, Dennis Joseph. *Shakespeare and the Students*. London: Chatto & Windus, 1970.

Epictetus. *The Discourses as Reported by Arrian, The Manual, and Fragments*. Translated by W. A. Oldfather. 2 vols. Cambridge, Mass.: Harvard University Press, 1966–67.

Fay, H. C. "Chapman's Materials for His Translations of Homer." *Review of English Studies* 2 (1951): 121–28.

――――. "Poetry, Pedantry and Life in Chapman's *Iliads*." *Review of English Studies* 4 (1953): 13–25.

Ferguson, Arthur B. *The Indian Summer of English Chivalry*. Durham, N.C.: Duke University Press, 1960.

Fisch, Harold. "*Antony and Cleopatra*: The Limits of Mythology." *Shakespeare Survey* 23 (1970): 59–68.

Fletcher, Angus. *Allegory: The Theory of a Symbolic Mode*. Ithaca, N.Y.: Cornell University Press, 1964.

Fly, Richard D. "Cassandra and the Language of Prophecy in *Troilus and Cressida*." *Shakespeare Quarterly* 26 (1975): 157–71.

――――. *Shakespeare's Mediated World*. Amherst, Mass.: University of Massachusetts Press, 1976.

Gabel, John B. "The Original Version of Chapman's *Tragedy of Byron*." *Journal of English and Germanic Philology* 63 (1964): 433–40.

Gerard, Albert. " 'Egregiously an Ass': The Dark Side of the Moor." *Shakespeare Survey* 10 (1957): 98–106.

Gilbert, Allen H. *Literary Criticism: Plato to Dryden*. New York: American Book Co., 1940.

Goddard, Harold C. *The Meaning of Shakespeare*. Chicago: University of Chicago Press, 1951.

Goldman, Michael. *The Actor's Freedom: Toward a Theory of Drama*. New York: Viking Press, 1975.

――――. *Shakespeare and the Energies of Drama*. Princeton: Princeton University Press, 1972.

Gombrich, Sir Ernst H. J. *Symbolic Images: Studies in the Art of the Renaissance*. London: Phaedon Press, 1972.

Gordon, Donald James. "Name and Fame: Shakespeare's Coriolanus." In *Papers, Mainly Shakespearean*, edited by George Ian Duthie. London: Oliver and Boyd, 1964. Pp. 40–55.

Greg, Sir Walter Wilson. *Dramatic Documents from Elizabethan Playhouses*. Oxford: Clarendon Press, 1931.

Guillén, Claudio. *Literature as System: Essays toward the Theory of Literary History*. Princeton: Princeton University Press, 1971.

Hallett, Charles A. "Change, Fortune, and Time: Aspects of the Sublunar World in *Antony and Cleopatra*." *Journal of English and Germanic Philology* 75 (1976): 75–89.

Harbage, Alfred. *Annals of English Drama, 975–1700*. 1940; rev. Samuel

Schoenbaum, Philadelphia: University of Pennsylvania Press, 1964.

Harrison, George B. *The Life and Death of Robert Devereux, Earl of Essex.* London: Cassel and Company, 1937.

Haydn, Hiram. *The Counter-Renaissance.* New York: Scribner's, 1950.

Heffner, Ray. "Essex, the Ideal Courtier." *Journal of English Literary History* 1 (1934): 7–36.

Heffner, Ray L., Jr. "The Messengers in Shakespeare's *Antony and Cleopatra.*" *Journal of English Literary History* 43 (1976): 154–62.

Heilman, Robert Bechtold. *Magic in the Web: Action and Language in Othello.* Lexington, Ky.: University of Kentucky Press, 1956.

———. *Tragedy and Melodrama: Versions of Experience.* Seattle: University of Washington Press, 1968.

Henslowe, Philip. *Henslowe Papers.* Edited by W. W. Greg. London: A. H. Bullen, 1970.

———. *Henslowe's Diary.* Edited by R. A. Foakes and R. T. Rickert. Cambridge, England: Cambridge University Press, 1961.

Hesiod. *Works and Days and Theogony.* In *Hesiod, The Homeric Hymns and Homerica.* Translated by Hugh G. Evelyn-White. Loeb Classical Library. London: William Heinemann Ltd., 1970. Pp. 1–155.

Hester, M. Thomas. "'Zeal' as Satire: The Decorum of Donne's Satyres." *Genre* 10 (1977): 173–94.

Heuer, Hermann. "From Plutarch to Shakespeare: A Study of *Coriolanus.*" *Shakespeare Survey* 10 (1957): 50–60.

Heywood, Thomas. "An Apologie for Actors," 1612. Introduced by Richard H. Perkinson. New York: Scholars Facsimiles & Reprints, 1941.

Hibbard, George R. "'Othello' and the Pattern of Shakespearian Tragedy." *Shakespeare Survey* 21 (1968): 39–46.

Highet, Gilbert. *The Classical Tradition.* New York: Oxford University Press, 1953.

Hirsch, Eric Donald, Jr. *Validity in Interpretation.* New Haven: Yale University Press, 1967.

Holaday, Allan. "Heywood's *Troia Britanica* and *The Ages.*" *Journal of English and Germanic Philology* 45 (1946): 430–39.

Homer. *The Iliad.* Translated by A. T. Murray. Loeb Classical Library. 2 vols. Cambridge, Mass.: Harvard University Press, 1924–25.

———. *The Odyssey.* Translated by A. T. Murray. Loeb Classical Library. 2 vols. Cambridge, Mass.: Harvard University Press, 1919.

Honigmann, Ernst A. J. *Shakespeare: Seven Tragedies: The Dramatist's Manipulation of Response.* London: Macmillan, 1976.

Horace. *The Odes and Epodes.* Translated by C. E. Bennett. Loeb Classical Library. Cambridge, Mass.: Harvard University Press, 1968.

———. *Satires, Epistles, Ars Poetica.* Translated by H. Rushton Fairclough. Loeb Classical Library. London: William Heinemann Ltd., 1966.

Hough, Graham. *A Preface to the Faerie Queene.* London: G. Duckworth, 1962.

Hunter, Robert G. "Cleopatra and the 'Oestre Junonicque.'" *Shakespeare Studies* 5 (1971): 236–39.

————. *Shakespeare and the Mystery of God's Judgment.* Athens, Ga.: University of Georgia Press, 1976.

Jacquot, Jean. "*Bussy D'Ambois* and Chapman's Conception of Tragedy." *English Studies Today* 11 (1961): 129–41.

————. *George Chapman: Sa vie, sa poésie, son théâtre, sa pensée.* Paris: Les Belles Lettres, 1951.

Jaeger, Werner W. *Paideia: The Ideals of Greek Culture.* Translated by Gilbert Highet. 3 vols. Vol. 1, *Archaic Greece: The Mind of Athens.* Vol. 2, *In Search of the Divine Centre.* Vol. 3, *The Conflict of Cultural Ideas in the Age of Plato.* New York: Oxford University Press, 1939–44.

Jeffrey, David L., and Grant, Patrick. "Reputation in *Othello.*" *Shakespeare Studies* 6 (1970): 197–208.

Jones-Davies, Marie Thérèse. "Discord in Shakespeare's *Troilus and Cressida*; or, the Conflict between 'Angry Mars and Venus Queen of Love.'" *Shakespeare Quarterly* 25 (1974): 33–41.

Jorgensen, Paul A. "'Perplex'd in the Extreme': The Role of Thought in *Othello.*" *Shakespeare Quarterly* 15 (1964): 265–75.

————. *Shakespeare's Military World.* Los Angeles: University of California Press, 1956.

Jusserand, J. J. "Ambassador La Boderie and the 'Compositeur' of the Byron Plays." *Modern Language Review* 6 (1911): 203–5.

Kaufmann, Ralph James. "Ceremonies for Chaos: The Status of *Troilus and Cressida.*" *Journal of English Literary History* 32 (1965): 139–59.

Kaula, David. "'Mad Idolatry' in Shakespeare's *Troilus and Cressida.*" *Texas Studies in Language and Literature* 15 (1973–74): 25–38.

————. "The Time Sense of *Antony and Cleopatra.*" *Shakespeare Quarterly* 15 (1964): 211–23.

————. "Will and Reason in *Troilus and Cressida.*" *Shakespeare Quarterly* 12 (1961): 271–83.

Kelso, Ruth. *The Doctrine of the English Gentleman in the Sixteenth Century.* Illinois Studies in Language and Literature, No. 14. Urbana: University of Illinois Press, 1929.

Kernan, Alvin. *The Cankered Muse.* New Haven: Yale University Press, 1959.

Kimbrough, Robert. *Shakespeare's Troilus and Cressida and Its Setting.* Cambridge, Mass.: Harvard University Press, 1964.

Kirschbaum, Leo. "The Modern Othello." *Journal of English Literary History* 11 (1944): 283–96.

Knight, George Wilson. *The Imperial Theme.* 3d Edition. London: Methuen, 1951.

Kristeller, Paul O. *Eight Philosophers of the Italian Renaissance.* Stanford: Stanford University Press, 1964.

————. *The Philosophy of Marcilio Ficino.* Translated by Virginia Conant. New York: Columbia University Press, 1943.

Laertius, Diogenes. *Lives of Eminent Philosophers.* Translated by R. D. Hicks. Loeb Classical Library. 2 vols. London: William Heinemann Ltd., 1970–72.

Leavis, Frank Raymond. *The Common Pursuit*. London: Chatto & Windus, 1952.

Lees, F. N. "*Coriolanus*, Aristotle, and Bacon." *Review of English Studies* 1 (1950): 114–25.

Levin, Harry. *The Overreacher: A Study of Christopher Marlowe*. Cambridge, Mass.: Harvard University Press, 1952.

Levitsky, Ruth. "All-in-All Sufficiency in *Othello*." *Shakespeare Studies* 6 (1970): 201–21.

Lipsius, Justis. *De Constantia. Two Bookes of Constancie*. Translated by Sir John Stradling. Edited with introduction by Rudolph Kirk and C. M. Hall. New Brunswick, N.J.: Rutgers University Press, 1939.

Lloyd, Michael. "Antony and the Game of Chance." *Journal of English and Germanic Philology* 61 (1962): 548–54.

————. "Cleopatra as Isis." *Shakespeare Survey* 12 (1959): 88–94.

————. "The Roman Tongue." *Shakespeare Quarterly* 10 (1959): 461–68.

Long, Michael. *The Unnatural Scene: A Study of Shakespearean Tragedy*. London: Methuen, 1976.

Lord, George deForest. *Homeric Renaissance: The Odyssey of George Chapman*. New Haven: Yale University Press, 1956.

Lowes, John Livingston. "The Loveres Maladye of Hereos." *Modern Philology* 11 (1913–14): 491–546.

Lyons, Charles. *Shakespeare and the Ambiguity of Love's Triumph*. The Hague: Mouton, 1971.

MacCallum, Sir Mungo William. *Shakespeare's Roman Plays*. London: Macmillan, 1910.

MacLure, Millar. *George Chapman*. Toronto: University of Toronto Press, 1966.

Mack, Maynard. "*Antony and Cleopatra*: The Stillness and the Dance." In *Shakespeare's Art*, edited with introduction by Milton Crane. Chicago: University of Chicago Press, 1973. Pp. 79–113.

Markels, Julian. *The Pillar of the World: Antony and Cleopatra in Shakespeare's Development*. Columbus: Ohio State University Press, 1968.

Marsh, Derick R. C. "Interpretation and Misinterpretation: The Problem of *Troilus and Cressida*." *Shakespeare Studies* 1 (1965): 182–98.

————. *Passion Lends Them Power: A Study of Shakespeare's Love Tragedies*. New York: Barnes & Noble, 1976.

McAlindon, T. "Language, Style, and Meaning in *Troilus and Cressida*." *Publications of the Modern Language Association of America* 84 (1969): 29–43.

————. *Shakespeare and Decorum*. London: Macmillan, 1973.

McCanles, Michael. "The Dialectic of Transcendence in *Coriolanus*." *Publications of the Modern Language Association of America* 82 (1967): 44–53.

McFarland, Thomas. *Tragic Meanings in Shakespeare*. New York: Random House, 1966.

Mitchell, Charles. "*Coriolanus*: Power as Honor." *Shakespeare Studies* 1 (1965): 199–226.

Montaigne, Michel de. *Essais*, 1580. *Essayes*, translated by J. Florio. London, 1603.

Morris, Brian. "The Tragic Structure of *Troilus and Cressida*." *Shakespeare Quarterly* 10 (1959): 481–91.

Muir, Kenneth. *Shakespeare's Sources*. 2 vols. Vol. 1, *The Comedies and Tragedies*. London: Methuen, 1957.

Nowottny, Winifred M. T. " 'Opinion' and 'Value' in *Troilus and Cressida*." *Essays in Criticism* 4 (1954): 282–96.

Oman, Sir Charles. *A History of the Art of War in the Sixteenth Century*. London: Methuen, 1937.

Ornstein, Robert. "The Ethic of the Imagination: Love and Art in *Antony and Cleopatra*." In *Later Shakespeare*. Stratford-Upon-Avon Studies, No. 8. New York: St. Martin's Press, 1967. Pp. 31–46.

———. *The Moral Vision of Jacobean Tragedy*. Madison: University of Wisconsin Press, 1960.

Ovid. *Metamorphoses*. Translated by Frank Justus Miller. Loeb Classical Library. 2 vols. Cambridge, Mass.: Harvard University Press, 1971.

Painter, Sidney. *French Chivalry*. Baltimore: Johns Hopkins Press, 1940.

Panofsky, Erwin. *Idea: A Concept in Art Theory*. Translated by Joseph J. S. Peake. Columbia, S.C.: University of South Carolina Press, 1968.

———. *The Life and Art of Albrecht Dürer*. 4th Edition. Princeton: Princeton University Press, 1955.

Parr, Johnstone. *Tamburlaine's Malady, and Other Essays on Astrology in Elizabethan Drama*. University, Ala.: University of Alabama Press, 1953.

Patterson, Annabel M. "Tasso and Neoplatonism: The Growth of His Epic Theory." *Studies in the Renaissance* 18 (1971): 105–33.

Payne, Michael. "Erotic Imagery and Polarity in *Antony and Cleopatra*." *Shakespeare Quarterly* 24 (1973): 265–79.

Perkinson, Richard H. "Nature and the Tragic Hero in Chapman's Bussy Plays." *Modern Language Quarterly* 3 (1942): 263–85.

Persius. *Satires*. In *Juvenal and Persius*. Translated by G. G. Ramsay. Loeb Classical Library. London: William Heinemann Ltd., 1969. Pp. 310–401.

Phillips, James E. *The State in Shakespeare's Greek and Roman Plays*. New York: Columbia University Press, 1940.

Phinney, Edward, Jr. "Continental Humanists and Chapman's *Iliads*." *Studies in the Renaissance* 12 (1965): 218–26.

Pico Della Mirandola, Giovanni. *Oration on the Dignity of Man*. Translated by Elizabeth Livermoore Forbes. In *The Renaissance Philosophy of Man*, edited by Ernst Cassirer et al. Chicago: University of Chicago Press, 1948. Pp. 223–53.

Plato. *The Dialogues of Plato*. Translated by B. Jowett. 2 vols. New York: Random House, 1937.

Plutarch. *Plutarch's Lives*. Translated by Bernadotte Perrin. Loeb Classical Library. 11 vols. London: William Heinemann Ltd., 1914–26.

————. *Plutarch's Moralia*. Translated by Frank Cole Babbitt. Loeb Classical Library. 14 vols. London: William Heinemann Ltd., 1927–76.

Presson, Robert K. *Shakespeare's Troilus and Cressida & The Legends of Troy*. Madison: University of Wisconsin Press, 1953.

————. "Wrestling with This World: A View of George Chapman." *Publications of the Modern Language Association of America* 84 (1969): 44–50.

Proser, Matthew. *The Heroic Image in Five Shakespearean Tragedies*. Princeton: Princeton University Press, 1965.

Puttenham, George. "The Arte of English Poesie." 1589; rpt. *Elizabethan Critical Essays*. Edited by George Gregory Smith. 2 vols. Oxford: Oxford University Press, 1904. Vol. 2, pp. 1–193.

Rabkin, Norman. *Shakespeare and the Common Understanding*. New York: Free Press, 1967.

————. "The Tragedy of Politics." *Shakespeare Quarterly* 17 (1966): 195–212.

Rebhorn, Wayne A. "Structure and Meaning in *The Praise of Folly*." *Publications of the Modern Language Association of America* 89 (1974): 463–73.

Rees, Ennis. *The Tragedies of George Chapman: Renaissance Ethics in Action*. Cambridge, Mass.: Harvard University Press, 1954.

Regel, H. M. "Über George Chapmans Homerübersetzung." *Englishe Studien* 5 (1881): 1–55, 295–356.

Ribner, Irving. *The English History Play in the Age of Shakespeare*. Revised edition. London: Methuen, 1965.

————. *Jacobean Tragedy*. New York: Barnes & Noble, 1962.

Riggs, David. *Shakespeare's Heroical Histories: Henry VI and Its Literary Tradition*. Cambridge, Mass.: Harvard University Press, 1971.

Robb, Nesca. *Neoplatonism of the Italian Renaissance*. London: Allen & Unwin, 1935.

Rodis-Lewis, Geneviève. *La morale stoicienne*. Paris: Presses Universitaires de France, 1970.

Romei, Annibale. *The Courtiers Academie*. Translated by I. K. London, 1598.

Rose, Mark. *Heroic Love: Studies in Sidney and Spenser*. Cambridge, Mass.: Harvard University Press, 1968.

Rosen, William. *Shakespeare and the Craft of Tragedy*. Cambridge, Mass.: Harvard University Press, 1960.

Rossiter, Andrew P. *Angel with Horns*. New York: Theatre Arts, 1961.

Rothstein, Eric. *Restoration Tragedy: Form and the Process of Change*. Madison: University of Wisconsin Press, 1967.

Roy, Emil. "War and Manliness in Shakespeare's *Troilus and Cressida*." *Comparative Drama* 7 (1973–74): 107–20.

Scapula, Johann. *Lexicon Graeco-Latinum novum*. Basel, 1615.

Schoell, Franck L. *Etudes sur l'humanisme continental en Angleterre à la fin de la Renaissance*. Paris: Librairie Anciennne Honoré Champion, 1926.

Schwartz, Elias. "Chapman's Renaissance Man: Byron Reconsidered." *Journal of English and Germanic Philology* 58 (1959): 613–26.

————. "Seneca, Homer, and Chapman's *Bussy D'Ambois*." *Journal of English and Germanic Philology* 56 (1957): 163–76.

————. "Tonal Equivocation and the Meaning of *Troilus and Cressida*." *Studies in Philology* 69 (1972): 304–19.

Seaton, Ethel. "*Antony and Cleopatra* and the Book of Revelation." *Review of English Studies* 12 (1946): 219–24.

Seneca, Lucius Annaeus. *Epistulae Morales. Seneca's Epistles*. Translated by Richard M. Gummere. 3 vols. New York: Putnam's, 1917–25.

————. *Moralia. Moral Essays*. Translated by John W. Basore. 3 vols. New York: Putnam's, 1928–35.

Serres, Jean de. *A Generall Historie of France*. Translated by Edward Grimeston. London, 1611.

Shakespeare, William. *Antony and Cleopatra*. The Pelican Edition. Edited by Maynard Mack. Baltimore: Pelican Press, 1960.

————. *Coriolanus*. The Cambridge Edition. Edited by John Dover Wilson. Cambridge, England: Cambridge University Press, 1960.

————. *The New Variorum Troilus and Cressida*. Edited by Harold N. Hillebrand. Philadelphia: J. B. Lippincott Co., 1953.

————. *The Riverside Shakespeare*. Edited by G. Blakemore Evans; Harry Levin; et al. Boston: Houghton Mifflin Co., 1974.

Shalvi, Alice. *The Relationship of Renaissance Concepts of Honour to Shakespeare's Problem Plays*. Salzburg: University of Salzburg Press, 1972.

Sicherman, Carol M. "*Coriolanus*: The Failure of Words." *Journal of English Literary History* 39 (1972): 189–207.

Sidney, Sir Philip. "An Apologie for Poetrie." Ca. 1583. 1595; rpt. *Elizabethan Critical Essays*. Edited by George Gregory Smith. 2 vols. Oxford: Oxford University Press, 1904. Vol. 1, pp. 148–207.

Siegel, Paul N. *Shakespeare in His Time and Ours*. South Bend, Ind.: University of Notre Dame Press, 1968.

Siemon, James E. " 'The Strong Necessity of Time': Dilemma in *Antony and Cleopatra*." *English Studies* 54 (1973): 316–25.

Simmons, James L. *Shakespeare's Pagan World: The Roman Tragedies*. Charlottesville: University Press of Virginia, 1973.

Smalley, Donald. "The Ethical Bias of Chapman's Homer." *Studies in Philology* 36 (1939): 169–91.

Smith, Hallett. *Elizabethan Poetry*. Cambridge, Mass.: Harvard University Press, 1952.

Smith, Irwin. *Shakespeare's Blackfriars Playhouse*. New York: New York University Press, 1964.

Smith, James. "George Chapman (II)." *Scrutiny* 4 (1935–36): 45–61.

Smith, Joyce Carol Oates. "The Alchemy of *Antony and Cleopatra*." *Bucknell Review* 12 (1964): 37–50.

Soellner, Rolf. *Shakespeare's Patterns of Self-Knowledge*. Columbus: Ohio State University Press, 1972.

Spencer, Terence J. B. " 'Greeks and Merrygreeks': A Background to *Timon of Athens* and *Troilus and Cressida*." In *Essays on Shakespeare and Elizabethan Drama in Honor of Hardin Craig*, edited by Richard Hosley. Columbia: University of Missouri Press, 1962. Pp. 223–33.

————. "Shakespeare and the Elizabethan Romans." *Shakespeare Survey* 10 (1957): 27–38.

Spens, Janet. "Chapman's Ethical Thought." *Essays and Studies* 11 (1925): 145–69.

Spondanus (see Sponde, Jean de).

Sponde, Jean de. *Homeri quae extant omnia . . .* Basel, 1583.

Steadman, John M. *Epic and Tragic Structure in Paradise Lost.* Chicago: University of Chicago Press, 1976.

————. *Milton and the Renaissance Hero.* Oxford: Clarendon Press, 1967.

Stein, Arnold. "The Image of Antony: Lyric and Tragic Imagination." *Kenyon Review* 21 (1959): 586–606.

Stempel, David. "The Transmigration of the Crocodile." *Shakespeare Quarterly* 7 (1956): 59–72.

Stirling, Brents. *Unity in Shakespeare Tragedy.* New York: Gordian Press, 1966.

Stockholder, Katherine S. "Egregiously an Ass: Chance and Accident in *Othello*." *Studies in English Literature, 1500–1900* 13 (1973): 256–72.

————. "The Other Coriolanus." Publications of the Modern Language Association of America 85 (1970): 228–36.

Stone, Laurence. *The Crisis of the Aristocracy, 1558–1641.* Oxford: Clarendon Press, 1965.

Swedenberg, Hugh Thomas. *The Theory of the Epic in England, 1650–1800.* Berkeley: University of California Press, 1944.

Tasso, Torquato. *Discourses on the Heroic Poem.* Translated by Mariella Cavalchini and Irene Samuel. Oxford: Clarendon Press, 1973.

————. *Jerusalem Delivered.* Translated by Edward Fairfax. 1600; 4th Edition, London: J. Purser, 1749.

Tatlock, John S. P. "The Siege of Troy in Elizabethan Literature, Especially in Shakespeare and Heywood." *Publications of the Modern Language Association of America* 30 (1915): 676–78.

Taylor, Frederick L. *The Art of War in Italy, 1494–1529.* Cambridge, England: Cambridge University Press, 1921.

Thomson, James A. K. *Shakespeare and the Classics.* London: George Allen & Unwin, 1952.

Tillyard, Eustace M. W. *Shakespeare's History Plays.* New York: Macmillan, 1946.

Traversi, Derek Antona. *Shakespeare: The Roman Plays.* Stanford: Stanford University Press, 1963.

Tricomi, Albert H. "The Revised Version of Chapman's *Bussy D'Ambois*: A Shift in Point of View." *Studies in Philology* 70 (1973): 288–305.

Ure, Peter. *Elizabethan and Jacobean Drama.* Edited by J. C. Maxwell. Liverpool: Liverpool University Press, 1974.

————. "A Note on 'Opinion' in Daniel, Greville, and Chapman." *Modern Language Review* 46 (1951): 331–38.

Vian, Francis. *La guerre des géants: Le mythe avant l'épôque hellénistique.* Paris: Librairie C. Klincksieck, 1952.

Waddington, Raymond B. "*Antony and Cleopatra*: What Venus Did with Mars." *Shakespeare Studies* 2 (1966): 210–27.

————. *The Mind's Empire: Myth and Form in George Chapman's Narrative Poems*. Baltimore: Johns Hopkins Press, 1974.

————. "Prometheus and Hercules: The Dialectic of *Bussy D'Ambois*." *Journal of English Literary History* 34 (1967): 21–48.

Waith, Eugene. *The Herculean Hero*. New York: Columbia University Press, 1962.

————. *Ideas of Greatness: Heroic Drama in England*. New York: Barnes & Noble, 1971.

Walker, Daniel Pickering. *Spiritual and Demonic Magic from Ficino to Campanella*. Leiden: Warburg Institute, 1958.

Watson, Curtis Brown. *Shakespeare and the Renaissance Concept of Honor*. Princeton: Princeton University Press, 1960.

Weidhorn, Manfred. "The Relation of Title and Name to Identity in Shakespearian Tragedy." *Studies in English Literature* 9 (1969): 303–19.

Weinberg, Bernard. *A History of Literary Criticism in the Renaissance*. 2 vols. Chicago: University of Chicago Press, 1961.

Whitman, Cedric H. *Homer and the Heroic Tradition*. Cambridge, Mass.: Harvard University Press, 1958.

Williamson, Marilyn L. "Fortune in *Antony and Cleopatra*." *Journal of English and Germanic Philology* 67 (1968): 423–29.

Wilson, Harold S. *On the Design of Shakespearean Tragedy*. Toronto: University of Toronto Press, 1957.

Wind, Edgar. *Pagan Mysteries in the Renaissance*. 2d Edition. London: Faber & Faber, 1968.

Witt, Reginald E. *Isis in the Graeco-Roman World*. Ithaca, N.Y.: Cornell University Press, 1971.

Yoder, R. A. "The Two Worlds of Othello." *South Atlantic Quarterly* 72 (1973): 213–25.

INDEX

Achilles, 11, 18, 23–31, 83, 115, 177, 184;
Homer's contrasted with Chapman's, 10,
22–23, 26, 28; "Predominant Perturbation" of, 23–24, 30, 76, 77, 78, 161; as
Chapman's exemplary hero, 24, 26–28,
32–33, 72, 77, 100; related to Hercules,
28, 100; Chapman's changing attitude
toward, 32, 75–76; contrasted with
Ulysses, 76–78, 160, 161, 162; as Ulyssean hero of *Iliads* (1598), 76, 100. See
also *Bussy D'Ambois*; Chapman, George;
Chapman and Shakespeare; *Iliads*
(1598); *Iliads* (1611); names of individual characters; *Troilus and Cressida*
Adelman, Janet, 222 (n. 25), 223 (n. 33)
Agrippa, Cornelius, 224 (n. 10)
Alexander the Great, 184, 224 (n. 12). *See
also* Byron; Coriolanus
Antony, Mark (Shakespeare's), 11, 102–31
passim; human heroism of, 48; contrasted with Bussy, 103–4, 129, 131; as
Mars, 104, 105, 107–8, 111, 113, 118,
119, 121; as Hercules, 104, 110, 113,
116, 118, 119, 120, 123, 124, 125, 129,
222 (n. 20); conflict with self (soldier
versus lover), 104, 107–8, 110, 113;
Roman conception of self, 104, 109, 113,
120, 121, 122–23; "Roman thought,"
109; as "soldier-servant" of love, 110–
11, 113, 115, 117–18, 119, 121, 124; as
surrogate dramatist, 118, 123; suicide
attempt, 120–21, 124; folly and grandeur at death, 122–24; associated with
Nature, 125. See also *Antony and
Cleopatra*
Antony and Cleopatra, xi, xvi, 7, 13, 72,
102–31, 168; related to *Bussy D'Ambois*, 102, 115, 128–31; *de casibus*
tragedy in, 103–4, 105–6, 197, 220–21
(n. 6); Roman historical perspective in,
103, 106–7, 116–17, 118, 126, 220–21
(n. 6); heroism and tragic grandeur in,
103–4, 115, 124, 129–31, 133, 160,
173; Octavius Caesar in, 103, 106, 107,
108, 114–26 passim, 197, 220–21 (n. 6);

Fortune in, 104, 106, 112–14, 115–16,
119, 123, 128; romantic and comedic
elements in, 105–6, 107, 112–13, 115,
126, 130–31, 133, 197; double perspective in, 106–7, 109, 116, 121, 123–24,
125–26, 130–31, 133, 197; Roman and
Egyptian time-senses in, 106–7; Roman
Fortune and Egyptian Nature in, 107,
114; Pompey in, 109; Octavia in, 110,
113; Enobarbus in, 111, 112, 115–17,
119, 124; Rome's antiquated ideals in,
111; grandeur versus success in, 111,
113, 114, 115, 116, 117; use of countergenres in, 113–14, 131; folly in,
114–17, 122–24, 131; paradoxes of love
in, 118, 222 (n. 23); clown as symbol in,
126–27; human nature as source of
heroism in, 128–29, 160. See also Antony, Mark; Cleopatra
Areté, 10, 46, 75, 77, 87, 141, 169, 178,
195, 219 (n. 26)
Ariosto, Lodovico, 201; *Orlando Furioso*,
xiv
Aristotle: conception of honor, 39, 218 (n.
12); conception of "god-beasts," 171;
conception of heroic pride, 182; *Poetics*,
205 (n. 8)

Bacon, Francis, 3, 224 (n. 18)
Barber, C. L., 218 (n. 15)
Barroll, J. Leeds, 208–9 (n. 21), 213 (n.
44), 220 (n. 6)
Barton, Anne, xv
Battenhouse, Roy, 226 (nn. 2, 3)
Bement, Peter, 217 (n. 7), 224 (n. 18)
Bergson, Allen, 219 (n. 19)
Berry, Ralph, 228 (n. 20)
Bethell, S. L., 221 (n. 10)
Bible, The: Isaiah, 146
Blackfriars Playhouse, 170, 227 (n. 8)
Bonjour, Adrien, 213 (n. 42)
Boynton, Lindsay, 206 (n. 5)
Bradley, A. C., 172
Brodwin, Leonora, 214 (n. 7), 215 (n. 14)
Brooke, Nicolas, 217 (n. 8)

psychology of, 11, 134–35, 161–62; as neo-Platonic dramatist, 13–14; principles of characterization, 14–15, 48, 130, 196, 208 (nn. 19, 20); related to Marlowe, 15; conception of "complete man," 16, 99, 161–63, 167, 199–200; as neo-Platonic poet, 22; attitude toward Homer, 23, 31, 77; rejection of Stoic apathy, 28, 134, 161; politics of, 31; heroic conception of himself, 33, 200–201; conception of heroic spirit, 46, 48, 77, 148, 160–61, 162, 167, 215–16 (n. 4); conception of heroism and tragic grandeur, 49, 100, 129, 198–99; supposed disenchantment with Achilles, 76, 160–61, 162, 167; so-called "Stoic period," 77, 162, 216 (n. 5); conception of heroic tragedy, 129, 169; so-called "heroic period," 160–61, 216 (n. 5); celebratory conception of epic, 167, 200; and comedy of humours, 201, 208 (n. 20); so-called "neo-Platonic" period, 216 (n. 5). See also Achilles; Chapman and Shakespeare; Chapman, works by; Coriolanus; Coriolanus; Heroic Tragedy; Tasso, Torquato; Tragedy

Chapman, works by: "Ovids Banquet of Sence," xv; The Gentleman Usher, xv, 85, 201; "Achilles' Shield," 20–21; "De Guinea," 31; The Tragedy of Chabot, Chabot in, 33; "The Teares of Peace," 145, 225 (n. 18); Iliads (1609), 170; The Widow's Tears, 201; Sir Giles Goosecap, Knight, 224 (n. 10). See also Bussy D'Ambois; Caesar and Pompey; Iliads (1598); Iliads (1611); Odysses; Conspiracy and Tragedy of Byron, The; Revenge of Bussy D'Ambois, The

Chapman and Shakespeare; interest in heroic tragedy, xiii–xiv; fascination with epic, xiv; dialogue on epic, xv, xvi, 199, 200; mutual negative influence, xv, xvi; competitive relationship, xv; uses of honor, 7, 207 (n. 9); conceptions of soldier's failure contrasted, 8–9; similarities in approach to heroic tragedy, 9–10; attitude toward pagan epic contrasted, 10–11, 36, 41, 124, 173, 199, 200; psychological theories contrasted, 11; attitude toward heroic passion contrasted, 11, 47; treatment of love contrasted, 12–13; heroic characterization contrasted, 13–19, 130, 196; dramaturgy contrasted, 15; dramatic *idea* contrasted, 16; conceptions of "the matter of Troy"

contrasted, 21, 77; conceptions of Achilles contrasted, 38, 198; attitude toward heroic spirit contrasted, 46–47, 87–88, 135–36, 148; ironic and tragic effects contrasted, 47; epic evocations contrasted, 47–48; conceptions of heroic tragedy contrasted, 48–49; conceptions of heroism and tragic grandeur contrasted, 100, 124, 129–30, 131, 193, 199–200; conceptions of Herculean heroism contrasted, 104, 129–30; conceptions of heroic love contrasted, 115, 131; conceptions of themselves contrasted, 201–2. See also Chapman, George; Shakespeare, William

Characterization: presentational, 15; naturalistic, 16–17. See also Chapman, George; Chapman and Shakespeare; names of individual characters; Shakespeare, William

Charron, Pierre, 164

Chaucer, Geoffrey, 20, 21

Chettle, Henry, 20

Children of Blackfriars, 170, 227 (n. 8)

Cicero, Marcus Tullius, 216 (n. 5), 218 (n. 11)

Clemen, Wolfgang, 214 (n. 3)

Cleopatra, 102–31 passim; human heroism of, 48, 105, 130; as Venus, 104, 105, 107, 108, 118, 128; related to Chapman's Tamyra, 105, 130; as Isis, 105, 112, 113, 127–28, 220 (n. 4); as Circe, 105; associated with Nature, 107, 108–9, 112, 128; magical decorum of, 108–10, 127–28; Roman heroic image of, 112–13; as surrogate dramatist, 118, 126; versus Caesar, 107, 125–26; as "soldier"-servant of love, 126, 128, 130; and the clown, 126–27; *concordia discors* of, 221 (n. 10). See also *Antony and Cleopatra*

Clermont D'Ambois, 16, 31, 160–63, 166; contrasted with Bussy, 160, 162; as Achillean hero, 162–63, 216 (n. 5); the "learning" of, 162–63; as Stoic sage, 162, 163; exemplary heroism of, 163, 199–200; as "complete man," 200

Colie, Rosalie, xii, 48, 73, 215 (n. 11), 214–15 (n. 10)

Comes, Natalis. See Conti, Natale

"Complete man." See Bussy D'Ambois; Byron; Chapman, George; Clermont D'Ambois; Ulysses

Conspiracy and Tragedy of Byron, The, xi, xvi, 15, 132–60, 161–62; Platonic

139–40; *magus*, 141; Pico's "miraculous man," 141; aesthetics in general, 144; creative melancholy, 144. *See also* Chapman, George; titles of individual works

Neo-Stoicism. *See* Stoicism

North, Sir Thomas, 169, 190

Odysses, xv, 22, 76, 160, 163–67, 200, 201; Nausikaa episode in, 22; epistle to Somerset, 76; Telemachus in, 163, 165; *prudentia* as "spirit" in, 165; Minerva as patroness of *prudentia* in, 165–66; rational control in, 226 (n. 31). *See also* Chapman, George; *Iliads* (1598); *Iliads* (1611); Ulysses

O'Neill, Hugh. *See* Tyrone, Earl of

Ornstein, Robert, 52, 214 (n. 4), 219 (n. 8), 223 (n. 35)

Othello, xi, xvi, 17, 50–74, 87; Desdemona in, 50, 51, 53–74 passim; Iago in, 50, 51, 53–66 passim; Brabantio in, 51, 52, 53, 56, 66; Venetian "courtesy culture" in, 53; Desdemona's amatory idealism in, 53–54; Cassio in, 54–66 passim, 74; comedic elements in, 55; Desdemona as Venus in, 55–56; sonnet elements in, 56, 73–74; Roderigo in, 56; Lodovico in, 57; related to *Troilus and Cressida*, 64, 68, 71; symbolism of the handkerchief in, 66; self-idolatry in, 67–68; love versus honor in, 68; contrasted with *Iliads* (1598), 72; tragedy as countergenre to epic in, 72–74; honor in, 213 (n. 2), 218 (n. 12). *See also* Othello

Othello, 7, 9, 11, 50–74; conflict with self (soldier versus lover), 12–13, 51, 57–58, 61, 63, 64, 68, 71, 72–74, 81–82, 99; progression in character, 17, 68; human heroism of, 48; heroic image as soldier-servant of Venice, 50, 53, 55–56, 57, 61, 70, 148; delusive heroic image, 50, 63–64, 67–68, 71–72, 73, 74, 160; heroic egomania, 50–51, 55, 67, 74; as racial and cultural alien, 50, 52, 60, 70; conception of honor, 50, 70, 71; as stereotypical Moor, 51, 62, 66; impersonal resolution of public man, 51, 52, 55, 58, 59, 62–63, 68, 70, 72, 81; love distinguished from Troilus's, 52; martial mentality of, 52, 55, 60, 214 (n. 6); social quest of, 52–53, 56; the quality of his love, 53, 54; as Mars, 55–56, 73; his "contentment," 56; the lover's passion,

55–56, 57–58, 65; the soldier's Stoic calm, 57, 214 (n. 3); betrayal of amatory ideals, 60; as revenger, 62–63, 67, 71; false conception of honor, 63; pretension to virtue and justice, 63–64, 67–68; his shame, 66; *anagnorisis* of, 69–71; unnaturalness of, 72, 99; as heroic lover at death, 73–74; final heroism of, 74, 95; contrasted with Bussy, 81–82, 87, 95, 97, 99; contrasted with Byron, 146. *See also Othello*; "Turn in character"

"Over-ruling Wisedome." *See* Ulysses

Ovid, 87; *Metamorphoses*, 150

Persius, 217 (n. 7)

Phillips, James E., 220 (n. 6)

Philotas: related to Essex, xiv, 5, 16, 144, 207 (n. 7); related to the *Byron* plays and *Coriolanus*, 132

Pico della Mirandola, Giovanni, 141

Plato, 92; social and psychological hierarchies, 11; distinction between *eros* and *thumos*, 172. *See also* Neo-Platonism

Plutarch, 17, 144; *Lives*, 115, 117–18, 129, 169, 190, 229 (n. 3); *Moralia*, 224 (n. 12)

"Predominant Perturbation." *See* Achilles

Presson, Robert, 21

Proser, Matthew, 8, 207 (n. 8), 214 (n. 3), 215 (n. 16), 222 (n. 31)

Puttenham, George: conception of epic, xi; contrast between epic and tragedy, 10, 11

Rabkin, Norman, 214 (n. 7)

Ralegh, Sir Walter, 31

Rees, Ennis, 11

Revenge of Bussy D'Ambois, The, xv; the Guise in, 33, 100, 200. *See also* Clermont D'Ambois

Riggs, David, 205 (n. 10), 208 (n. 19)

Robb, Nesca, 224 (n. 14)

Rosen, William, 222 (n. 32)

Rothstein, Eric, 208 (n. 19)

Scaliger, Julius Caesar, 22

Schoell, Franck L., 224 (n. 12)

Seneca, 24, 28, 32, 33, 87, 92, 161, 199, 216 (n. 5), 217 (n. 10); conception of primitive man, 84–85; *Hercules Oetaeus*, 216 (n. 5); Stoic retirement, 217 (n. 7); *Hercules Furens*, 223 (n. 7)

Serres, Jean de, 132

Shakespeare, William: attitude toward Essex, 6, 18, 98; use of symbolic geography,